Popular Receptions
of Classical Antiquity

Aarhus Studies in

Mediterranean Antiquity

(ASMA)

XVI

ASMA is a series of monographs and anthologies published by the research programme "Classical Antiquity and its Heritage" in the School of Culture and Society, Aarhus University, Denmark. The programme includes researchers from a wide range of disciplines studying Graeco-Roman Antiquity, such as Classical Archaeology, Classical Philology, Ancient History, the Study of Religion and Theology. The aim of the series of the series is to publish significant new research in Classical Studies and to provide an interdisciplinary platform for the study of the ancient world.

ASMA Editorial Board:
Christian Thrue Djurslev, Jakob Engberg, George Hinge, Vinnie Nørskov, Adéla Sobotkova, Elisa Katariina Uusimäki

ASMA Advisory Board:
Rasmus Brandt, Björn Forsén, Lin Foxhall, Tobias Georges, Thomas Heine Nielsen, Cornelia Isler-Kerényi, Inge Nielsen, David Pritchard, Jörg Rüpke

Popular Receptions of Classical Antiquity

The Aarhus Studies in Mediterranean Antiquity Conference 2021

Edited by
Christian Thrue Djurslev,
Jens A. Krasilnikoff
and Vinnie Nørskov

Aarhus University Press |

Popular Receptions of Classical Antiquity
© The Authors and Aarhus University Press 2024

Cover: Jørgen Sparre
Cover illustration: Front: Life in the City, embroidery and crochet flower by Eva Blom, from the exhibition Embrodering the City, Museum of Ancient and Archaeology, Aarhus University, 2016.
Back: Stiching in a Classic: Afro-Ditte by Anne Ditte Høi, from the exhibition Embrodering the City, Museum of Ancient Art and Archaeology, Aarhus University, 2016.

Layout and typesetting: Narayana Press
Publishing editor: Sanne Lind Hansen
This book is typeset in Adobe Garamond and LTSyntax and printed on 130 g Arctic Volume
Printed by Narayana Press, Denmark
Printed in Denmark 2024

ISBN 978 87 7597 227 2 (printed book)
ISBN 978 87 7597 567 9 (e-pdf)
ISBN 978 87 7597 568 6 (epub)

ISSN 1399 2686

Aarhus University Press
aarhusuniversitypress.dk

Published with the financial support of:
Aarhus University Research Foundation
The Carlsberg Foundation

International distributors
Casemate UK, casemateuk.com
ISD, isdistribution.com

PEER REVIEWED

/ In accordance with requirements of the Danish Ministry of Higher Education and Science, the certification means that a ph.d.-level peer has made a written assessment which justifies this book's scientific quality.

Contents

1 Introduction
In Memoriam Jens Krasilnikoff (5 April 1962 – 14 February 2024)   7
Christian Thrue Djurslev & Vinnie Nørskov

2 What's behind the label?   13
Lorna Hardwick

3 Orality, literacy, and authority in Eudocia's
Martyrdom of Saints Cyprian and Justina   37
Andrew Faulkner

4 The vernacular Alexander   49
Marianne Pade

5 Finding Pericles lost
Indicators of the meaning of Danish travel accounts and nostalgic encounters with nineteenth-century Greece in transition   61
Jens Krasilnikoff

6 *Ór na Gréige is stór na hÉigipt*
Classical antiquity in Irish-language popular poetry of the eighteenth and nineteenth centuries   81
Gregory R. Darwin

7 From the Rubicon to Stevns and back
Intertwined receptions of Caesar in *Elverhøj* and *Asterix* in Danish   101
Trine Arlund Hass

8 Wronged imperialists, primitive Romans, and advanced barbarians (and vice versa)
The Romans and the Roman Empire in Claus Deleuran's *The Illustrated History of Denmark – a People's History*   123
Jakob Engberg

9 Hercules and the Incredible Hulk
Myth meets Marvel's megatext   141
C.W. Marshall

10 Ancient history amplified
   Herodotus, heavy metal and the Iron Maiden   167
   Christian Thrue Djurslev

11 The unruly power of myth
   Classical narratives in contemporary Danish art   187
   Vinnie Nørskov

12 The *Iliad* and the twenty-first-century apocalyptic imagination   205
   Edith Hall

1

INTRODUCTION

IN MEMORIAM JENS KRASILNIKOFF (5 APRIL 1962 – 14 FEBRUARY 2024)

CHRISTIAN THRUE DJURSLEV & VINNIE NØRSKOV

The present volume is a paradigmatic example of the series "Aarhus Studies in Mediterranean Antiquity" at Aarhus University Press, which seeks not only to publish significant new research in the field of Classical Studies but also to provide an interdisciplinary platform for the study of the ancient world as a whole. The theme is classical antiquity in popular culture, broadly construed. This has been one of the most productive avenues within Classical Studies, reflected in a buzzing community, book series at established presses, academic journals, scholarly networks, media sites, blogs, and many other venues. "Popular culture (modern)" even has its own free entry in the online edition of the *Oxford Classical Dictionary* (Gideon Nisbet, 2015). Given the incredible interest in the ancient world, this topic has endless potential, including for interdisciplinary interactions, as this volume shows. Contributors to this volume were asked to explore the ways in which classical antiquity has been received and interpreted in popular culture across different time periods and geographical locations. Their responses showcase some established trajectories but also add a range of new areas to the subject, particularly the Danish dimension.

This volume is based on another Aarhus venture, as the papers originated from an international hybrid conference held at the Aarhus Institute of Advanced Studies (AIAS) on 2 and 3 September 2021. The event was a collaboration between different research groups at Aarhus University – most prominently, the research programme "Classical Antiquity and its Heritage", the Centre for the Study of Antiquity and Christianity (C-SAC), Museum of Ancient Art and Archaeology, and AIAS. It was organized by a committee of local academics comprising members from various departments, including Archaeology, Classics, English, History, and Theology. They were complemented by an international cast of speakers, some of whom attended in person while others joined virtually. The virtual space also sparked lively discussion among participants from a wide range of disciplines. The interdisciplinary nature of the event highlights the manifold aspects of classical reception and its relevance to various academic fields; it also attests to the academic interest in popular culture as a place for intellectual engagement. The editors and organizers would like to thank everyone involved for their contributions, especially the staff at AIAS for providing the conference with a stimulating space for reflection, receptions, and discussion.

Most of the papers delivered at the conference were rewritten for this volume, and incorporate the conversations that were had during the conference. No restrictive definitions of "classical antiquity" or "popular culture" were imposed. This approach allowed for a broad range of perspectives and interpretations, reflecting the multidimensional nature of the topic. It also raised a number of immediate questions, such as: How can we talk about "popular culture"? In what ways can we detect it? How recent is the mass consumption and commercialization of antiquity? Where do such activities take place? What are the kinds of "classical antiquity" that have drawn interest from the wider public? How does popular culture express these antiquities? Do different media change the medialization of classical antiquity? And why does antiquity continue to interest people beyond the academy?

Readers of this volume will recognize that different periods, people, and spaces convey classical antiquity in their own ways, which is why the contributors embrace such polyphony. Obviously, it is not possible to be comprehensive, and readers will have to look elsewhere for frontier topics such as classical antiquity in video games. Nevertheless, we the editors believe several exciting areas are covered here, divided into three principal areas of interest. The first is the popular reception of classical antiquity before the twentieth century, with special attention to the dynamic relationship between different layers of society and their cultural production. The second area of interest is classics and comics. The third is contemporary society, with a focus on art, literature, and music. We urge readers not to consider these labels a rigid selection, as some common themes will inevitably emerge and overlap across the chapters. Indeed, it is hoped that the volume will be more than a sum of its constituent parts in that they collectively seek to contribute to the ongoing conversations about what classical antiquity and popular culture might mean.

Here follows an outline of the contents. In the introductory chapter, Lorna Hardwick offers a broad theoretical sweep of reception studies. She lays out the implications of key terms used in the area, primarily the labels that carry with them assumptions about cultural value and appropriate methodology and epistemology. The study of Greek and Roman antiquity throughout the centuries has largely focused on extant sources, both written and material, created by and for elites. Shifts in terminology are markers of deeper cultural and geo-political shifts. The development of theories and methods for investigating popular culture within antiquity and in its subsequent reception therefore deserves scrutiny both on its own account and for its place in a wider dynamic. Hardwick explains that the study of popular culture in the modern world extends from the specific impact of modern technologies and new genres (from print to computer games) to how these situate material from antiquity and act as a conduit for its transmission into the public imagination. In terms of relationships with antiquity, a focus on the 'popular' in contemporary culture is sometimes seen as a counterbalance, even an antidote, to perceptions of antiquity that have been skewed by transmission and labelling in elite contexts. Hardwick questions rigid polarizations between 'high' and 'popular' culture in the creative and scholarly practices involved in the reception of antiquity. Discussion of specific examples will draw out how new 'labels' are constructed and disseminated, by whom, for whom, with what purpose, and with what effect over time. It is Hardwick's ambition that this approach not only suggests critical tools for the study of antiquity and its reception, but also opens the way for the perhaps urgent resetting of teaching and research.

The next four papers comment on popular receptions from before the twentieth century, in chronological order. We begin in antiquity. Andrew Faulkner examines stories about local saints and their martyrdoms, which were widely popular in late antiquity. While these prose narratives were closely connected to cultural and civic identity, they also inspired poetic productions. Faulkner focuses on one particular instance in early Christian paraphrastic poetry: the hexameter version of the hagiographical *Acts of Saints Cyprian and Justina* by the fifth-century empress Aelia Eudocia, consort of Emperor Theodosius II. He considers how Eudocia negotiates scholarly and popular reception of the classical in this paraphrase, with special attention to the question of Eudocia's audience and the enactment of popular performance within her narrative, especially the tension between orality and bookish learning. Popular public traditions are thus reinterpreted and reworked for new literary settings and circles.

Marianne Pade explores the inverse of the phenomenon addressed by Faulkner – how a local elite could disseminate popular collections of texts into the steady stream of the vernacular. Pade takes us to the Renaissance, analysing Pier Candido Decembrio's *Istoria d'Alexandro Magno* and its impact. This text was commissioned by Filippo Maria Visconti († 1447), the Duke of Milan, who was interested in ancient history but not proficient in Latin. He therefore had his secretary Pier Candido Decembrio produce vernacular versions of ancient historians, among them Julius Caesar. But Visconti also wanted to read about Caesar's traditional foil in the 'Hall of Fame', Alexander the Great. Accordingly, in 1438 Decembrio translated Curtius' *Historia Alexandri Magni* into the Lombard language, filling in the *lacunae* in Curtius' narrative with passages from Plutarch's *Alexander*. He also included the comparison between Alexander and Caesar that was missing in the Plutarchan pairing. The two texts circulated together under the title *Istoria d'Alexandro Magno*, which became hugely popular, as is evident in the many other vernacular translations and numerous printings in various languages.

Gregory Darwin takes a bottom-up approach to popular culture in Ireland during the eigthteenth and nineteenth centuries. He examines the lyrical themes of Irish-language songs, with all their references and allusions to classical figures, events, and landscapes. While many of these songs were composed by scholarly poets, their dissemination, transmission, and reception among the general population were facilitated by itinerant teachers at hedge schools. This indicates a strong public interest in classical antiquity. Darwin provides a comprehensive overview of the classical allusions and references found in both anonymous and authored songs dating from this era. He demonstrates that these songs predominantly employ comparisons between the contemporary world and the classical realm. The allusions are not simply ostentatious displays of learning, but part of a larger cultural logic that sees Irish as a classical language alongside Latin and Greek. Additionally, Darwin contemplates the significance of these allusions within the context of expanding British influence and the cultural dominance of the English language.

Jens Krasilnikoff employs a diachronic approach to the representation of Greece in nineteenth-century Denmark by collating Danish travel accounts of the Mediterranean country. Throughout this period, scholars and artists embarked on journeys to Greece and produced narratives that depicted a nation in the process of formation. The texts cover a wide range of topics, from elevated expectations of encountering "the descendants of Pericles" to disillusionment stemming from the perceived degradation of "modern" Greek society under Ottoman rule in the 1830s. Some authors contemplated strategies to rescue Greece from internal challenges while preserving its classical heritage, which they believed was endangered by the influences of the East. Subsequently, from the 1860s to the 1880s, frustrations emerged concerning the Greek population's perceived failure to adhere to legal principles. At the end of the century, Danish journalists engendered the most dominant image by rediscovering the lost Pericles in their coverage of the War of Independence in Crete.

The next trio of contributions deals with mythic and historical topics in comics. Trine Arlund Hass identifies a novel interaction of popular receptions in a comic and a Danish play. She focuses on the representation of Julius Caesar in an issue of the Asterix comic book series and its precedent in what is perhaps the most famous instance of Caesar's Danish reception, the play *Elverhøi* (Elven Hill, 1828). The former is one of the most popular receptions of classical antiquity throughout Europe. The latter is one of the most famous plays of Danish Romanticism, written by the influential and renowned playwright and critic J.L. Heiberg for the wedding of the crown prince. It is a narrative of mistaken identities situated during the reign of King Christian IV (1588/1596-1648). Hass specifically focuses on a scene in which the king crosses a stream and utters the famous phrase "I may not be Caesar and these waves not the Rubicon, and yet I say: *Jacta est alea*". She argues that this very utterance is appropriated in the Danish translation of *Asterix and the Chieftain's Shield* (1972; orig.: *Le bouclier arverne*, 1967), the eleventh volume in the series.

Jakob Engberg investigates the reception of Roman history in a multi-volume work that has had a major impact in Danish society. In 1987, the cartoonist Claus Deleuran published the first volume of his *The Illustrated Danish History for the People*, planned to detail the history of Denmark from the World's creation in the middle of Ginnungagap up to the present day. By Deleuran's death in 1996, he had managed to complete nine volumes that covered the chronology until 1100 AD. Engberg discusses Deleuran's reception of Roma and the Romans, especially in volumes three to five, in which several pages are devoted to the Roman Empire. His analysis centres on Deleuran's representations, his approach, his sources, and his scholarship. Another major focus is how Deleuran's text and illustrations satirized their sources, as well as (some of the more far-fetched) scholarly theories.

C.W. Marshall takes on a sprawling series of comics based on Greek myth. Specifically, Marshall's investigation centres on *The Incredible Hercules*, which was published serially by Marvel between 2007 and 2011 and offers thoughtful and meaningful engagement with the processes of classical myth-making in the context of comics. The series incorporates the Greek god Heracles (known in the series by his Latin name, Hercules) into the expansive fictional world of the Marvel Universe. Marshall explains this successful incorporation by situating *The Incredible Hercules* and its associations with Greek mythology in terms of what has been called a "megatext". This concept refers to a vast interconnected network of narratives that together form a coherent and fictional universe. Despite occasional contradictions, the Marvel megatext intertwines multiple classical storylines, characters, and themes, thereby creating a cohesive narrative tapestry for *The Incredible Hercules*.

The final trio of contributions transport us to the twenty-first century and the contemporary world. Christian Thrue Djurslev brings the music genre of heavy metal into the conversation. Heavy metal is an offspring of rock music, characterized by its clamorous sound, provocative counterculture, and aggressive machismo. In recent years, however, artists have embraced an ever more diverse cast of characters and stories from the ancient world, and Djurslev explores two receptions of the renowned Queen Tomyris, the "iron maiden", who first appeared in the historical narrative of the ancient Greek storyteller Herodotus (1.205-14). In the first case study, he considers the way in which Tomyris is represented as a national hero of Romania in the track "Tomiris", the first song on the album Naemul Dacilor (2016) by the folk metal band Ka Gaia An from Bucharest. In the second case study, he examines the representation of Tomyris as a powerful female ruler and fierce fighter in the track "Tomyris" released on the album *It was Metal* (2018) by the American band A Sound of Thunder. Both case studies investigate novel receptions that, taken together, say something significant about antiquity's polyvalence and heavy metal's polyphony in contemporary popular culture.

The popularity of classical myth in contemporary art has been increasing in recent decades, and Vinnie Nørskov discusses two different types of receptions in contemporary Danish art production. In the first part of her chapter, she analyses a popular television programme that follows a group of artists over two weeks. It provides insights into how artists choose and transform motifs and myths from classical antiquity into their own productions. In the second part, she focuses on the work of contemporary artists who have exhibited at the Museum of Ancient Art and Archaeology at Aarhus University since 2011. The museum's exhibition programme operates on an artist-driven approach, meaning that the museum does not actively invite artists, but rather that hosts propose exhibitions based on the participatory model of Nina Simon. Nørskov identifies classical myths as a significant focal point, emphasizing the strong transformative element that drives artists to reinterpret and engage with these myths in their own artistic practice. In her analysis, she sheds light on the motivations, processes, and transformations that characterize contemporary Danish artists' engagement with classical mythology. She thus shows the diverse ways in which classical myths become part of the contemporary artistic production in Denmark.

Edith Hall turns to the notable preoccupation of contemporary English authors with Homer's *Iliad* and endeavours to uncover the reasons behind its remarkable prominence.

While acknowledging recent historical and political factors, Hall asserts that the issue is far more complex. She highlights the recent resurgence of the text's overarching theme of continents in mortal combat. Also troubling is the text's nexus of war crimes, captivity, and migration. These focal points carry an ominous potential, a shared anticipation of an apocalyptic near future, and the looming threat of humanity's extinction. Hall discusses works by acclaimed authors, such as David Malouf, Alice Oswald, Madeline Miller, Bettany Hughes, Pat Parker, and Nathalie Haynes. Their engagements with Homer's poem are emulative, resistant, tonal, and self-consciously aesthetic – the four basic modes of reception identified by Hall. They make the *Illiad* a poem of the twenty-first century, or, as she concludes, "it's an ancient poem whose modern time has truly come".

As stated at the outset, the present volume contributes to our local series, and we the editors are grateful for all the support we have had from Sanne Lind Hansen at Aarhus University Press in bringing this latest instalment to completion. We are also very grateful to Taylor Grace FitzGerald for helping us with the editing. The publication has been made possible by generous grants from the Aarhus University Research Foundation and the Carlsberg Foundation, for which we are immensely grateful. The original conference was funded by the Carlsberg Foundation and various funding bodies in the departments and the School of Culture and Society, Aarhus University. We would also like to thank our fellow co-organizers of the conference: Marianne Pade, Isabelle Torrance, Troels Myrup Kristensen, and Jakob Engberg.

One person who is sadly no longer with us to thank in person is Jens Krasilnikoff. He died unexpectedly this spring. He was hired by Aarhus University in 1998 as an ancient historian and worked primarily on Greek history with a focus on agriculture, gender, and reception studies. A central area of his research and teaching was the use and reception of ancient Greece in historical films, a hugely popular subject among his students. Jens was in all respects a highly valued colleague and will be sorely missed by his immediate coworkers, as well as by the ancient history community in Denmark and abroad. He was one of the prime movers for organizing the conference in the first place, as well as one of the principal editors of the present volume. We hereby dedicate this book to his memory.

Christian Thrue Djurslev
Vinnie Nørskov
Aarhus, August 2024

2

WHAT'S BEHIND THE LABEL?

LORNA HARDWICK

If classicists are to make their full contribution to what Adorno has called "seriously working upon the past", then this publication and the conference that led to it give a crucial lead in asking us to re-examine and reflect on what may be understood by the term 'popular'. The multi-directional cultural agency offered through study of Greek and Roman antiquity and its reception has been opened up by the displacement of classics from its hegemonic position in education and in the historical understanding, critical thinking, and imagination of the wider public. Modes of encountering Greek and Roman material have been revolutionized. As a result, scholars are developing a range of strategies that recognize that practitioners, readers, and the wider public have a myriad of entry points into this rich field. When ancient cultures are recuperated into contemporary consciousness they once again, but in very different ways, contribute to understanding of the past and its roles in the construction of cultural memory, and also to perceptions of the present and aspirations about the future. Brooke Holmes has referred to a new *cosmopoiesis* (2016, 285). The Postclassicisms Collective has proclaimed the positive advantages of the dismantling of the "traditional supports" that actually restricted appreciation of what the study of antiquity has to offer (2020, 201). Jacques Bromberg has called for a "global" frame to the study of antiquity, emphasizing comparative analysis, ethics, and community engagement (Bromberg 2021, 1-15). Ngugi wa Thiong'o has discussed and advocated the role of translation and network theory in enabling and evaluating local and global interactions (Ngugi 2012, 60-62). Edith Hall has documented the importance of translations in providing a route into knowledge about antiquity (Hall 2008; see also Hardwick 2021a on adaptations). The challenge now is to bring forward new narratives that engage with the old, challenging weaknesses and recognising strengths. Doing this requires scholars to practise and promote subtlety of reading and discussion, and to recognize that 'popular' engagements between the public imagination and Greek and Roman material and its mediations are crucial not only to "working seriously on the past" but also to working seriously with the future.

One of the necessary starting points for that endeavour is a focus on the implications of key terms used in classical reception studies. Key terms – and 'popular' is one – encode imperatives about what participants should look for, in both content and medium. They direct the gaze and the intellectual and affective responses. Yet (or perhaps therefore), cultural historians are continually reconstructing and adapting these concepts. For instance, recent and current debates have revealed the cultural freight around use of the term 'Neo-Latin', as opposed to 'Early Modern Latin'. Another example is the tension between the designations 'classical tradition' and 'classical reception'. Indeed, the terms 'classics' and 'classical' are themselves increasingly perceived as problematic. I think that the term 'popular' requires similar attention.

Key terms often operate as labels, carrying with them assumptions about cultural value and appropriate epistemology, which in turn governs methodology. Key terms reflect and shape the questions that are considered to be worth asking and the means of tackling them. The study of Greek and Roman antiquity throughout the centuries has largely focused on extant sources, both written and material, that were created by and for an elite – that has become a conventional wisdom.[1] People who have inherited that conventional wisdom have also inherited its perspectives and terminology. The study of popular culture in the modern world includes attention to the specific impact of modern technologies and new genres, from print to film to computer games. Further questions then arise concerning how these select and situate material from antiquity, and how they might act as a conduit and shaper of its transmission into the public imagination. In terms of relationships with antiquity, a focus on the 'popular' in contemporary culture is sometimes seen as a counterbalance, even an antidote, to perceptions of antiquity that have been skewed by restricted routes for transmission and labelling in elite contexts.

Shifts in terminology are markers of deeper cultural and geopolitical shifts. The development of theories and methods for investigating popular culture within antiquity and in its subsequent reception therefore deserves scrutiny both on its own account and for its place in a wider dynamic. For example, as fellow contributors and other colleagues have shown in their research and publication, ancient epic, drama, and mythology were part of a broad-based culture; Greek tragedy and comedy were part of the community culture associated with and refined by democracy (but a democracy that excluded women, slaves, and non-citizens from its deliberations). In the history of the reception of Greek and Roman material, particular texts, images, and ideas have moved in and out of mainstream and sub-cultures at different times. Recent research on the relationship between ancient culture and, for example, nineteenth-century burlesque; film in the twentieth and twenty-first centuries; animations and comics; and poetry gigs indicates that rigid polarization of 'popular' culture and 'elite' culture is misleading.[2] It is rather that modern cultural phenomena are broad-based in terms of participation and audience/spectator cohorts. They are also multi-faceted in how the creators and the

---

[1] How an elite is defined, and by whom, and how it is constituted, and by whom, is of course another thorny question. It is not the main concern of this essay, but the problem usefully reminds us of the pitfalls of setting up a straw-man 'other' against which to define and promote our own concerns.

[2] For discussion of how classical material in burlesque actually brought together ante-texts, myth, and new genres in leisure activities that included different social classes, see Hall & Macintosh 2005, especially chs 10-15. Similar points could be adduced in respect of modern comics and computer games.

participants conceive and understand the relationship between ancient and contemporary. The 'dark side' of this aspect has been probed in the analysis of appropriation of Greek and Roman material by imperial, fascist, and other totalitarian regimes.

Researchers have analyzed some of the ways in which modern media have selected and deployed Greek and Roman material for mass audiences and for 'niche' users. As is usual with new-ish areas of research and teaching, emphasis tends to be on case studies (and I know that many of the chapters in the present publication will supply detailed analysis and discussion of key examples). These case studies in their turn influence scholarship, theoretical frames, and the key terms used in further research and in teaching. In a short essay I cannot hope to do justice to the acuity of these investigations. Instead, I shall try to stand back and identify some key areas that may provoke debate and which will need to be tested through scholarly practice. This aim involves attention both to 'framing' (how patterns are constructed and interpreted) and to 'experience' (how people actually access and interact with Graeco-Roman antiquity, the ways in which it is presented to them, and the contexts in which they reflect on it). The scope of 'framing' and the agency it delivers have been helpfully summarized by Maarten De Pourcq, Nathalie de Haan, and David Rijser:

> Framing refers to the set of terms, paradigms, theories or frames of reference according to which we reflect and speak when we are teaching, doing research or criticizing. It defines the sort of questions that we ask and the ways in which we try to find answers to them. The term 'framing' points to the importance of 'perspectives', of the stances taken when considering any material …. 'Framing' implies an awareness of relativity: to assess the value of our findings, it is important to be conscious of the identity of our position, our collaborators and intended public. (De Pourcq et al. 2020, 1)

One of the major aims of this chapter, therefore, is to probe the range of associations, in academia and beyond, that are triggered by the term 'popular', both in itself *and* in its elasticity when it is linked to Graeco-Roman antiquity, the associated scholarship and receptions, and the cultural phenomena that all of these generate. In particular, I want to question rigid polarizations of 'high' and 'popular' culture in the creative and scholarly practices involved in the reception of antiquity. I shall also try to show how rigid distinctions between 'inside' and 'outside' the academy can be problematic. By discussing some so-called 'key' terms in the light of specific examples I hope to reveal some elements of the infrastructure that underlies how 'labels' are constructed and disseminated – by whom, for whom, with what purpose, and with what effect over time. I hope that this approach not only suggests some critical tools for the study of antiquity and its reception but also opens the way for the perhaps urgent resetting of teaching and research, so that they take account of new situations and insights. Such analysis requires probing of the layers and lateral dynamics that constitute 'thick' receptions. Among the helpful recent scholarship on this aspect is *Deep Classics: Rethinking Classical Reception*, edited by Shane Butler. In his introduction, Butler proposes that the multi-layered processes involved in reception studies – processes that involve reading and thinking laterally and well as temporally – constitute a "deep exploration – and, when needed, a close interrogation – of our whole discipline's raison d'être" (Butler 2016, 16).[3]

The recent context for the discipline of classics as a whole has sometimes been precarious. Much attention has been paid to pressures on teaching and research, and to the unwillingness of some universities to continue teaching classical subjects and/or their desire to remove advanced language study from the undergraduate curriculum. Sometimes this has led to mergers of departments in the arts and humanities; sometimes it is the arts and humanities themselves that have been under threat. Furthermore, within and beyond institutions, classics has been discredited by association (real and imagined) with exclusive social and political elites and with the ideologies of modern empire. Responses to this situation within academia have varied from the constructive to the pessimistic, but in many cases have embraced changes in the curriculum and aspired to broaden constituencies of students. It is salutary to note the wise comments of the editors of a recently published collection of essays on crises and recovery in antiquity: "the crisis of one group can be the desirable 'normal' of another. Crises do not simply happen, but are in large part created when influential actors decide to present an event or a state of affairs as such. When such labelling is successful, the target audience will experience the events affecting them as a crisis" (Klooster & Kuin 2020, 3). The subtitle of the book concerned is *Remembrance, Re-anchoring and Recovery*, all of which are emotive and complex concepts, intensively researched by classical reception scholars and beyond.

If notions such as 'crisis', 'watershed', 'recovery', and 'receptivity' are in themselves aspects of 'framing', it follows that the times, places, and contexts of use need further examination. Analysis may even point to dynamic 'hot spots' in which particular texts and themes from antiquity converge with contemporary experiences and aspirations, resulting in heightened receptivity to particular issues and particular texts that may even assist in the recuperation of classical studies (Hardwick 2018a; 2021b). Recent examples include the focus on Sophocles' tragedy *Antigone* and its receptions, translations, and adaptations in mainstream and community theatre in Ireland, especially in the context of the Troubles (Torrance 2020; and more generally the essays in Mee & Foley 2011), and the re-awakening of interest in the historian Thucydides in the contexts of modern international relations theory and responses to conflict within nations (Lee & Morley 2015).[4]

In my initial pairing of 'framing' and 'experience', I mentioned the importance of interaction. Brett Rogers and Benjamin Stevens focused on this in the introduction to their 2015 edited collection *Classical Traditions in Science Fiction*. They were well aware that the introduction of options in modern science fiction writing and film into the

---

3   Richardson 2019 broadens this perspective by investigating 'Classics on the Edge'.
4   There are many similar examples. For instance, 2004 became known as 'the year of the Hecubas' because of the number of different productions of Euripides' play, often interpreted in the context of the wars and civic violence in the Balkans and the ways in which this fed into cultures of revenge (Hardwick 2022).

undergraduate classical receptions curriculum might be regarded by cynics as a way of getting 'bums on seats', and even of indulging fan culture among lecturers. Rogers and Stephens tackled this head-on by asking three fundamental questions: How might a comparative study of ancient classics and modern science fiction proceed? Could there be more at the intersection of these two seemingly disparate fields than a few signal texts – beyond individual stars, were there whole galaxies awaiting discovery? Above all, could such a comparative study be put on a firm conceptual or theoretical basis so that research could move beyond mere 'scopophilia', Freud's term for a love of looking that is pleasing but ultimately pointless (Rogers & Stevens 2015, vii). They went on to propose that "ancient classics and modern science fiction have in common a deep epistemological similarity, that is in how each imagines the basic functioning of human knowledge". They suggested that the joint study of classics and science fiction facilitates awareness and analysis of both the fictional future and the undiscovered past, an enmeshment that raises urgent ethical and epistemological questions about the relationship of the humanities, science, and technology, including whether technoscientific understanding of the world should be allowed to shape or even replace deliberative philosophy (Rogers & Stevens 2015, 7-9).

These three examples from recent scholarship point unequivocally to the potential of classics and 'popular' culture (ancient and modern) as interlocutors in the experiential, ethical, and epistemological fabric of the humanities. In the next section of the discussion, I briefly consider some possible implications of the concept 'popular'.

I hinted above that simply distinguishing between inside and outside academia does not provide a secure site for discussing the relationship between 'popular' and 'scholarly', although mapping the growing dynamics of exchange between the two does reveal illuminating material (see Hall in this volume). Within academia, the shorthand 'popular' can refer to choices made about teaching texts, to experimentation with methods of analysis, and to the development of research initiatives. Academics, increasingly, figure in the media not just as 'public intellectuals' or 'advisors' but as presenters, commentators, and creative practitioners. When Greek and Roman material becomes better known and more 'popular' in the wider world, the process can refer to a range of aspects, from simplistic and cynical (mis)readings and appropriations to catalysts for creativity and the transformation of the public imagination. Public outreach is increasingly a means through which academics strive to recuperate the texts and contexts of antiquity, mining ancient popular culture to build bridges between antiquity and modern culture. There is rich material on which to draw – drama festivals, Aristophanes' plays, Roman comedy, debate and decision-making in the Athenian Assembly, and public rituals such as funerals. The feedback loops operate in both directions. It is especially worth noting that the receptions of antiquity mediated through newer media are not necessarily more or less 'popular' on that account, and their place on the spectrum between 'elite' and niche' may change over time. Film, for example, provides an interesting range from silent film ('popular' culture at the time of its first appearance and now a specialized area of study; see Michelakis & Wyke 2013) through to art films (Michelakis 2013), 'sword and sandals' blockbusters that have been box-office hits (Wyke 1997; Paul 2013; and in this volume), film poems for TV and cinema (Byrne 2022), and radio broadcasts (Wrigley 2015).[5] The ways and situations in which a subliminal or understated awareness of Greek and Roman antiquity can function as an almost unacknowledged touchstone corresponds to the 'low intensity' model that has been used to characterize the grey areas across and between spheres of cultural frameworks and confessional identities. These grey areas may carry implications of membership of a community or simply point to a shared cultural repository of allusions and metaphors, without implying that these bear the added freight of political affiliation or theological or academic orthodoxy. This 'soft', even 'passive' recognition of cultural hinterlands is often referred to as 'low-intensity' awareness and does not imply assent to an ontological or epistemological basis. However, 'low-intensity' adherence or complicity does serve to underpin processes and practices that can, in certain circumstances, become 'high intensity', either because they are perceived to be central to the material, emotional, or imaginative world of an individual or group, or because they resonate with heightened receptivity and sensibility in particular times and places. When there is conscious awareness of this material, and especially when it is accompanied by valorization of its authority and significance, the level rises to 'high intensity'.[6] This transformation can be brought about through interaction between personal and group experience and response to externally generated stimuli, including deployment of classical material.

By way of further ground-clearing, therefore, it is necessary to distinguish between 'popular' and 'populist'. 'Popular' establishes common ground for experience, communication, and imagination inside and outside academia and at its best has a multi-directional transformative effect. 'Populist' attitudes and practices tend to undervalue (or reject) this richness, and sometimes positively attack cultural relationships that reach across the constructed markers of class, ethnicity, gender, language, and religion. It would be tempting, but too easy, however, to omit mention of one extreme aspect of populist activity – the appropriation of Greek and Roman figures and themes as embodiments and justifications of hate language and violence.[7]

The website *Pharos*, based at Vassar, has been at the centre of the identification and rebuttal of appropriations of classical figures and myths by hate groups (https://pharos.vassarspace.net). *Pharos* has three main aims: to document examples of the appropriation of Greek and Roman culture by hate groups (for example for purposes of white supremacy, misogyny, antisemitism, violence, and terrorism); to expose the fundamental weakness of these appropriations; and to provide a locus for people who wish to resist

---

5   Michelakis 2013, 6-9, discusses the diversity of models in terms of their aesthetic, public, and economic reach.
6   Eidinow 2019a and 2019b discuss this in relation to religion, but the model can accommodate a range of cultural memes and agencies.
7   Vandiver 2022 discusses the modern context of right-wing nationalist movements in the USA as a prelude to her analysis of the pitfalls facing modern translators of key excerpts from Herodotus, in which ancient and modern meanings and associations of violence and racial and sexual abuse may vary.

them and to problematise them. The *Pharos* team also recognizes that such appropriations not only distort and misrepresent but may also draw on authentic aspects of the Graeco-Roman past that are congenial to hate-orientated polemic in the present – for example, ancient xenophobic practices, misogyny, hypermasculinity, violent imperialism, and antisemitism. The discussions on the site also recognize that these aspects of antiquity sometimes reappear in mainstream outlets that involve receptions of antiquity, such as film (*300*; *Gladiator*).[8] By providing teaching resources and the opportunity for debate, *Pharos* also aims to serve the needs of educators who wish to make students aware that the traditional idealization of the Graeco-Roman past overlaps with white supremacist and misogynistic interpretation of the past, use of its emblems, and other associations.[9] These cannot be ignored and are not the only objectionable threads in the relationship between antiquity and modern popular culture.[10] They are the dark underbelly to the better-known histories of appropriation of antiquity by ruling hegemonies.[11]

In recuperating ancient popular culture into discussions about modern receptions of antiquity, I also want to avoid the temptation to elide 'popular' and 'democratic'. Instead, I will be drawing on the associations between 'democratic' and 'deliberative' – in the sense that both the classical ante-texts themselves and the modern receptions are subject to readings and interpretations that are contested and may vary in content and emphasis over time, as well as between places, contexts, and languages. Equally important, I am not drawing an artificial polarity between 'popular' and 'elite' culture (which, although it may carry varying associations, is not necessarily 'unpopular' and may actually be an aspirational target, as discussed in Hardwick 2015a). To do so would not only be misleading conceptually; it would also close down discussion of important aspects of contemporary changes in cultural hegemonies and the role in these of attitudes in Greek and Roman antiquity and its receptions. Indeed, the associations between Greek and Roman culture, its receptions, and modern cultural and political hegemonies have been tested to the point at which they are no longer hegemonic.[12] However, there is invariably a gap, sometimes a very long one, between tectonic cultural shifts and public awareness. When I use the term 'The Label' in the title of this chapter, I refer to

---

8   Selection, stereotyping, and the impact of modern cultures of 'stardom' may be intertwined. The box-office success of these cultural artefacts may be aligned with moments of heightened receptivity to themes and situations derived from antiquity. In the process a 'low-intensity' public awareness of classical material may be transformed into a 'high-intensity' impact, which is damaging both to understanding of antiquity and to modern social attitudes.

9   The summary of aims is taken from the *Pharos* website. The *Pharos* project was also launched on the *Eidolon* website, which includes some of the resulting comments and blogs (*Eidolon.pub*).

10 Hardwick 2021b discusses some issues classicists and ancient historians have in getting to grips with the ancient past and the histories of its receptions, including the positive and negative aspects of identity scholarship.

11 See further Nelis 2011; Van Steen 2015; Roche 2021.

12 I recently discussed some of these issues at the Gramsci Network conference *Democratizing Classics*. My paper 'Cultural Hegemonies: Subaltern Agency through Greek and Roman Texts' has been made available on You Tube and as a heavily revised published version Hardwick 2024a).

the terms used by scholars that seep into the public imagination, and the terms used by practitioners, media, journalists, and the person in the pub that seep into the work of scholars. These labels may provide headers but they are not uncontested definitions. They are shaped by and carry with them the infrastructures from which they grew – as James Porter has put it: "Histories of words can only take us so far …. What histories of words and concepts reveal is at best the history of struggles over definition …. More significant than words and the concepts they name are the patterns of logic that underlie the deployment of both" (Porter 2006, 13). Porter was referring to the problematic notion of 'the classical'. Narrowing the lens on that huge field includes focusing on the nexus between Greek and Roman antiquity and its reception in popular culture. This brings into play the relationships between agencies of different kinds and origins, including in antiquity, through mediating contexts and in the contemporary world. All of these include triangularities of authors/practitioners (who are also readers), readers in various contexts and times, and scholars (who are also readers and may be authors). Therefore, to the logic of relationships to which Porter rightly refers must be added the range and density of material and the changing lenses through which it is generated and approached.

The next section of my discussion focuses on three guiding concepts that I take to be indicative of the deliberative aspects of the reception of popular culture: narratives; subtlety; and connections. For each, I sketch briefly why I think they are important for the relationship between ancient and modern and then suggest how they might usefully be explored. The underlying link between these three areas is 'mediation', which includes not only 'medium and media' in the technical sense but also the entire processes of negotiating, transmitting with revisions, adaptations, accretions, and transplantations across times, places, and languages. Those processes constitute a new ground on which similarities and differences meet. I follow up the conceptual discussion by looking briefly at three different examples that provide 'test' sites.

1. Narratives

Here is an extract from a discussion by Katherine Harloe:

> Stories about the classical past continue to shape contemporary cultural, political and social ideas and practices; consequently, there is a role for critical questioning of those stories … a 'democratic' researcher ought to be committed to using his or her authority to complicate those stories, widen their cast of characters, and open up debates over their meaning, rather than to close them down. (Harloe 2013, 12)

Harloe's point highlights the need to be aware of different kinds of 'narrative' that can be put alongside and challenge the traditionally hegemonic ones about Greek and Roman societies and values, and about how these relate to subsequent societies. Her analysis is reflected in the theoretical frames and detailed content of recent investigations about the connections between classical studies and newer and ongoing research in areas such as fugitive studies, nomadology, travel and frontiers, border theory, and colonially imposed differences. One way of creating new narratives is to use the ancient material as a springboard for new material, perhaps filling in gaps and envoicing those who have been excluded – good examples in popular fiction are Pat Barker's novels *The Silence of the Girls* (2018) and *The Women of Troy* (2021). The former is a response to the silencing of the young women used as pawns in the quarrels between the heroes in Homer's *Iliad*, while the latter explores the afterlives of the Trojan women who became spoils of war. However, for this chapter I have chosen a different path and will instead consider how material drawn from antiquity is folded in to create new narratives, not only about the ancient material but also about the receiving culture.

Traditional 'narratives' about classical texts, scholarship, and classical studies in general often include value-laden generalizations, that can pass unexamined into public perceptions. Examples include the ideas that: classical texts were produced by an elite for an elite and exclude the voices of women, subalterns, and workers; any study of classical material, including its receptions, inevitably embeds the same power structures; Homer is a poet of war; Pericles was a democratic leader of a culturally enlightened empire; and the poets of the First World War were classically educated and deployed figures and motifs from Homer and Horace to glorify death in battle. I could go on to list more, but you will recognize the pattern and can add your own examples. These generalizations are of different kinds but they have in common that although they contain elements of truth, they lack subtlety and they often assume a direct connection, unmediated comparison, or mutual applicability between ancient and modern. Therefore, my next question is: How can subtlety be recognized and communicated?

2. Subtlety

In a recent publication, Karin Harrasser posed the question "Can subtlety be depicted?" (Harrasser 2020, 168). The context was visual representation, but the notion applies to various kinds of representation and communication. Harrasser points out that 'subtle' is derived from the literal 'subtextilis' (from the Latin *texere*), something that is delicately woven or plaited under something else. This has multi-directional implications. The two most notable for my purposes are for the analysis of texts themselves – their warp and weft, their density of content and implication, their networks of construction and possible meaning, and their many points of entry. Digging beneath the surface text then leads to layers of mediations that have come into play in the intervening centuries: creative works, scholarly analyses, and readerly interpretations. Not all agents in these processes will be aware of how the material that comes to them, and their own insights on it, have been refined and elaborated. Receptions work forwards and backwards and sideways, not always in temporally tidy ways.

A collection of essays edited by Pantelis Michelakis (to which Harrasser was a contributor), *Classics and Media Theory* (2020), addresses these issues through examination of media. In his thought-provoking introduction, Michelakis discusses what is involved in the notion and processes of 'mediation', a central concept for classical reception studies. His overview is highly relevant to the overall theme of the present publication, since it analyses the impact in the digital era of new technologies and media that have been developed since antiquity. In addition, in offering a perspective on the relationships in the three-pronged approach of 'narratives', 'subtlety', and 'connections', Michelakis' discussion neatly expresses how:

> the media of and around Greece and Rome can be situated discursively on a spectrum … they can be celebrated and demonized, fetishized and commodified, politicized and moralized, gendered, and infused with nostalgia …. Reflections on the multiplicity of media as channels, languages, or environments can be sought in the metaphors of poetic composition as craftsmanship that abound in Greco-Roman poetry; in the political, financial, and social networks for the reproduction and dissemination of artistic works and values …. [Media] can also shape the presence and enduring worth of different cultural forms and practices in ways that are not always foregrounded. (Michelakis 2020, 6-7)

In my discussion, media and mediation are core aspects, both in reception and in scoping what may be regarded as 'popular'. In the next section, I look at how subtle connections can be made and read, at how these may suggest different narratives, and at some of the implications for scholarship. Analysis of the subtleties of mediation and reception requires 'thick' analysis, both of texts and in scholarship.

3. Making Connections[13]

Of course, Gallipoli is not Tomis or vice versa. But between these two poles, poetry can make its own connections. (Balmer 2009, xiv)

Thus Josephine Balmer wrote of how her receptions of Ovid's poetry of exile were folded into her own poetic response to the experience of a local soldier in the First World War.

The capacity of poets and readers to "make connections" provides the rationale for the development of new types of commentary which aim to reflect the differences in

---

13 This section draws on some of the material in preparation for *Oxford Classical Reception Commentaries* (edited by Lorna Hardwick, Stephen Harrison, and Elizabeth Vandiver). *OCRC* is a long-term digital and print project which aims to develop annotated commentaries on modern receptions of classical texts, using digital links to texts in the original languages, to literatures in English, and to textual and visual paramaterial. *OCRC* involves some bold and experimental scholarship in order to produce commentaries that take account of the different ways in which subsequent writers accessed Greek and Roman material and also to map the different perspectives and knowledge bases brought by modern readers who read ancient and modern texts in the light of one another. To further this aim an extended taxonomy is being developed. See further, Hardwick, Harrison and Vandiver 2024a, 7-13 & 2024b, 12-18.

range and intensity of the types of connection brought to the material by writers, readers, and scholars.[14]

The outline taxonomy included below helps to indicate the range of possible connections with Greek and Latin texts. Different forms of agency come into play – some connections might be 'seeded' by the ancient author; some noticed and developed by subsequent writers; and some brought or activated by readers of either or both texts. Not all categories of connection will be equally applicable to all authors – the differences and the reasons for these are likely to be illuminating.[15]

Allusion

Historically, many classicists have adopted an approach to reading receptions of classical texts that is based on analysing allusions and their role in the relationships between different poems (ancient and modern). This approach usually privileges the ancient author and implies that the formal and lexical aspects of a poem 'carry' a meaning that was in some sense intended, although scholars such as Stephen Hinds have emphasized that this type of analysis should not close down possibilities of pluralities of meaning (Hinds 1998, ch. 2). Allusion-based approaches also privilege the skills, education, and knowledge of the reader, who is expected to 'pick up' the allusions, whether they are openly signalled or subtly placed beneath the surface meaning (or both).

Any allusion-based analysis has to operate with a number of possible relationships, from direct allusion to allusion mediated through other texts and traditions (in the source language; in the language of the reception text; in other languages; through quotation in the original language or in translation). Indirect allusions might be tagged as indirect either because they have travelled through multiple mediations or because they hang on a cultural emblem, rather than a specific literary text, and therefore need to be recontextualized (for example Achilles as hero; Dido as deserted lover; Aeneas as the founder of a new nation).

Allusion that goes beyond a simple 'name-dropping' of a cultural figure or emblem is usually referred to as *intertextuality*, that is, moving across and between texts. Intertextuality can also involve moving between ancient texts, mediating texts, and texts

---

14 Stead 2022, x, usefully draws attention to the ways in which 'learned' and 'popular' allusions and resonances can work together in a particular text. Hardwick 2011 offers and introductory discussion.

15 The poetry of Isaac Rosenberg provides one important 'test site' for how far the taxonomy might stretch, in order to accommodate both the nuances of his poetry and the 'deep classics' that goes beyond acknowledged intertextuality. Rosenberg was not classically educated. He was a private soldier from a very poor background who accessed the ancient authors through reading translations and through mediations in English literature. He used classical allusions and motifs to complicate simple certainties and narratives of war and in so doing made a distinctive contribution to two rather different aspects of First World War poetry – the poetics of unease and of survival. See further, pp 27-29 below.

that are less obviously classically orientated but which are part of the literary tradition of the new writer.

Reader-response theory, for its part, has extended the agency of the reader in making connections. Readers may bring to the poem echoes and interpretations that are grounded in other texts familiar to the reader but not necessarily known to the original writer (including texts which may have been produced later). For example, twenty-first-century classicists would find it impossible to teach Horace *Odes* 3.2 without the intervention of Wilfred Owen's poem 'Dulce et decorum est'.

Intratextuality refers to connections made by the poet either within a *poem* or between it and other texts in the writer's oeuvre. Intratextuality often operates alongside intertextuality, enhancing the writer's self-referentiality and highlighting metalepsis.

These predominantly text-based connections imply a fairly detailed knowledge of the ancient texts by subsequent writers and their readers. The scholarship of classical receptions in popular culture should enlarge this taxonomy. Here are some possibilities:

Affinities: Affinity contributes to connection. The writer helps readers to feel empathy for the text and for its antecedents, as well as for other readers, possibly through the use of familiar vernacular terms or situations. For example, in his letters from the Front Isaac Rosenberg discussed the affinity between Aeschylus and himself because as serving soldiers both would have encountered lice (referred to by the Herald in *Agamemnon*).

Associations: The writer can build associative triggers into a poem to create for the reader a means of bridging ancient and modern; equally the reader can bring associations that are activated by contemporary language and situations. Sometimes associations imply parallel situations that cross times and places (for example war, death, love, loss, and motifs or tropes that recur in many literatures – for example the association between death in battle and the hanging motif of the poppy, from Homer's simile on the death of Gorgythion in *Iliad* 8 to the poppies Flanders that were assimilated into the iconography of remembrance). Sometimes apparently disparate experiences can be brought into association by a metaphor, simile, or key word that triggers an ongoing sequence of associations.

Associations of place are sometimes linked with the development of a sense of affinity. This is an important aspect of First World War poetry, especially by writers immersed in Greek literature. It is evident in the links drawn by soldiers voyaging to Gallipoli with places in the Homeric poems, and their location in the Greek islands and on the Trojan plain. Modern readers may respond readily to such associations because of their own travel experiences (see the discussion of Heaney's poem below, pp 29-30).

Glancing: This is a term for a brief encounter in which neither text is absorbed into the other but they touch briefly, perhaps through a shared word or experience, and then go their separate ways, although readers' understanding of both may be affected. In creative terms, one analogy is with the tangent to a circle – its velocity takes it away from the circle but they nevertheless touch. Another analogy with glancing is with a sideways look that notices briefly, but quickly resumes its main focus. In poetic terms, 'glancing' can imply an apparently off-the-cuff reference that also involves a subtle steer to the reader or listener to notice something that might otherwise have passed them by. So 'glancing' actually has effects on the poem, on the reader, and even on the onward trajectory of the apparently extraneous partner which is deflected in the encounter. Alice Oswald's May Lecture "Sidelong Glances" in her *Oxford Professor of Poetry Series* (27 May 2021) discussed how literature has "a back door". She identified aurality and orality (often exemplified by subaltern groups such as women and ethnically marginalized groups) as rich sources of unexpected ways into a poem. Oswald's 'glancing' is a lateral and associative movement, allowing poetry to be made from a patchwork of remarks and voices, rather than it being a link in a great chain of literary development. She used the technique in her 2011 work *Memorial*, in which she aimed to translate the atmosphere of the *Iliad* to give status to those killed who were not accorded an *aristeia* in Homer (Oswald 2011, 1-2).

Ghosting: This term is used to point to traces of an ancient text that survive into the subsequent reception but lie dormant, lurking beneath the surface and the readers' understanding until they rise, perhaps only to recede again. More formally, many receptions of Greek and Roman poetry use literary devices such as *katabasis* to activate these traces, both materially and metaphorically. Wilfred Owen's WW1 poem 'Strange Meeting' is an example of both aspects, as in different ways is Derek Walcott's *Omeros* (1990).

Improvising and riffing: These are critical terms borrowed from music. They describe how a modern writer may take a theme or passage from an ancient author and work with it, exploring its creative possibilities and variations before returning to the base theme.

Metalepsis: Metalepsis has been deployed as a concept in modern narratological scholarship to indicate how writers signal their own presence in the text and even directly highlight their intervention as narrators. Metalepsis is also a useful lens for examining the presence and direct interpretative agency of the author in classical receptions of poetry that are not confined to extended narrative. Sometimes the author appears in person, for instance Isaac Rosenberg in 'Break of Day in the Trenches' implants himself and his perspective into the scene (text in Noakes 2008, 106). However, metalepsis is not always indicated by the use of the first person 'I' – Christopher Logue in his *War Music* apostrophizes, addressing the reader as though he himself were a film director, and in this way directs the reader's gaze and imagination (Logue 2015, 9). Once readers are brought into the poem in this way, they can have a role in shaping how the story is perceived (see further Matzner & Trimble 2020, ch. 1).

Trace is a critical term used in two senses, as a verb and as a noun. As a verb it denotes ways in which a critic investigates and maps how a writer works and how connections are made. As a noun it denotes elements of other texts and of ways of looking identified by the critic, or a new writer, or a new reader, that persist into the new work. These residual elements may seem disconnected but also provide raw material for making new connections and questioning assumed ones.

The distinction between narratives, subtlety, and connections is a starting point rather than a *telos*. The most interesting classical receptions draw on each of these concepts, although in varying proportions and emphases. However, by way of 'test and experiment' for my model, here are three examples of receptions that illustrate the varied possible scope and realization of the label 'popular'. Each starts from one of the three nodal concepts but also, in different ways, embraces the others:

1. Narrative: Thucydides, *History of the Peloponnesian War*

Thucydides' *History* – composed on the basis of his experiences of the war between the Athenians and the Spartans and their respective allies in the second half of the fifth century BCE and its political and social repercussions – has generated multiple strands of reception in public life (Lee & Morley 2015, which has extensive bibliographies). These receptions extend far beyond historiographical writing and include shaping the theory and practices of internal politics and international relations, informing the curriculum in military and strategic academies, and contributing to media discussion of contemporary events and debates, for example on modes of leadership, concepts of democracy and empire, national and international strategies, civil strife, attitudes to citizenship and non-citizens, participation in institutions, and decision-making. Standout episodes in Thucydides have also crossed the boundaries between specialized political and military groups and provided the basis for wider debates in the media. The Plague narrative, the Mytilene Debate, the Melian Dialogue, the Periclean *Epitaphios* Funeral Speech on the occasion of the communal rites for the war dead, the departure of the Sicilian Expedition and its fate, the *stasis* (civil strife) in Corcyra, and the erosion of the democratic system in Athens have all functioned as touchstones. In addition, the Athenian *strategos* Pericles, in particular, has become an iconic symbol of the aristocrat who became a populist leader, was deposed and fined but returned to power, continuing to be associated with the adornment of public buildings financed by the spoils of the Athenian *arche* (empire). Once brought into the domain of modern public debate, some Thucydidean subtleties either fail to enter public consciousness or are marginalized.

In the aftermath of the invasion of Iraq by a US-led coalition of Western powers in 2003, public intellectuals and commentators drew on the episodes and paradigms in Thucydides, sometimes to advocate particular policies but more often to foster public consciousness. One example was the rehearsed reading of extracts from Thucydides presented at the Novello Theatre in Aldwych, London, on 12 February 2006, a Sunday afternoon, organized by the dramaturg and theatre director John Barton in collaboration with the Royal Shakespeare Company.[16] Thucydides' text contains little overt metalep-

---

16 Published text: *The War that Still goes on* (Barton 2006). The occasion is discussed in detail in Hardwick 2015.

sis but the power of the authorial voice was communicated by the actor who voiced Thucydides, sitting at a side-desk that conveyed his status as author/commentator. There was an audience of some five hundred people, including classicists, political scientists, and a wide constituency of members of the public interested in current affairs. Many seemed to have little previous detailed knowledge of Thucydides and there were frequent loud gasps of amazement, sometimes leading to shouts of assent. The theatricality of the event was followed by a discussion panel of scholars with specialisms in ancient history, the Middle East, Iran, law, and broadcasting. In this way, performative and deliberative aspects of Thucydides were intertwined, although the selection of the extracts and the use of modern idioms that triggered audience responses sometimes veered towards a narrow didactic function rather than fulfilling deliberative aims. The event did, however, construct a narrative that related ancient and modern experiences of war, the extent of citizen involvement in decision-making and fighting, the multiple causes and strategic aims of war, the relationship between external power and internal political competition, and the implications regarding loss of life, destruction of communities and the material environment, civic instability, and the longer-term effects of fear and desire for revenge. This particular example managed to move material in Thucydides outside academia and into the wider public domain, while presenting enough of the complexity and the arguments to prevent 'popular' sliding into 'populist'.

2. Subtlety: Isaac Rosenberg

There are several reasons why Rosenberg is especially interesting in a study of the inadvisability of polarizing popular culture and other types of classical receptions. First there is his own background – immigrant, poor, object of antisemitism (in his war service, from critics such as Ezra Pound, and from potential publishers). Unlike other First World War poets such as Rupert Brooke, Charles Sorley, and to a limited extent Wilfred Owen, Rosenberg did not have even a basic classical education. He was an autodidact who read Homer and Aeschylus in translation. He enlisted and served as a private soldier in the First World War (to get an allowance for his mother, which she then did not receive). Second, there is the paradox that the poetry of the First World War, much of it published after the war, was influential in the popular imagination, both in terms of influencing attitudes to the war and in embedding cultural emblems in memorials and nostalgic narratives. It also prompted counter-narratives that challenged the notion that the war was an heroic national enterprise. Third, Rosenberg, the autodidact, produced a number of outstanding poems which are distinctive for combining traces of classical and biblical texts in a multi-layered 'thick' poetics that is both immediately accessible to readers who may not be aware of the sources of the allusions, and that also repays classical reception analysis.

Isaac Rosenberg lived from 1890 to 1918, when he was killed in France on the night of 31 March/1 April. He was born in Bristol to an immigrant family from Lithuania. They were poor Jewish refugees who moved to the east end of London in 1897, partly in the hope of improving his educational opportunities. Rosenberg's father had a rabbinic education and Rosenberg's early poetry shows that he was steeped in the images and poetry of the Hebrew Bible.[17] Rosenberg's grounding in Hebrew poetry provides significant comparative insights in analysis of the Greek and Roman material that he threads into his war poetry, and which becomes dominant at key points.

'Dead Man's Dump' was composed by May 1917 and published in 1922. It is a fine example of the subtle multi-valency of pivotal words and images. The poem narrates the experiences of soldiers who had to take wire up to the front line at night and whose wagons (or *limbers*) then returned on a rough track that was littered with the dead and dying. Rosenberg had been transferred to the Royal Engineers in January 1917 and wiring was among their duties, so the poem was written out of his lived experience as a private soldier.

The intertextualities in the poem are of three main kinds: biblical, Homeric, and with literature in English (both predecessors and contemporary). The specifically classical referents are mainly Homeric. They occur at nodal points in the narrative and mark shifts of narrative voice and perspective in the poem. Pivotal motifs include ambrosia, wheels, a pyre (with funerary associations), and grass/earth. All of these work together to create an implicit contrast between the treatment of the dead soldiers and the contemporary stereotypes about the glorious deaths of heroes at Troy that underlay some of the early poetry of the First World War.[18]

Lines 34-35 of the poem refer to the unthinking optimism of soldiers that they will escape death "as on ichor fed". Ichor was the ambrosia flowing in the veins of the gods in Greek mythology. The fallacy of that hope is intensified by the images of wheels and fire – the soldiers, alive and dead, are flung on the "shrieking pyre" (line 32), in a travesty of the funerary ritual for dead heroes in Homer. The dominant allusion underlying the motif of the wheels driving over the dead (lines 62-79) is to the sequence in Homer's *Iliad* when the body of the Trojan hero Hector is defiled by being attached to the wheels of Achilles' chariot and dragged round the battlefield outside the walls of Troy in the sight of his mother (Homer, *Iliad* XXII, 395-440). In contrast with the lumbering wagon in Rosenberg's poem, Achilles' horses were whipped into a gallop and "A cloud of dust rose where Hektor was dragged, his dark hair was falling / about him and all that head that was once so handsome was tumbled / in the dust". Only through the intervention of Apollo was Hector's body not irredeemably mutilated and destroyed. *Iliad* XXIV lines 18-23 recount how the dead man was to be thrown down

---

[17] According to Noakes 2008, Rosenberg probably read the English translation of the Old Testament in the Authorised Version of 1611 (the 'King James' Bible, which had lexical and tonal influence on the diction, metaphors, and motifs of subsequent literatures in English).

[18] The text of the poem is in Noakes 2008, 113-16, together with an image of an early pencil draft (Rosenberg's trench poetry was written in battle conditions). Noakes 2008, xxviii-xxx discusses earlier editions of Rosenberg's work and the difficulties of retrieving, dating and preserving the mss. She also discusses editorial decisions and outlines her largely non-interventionist strategy (Noakes 2008, xxi–xxvi). Noakes' text is also included with detailed commentary in Hardwick, Harrison and Vandiver 2024 (forthcoming). See also Appendix A, pp 31-33 below, for the full text of the poem (Gutenberg version)

and left "to lie sprawled on his face in the dust. But Apollo / had pity on him, although he was only a dead man, and guarded his body from all ugliness". Rosenberg's poem denies the possibility of divine intervention but adds additional elements. The bodies in the opening sequence are of men who are dead – the wheels "pained them not … / Their shut mouths made no moan". However, in the closing lines it is an open question whether it is the wheels that crush the last hope and the last breath out of the wounded man: "We heard his very last sound, / And our wheels grazed his dead face". The desecration portrayed in Homer is transplanted by Rosenberg to show the fate of the soldiers' bodies in the contemporary war.

3. Connections: Seamus Heaney's 'Stone from Delphi'

My third example is of a material object that becomes the focus of a poem by Seamus Heaney.[19]

In Heaney's personal and public odyssey, a pivotal point occurs in his collection *Station Island* (1984), in which he reflects on his religious and cultural hinterland, converses with interlocutors from history and literature, and comes to an understanding that his activity as a poet is an expression of vocation – a vocation that contrasts with the trivia and constraints of the established organization and norms of the Catholic Church.[20] The poems in the first section of *Station Island* depict and reflect on key points in the poet's life. Important among these is the short lyric 'Stone from Delphi', which is the fifth poem in a sequence entitled 'Shelf Life' that takes as its initial inspiration material objects, with associated memories and aspirations that are part of the poet's lived experience (Heaney 1984, 21-24). The other objects are: a 'Granite Chip' (an "Aberdeen of the mind", "a Calvin edge in my complaisant pith"); an 'Old Smoothing Iron' (used by his mother); 'Old Pewter' (a "dented hand-me-down", associated with a scary incident from his childhood); an 'Iron Spike' (a rusty object excavated from an old railway line); and a 'Snowshoe' (that "hangs on a wall in my head" and opens the poet's imagination to a vast unsullied expanse). Among these everyday objects, familiar to most of his readers, is a stone originating from the Greek sacred site of Delphi. The stone, with all its associations, prompts the desire to "make a morning offering" that will enable the poet to escape the pollutions of bloodshed, "govern the tongue", and become a conduit for the combination of warning, prophecy, and conflict resolution associated with Delphi.[21] The object combined sensory materiality with the status of an ancient Greek oracle that was the source of insights and guidance but uncomplicated by a theology. It is also one among several sources of Heaney's exploration of the mysterious and numinous.

The connections stated and implied in the sequence of poems are multi-directional. They include the connection with the poet himself, his feelings and aspirations, and

---

19 Heaney lived 1939-2013 and was a Nobel Laureate for Literature. His engagement with classical material was extensive (see in detail Harrison, Macintosh & Eastman 2019).
20 See further, Hardwick 2025 (forthcoming).
21 *The Government of the Tongue* became the title of a collection of Heaney's prose writings (1988).

the place of the stone alongside other significant material objects connected with his life. Then there is the connection with Delphi, the sacred site in Greece that was the home of the oracle, the source of often gnomic pronouncements uttered in response to questions posed by devotees and by those seeking sanction or advice in respect of personal or public problems. The further sphere of connections – the outer rim that connects with readers – embraces the associations of Delphi and its mementos in the experiences of modern tourists, together with the appeal to the underlying sensitivity of many readers to low-intensity religious norms that can function as guides to human behaviour. Heaney regarded the existence of a religious "sub-culture" as a shared feature in Irish life – a feature that crossed sectarian divides. For example, in commenting on his choice of title *The Cure at Troy* for his adaptation of Sophocles' tragedy *Philoctetes*, he said that the title was chosen because "in Ireland, north and south, the idea of a miraculous cure is deeply lodged in the religious sub-culture, whether it involves faith healing or the Lourdes pilgrimage" (O'Driscoll 2008, 422). In the poem inspired by the Stone from Delphi, Heaney reflected on how he shared the human urge to "make an offering", to escape "the miasma of spilled blood", to initiate a transactional relationship with the oracle in the hope of obtaining enlightenment. In offering its connectivity, the poem draws on personal and social narratives and reaches out with subtlety to its readers.

Coda

Framing and lived imaginative experience are intertwined in the relationships between Graeco-Roman material and popular culture, ancient and modern. These relationships are not only temporal but also lateral. Scholars who research and teach classics work with a discipline that is continually evolving. Part of this development embraces receptions of popular culture that reach out to additional constituencies of students and to the wider public. That trajectory, however, is not only from the inside of academia outwards. It is also from the outside to the centre. Openness to this counter-intuitive situation enables scholars to listen and discuss, to discover how and in what contexts people encounter classical material, and to learn about how they connect it to their own cultural and imaginary worlds. This in turn imposes new challenges and obligations on scholars as they revise theoretical frames and experiment with enlarged taxonomies. Narratives, subtlety, and connections provide nodal points that interact in the spheres of deep classics, heightened receptivity, and the transformations of sensibility that underlie shifts from low to high intensity in public awareness of the role of Greek and Roman material. In this process, rigid polarities of 'elite' and 'popular' become grey areas. The label 'popular' can come instead to signal overlapping spaces that are shared, diversely populated, and offer a springboard for a fuller range of deliberative and aesthetic reciprocities.

Acknowledgements

Many thanks to the editors of this volume for their far-sightedness and patience. Special thanks to all the organizers of the conference from which the publication grew for all their work in such adverse circumstances, and to the participants for their constructive comments. I would also like to thank my extended network of 'critical friends' for their long-term support in subjecting my ideas to critical scrutiny, especially Richard Armstrong, Sandie Byrne, Edith Hall, Stephen Harrison, Alexandra Lianeri, Fiona Macintosh, Henry Stead, and Elizabeth Vandiver.

APPENDIX A

DEAD MAN'S DUMP[22]
Isaac Rosenberg

The plunging limbers over the shattered track
Racketed with their rusty freight,
Stuck out like many crowns of thorns,
And the rusty stakes like sceptres old
To stay the flood of brutish men
Upon our brothers dear.
The wheels lurched over sprawled dead
But pained them not, though their bones crunched;
Their shut mouths made no moan.
They lie there huddled, friend and foeman,
Man born of man, and born of woman;
And shells go crying over them
From night till night and now.
Earth has waited for them,
All the time of their growth
Fretting for their decay:
Now she has them at last!
In the strength of their strength
Suspended—stopped and held.
What fierce imaginings their dark souls lit?
Earth! Have they gone into you?
Somewhere they must have gone,
And flung on your hard back

---

[22] The text of Rosenberg's poem is reproduced by permission of the Project Gutenberg eBook of Poems by Isaac Rosenberg (www.gutenberg.org). There are two variants from the text published in Noakes 2008: Noakes has a stanza break after line 70, and Gutenberg has a stanza break after line 75 which is not in the Noakes text. See n. 18 above for Noakes' editorial strategy.

Is their souls' sack,
Emptied of God-ancestralled essences.
Who hurled them out? Who hurled?
None saw their spirits' shadow shake the grass,
Or stood aside for the half used life to pass
Out of those doomed nostrils and the doomed mouth,
When the swift iron burning bee
Drained the wild honey of their youth.
What of us who, flung on the shrieking pyre,
Walk, our usual thoughts untouched,
Our lucky limbs as on ichor fed,
Immortal seeming ever?
Perhaps when the flames beat loud on us,
A fear may choke in our veins
And the startled blood may stop.
The air is loud with death,
The dark air spurts with fire,
The explosions ceaseless are.
Timelessly now, some minutes past,
These dead strode time with vigorous life,
Till the shrapnel called "An end!"
But not to all. In bleeding pangs
Some borne on stretchers dreamed of home,
Dear things, war-blotted from their hearts.
A man's brains splattered on
A stretcher-bearer's face;
His shook shoulders slipped their load,
But when they bent to look again
The drowning soul was sunk too deep
For human tenderness.
They left this dead with the older dead,
Stretched at the cross roads.
Burnt black by strange decay
Their sinister faces lie,
The lid over each eye;
The grass and coloured clay
More motion have than they,
Joined to the great sunk silences.
Here is one not long dead.
His dark hearing caught our far wheels,
And the choked soul stretched weak hands
To reach the living word the far wheels said;
The blood-dazed intelligence beating for light,

Crying through the suspense of the far torturing wheels
Swift for the end to break
Or the wheels to break,
Cried as the tide of the world broke over his sight,
"Will they come? Will they ever come?"
Even as the mixed hoofs of the mules,
The quivering-bellied mules,
And the rushing wheels all mixed
With his tortured upturned sight.
So we crashed round the bend,
We heard his weak scream,
We heard his very last sound,
And our wheels grazed his dead face.

Bibliography

Balmer, J. 2009. *The Word for Sorrow*. Cambridge: Salt.
Barton, J. 2006. *The War that Still Goes On: Adapted from Thucydides' History of the Peloponnesian War and Plato's Dialogue with Alcibiades*. London: Oberon Books.
Bromberg, J.A. 2021. *Global Classics*. London & New York: Routledge.
Butler, S. (ed.) 2016. *Deep Classics: Rethinking Classical Reception*. London: Bloomsbury.
Byrne, S. (ed.) 2022. *Tony Harrison and the Classics*. Oxford: Oxford University Press.
De Pourcq, M., de Haan, N. & Rijser, D. 2020. *Framing Classical Reception Studies: Different Perspectives on a Developing Field*. Metaforms: Studies in the Reception of Classical Antiquity. Leiden: Brill.
Eidolon, eidolon.pub. (Ceased to publish new material December 2020, last accessed 20 July 2022.)
Eidinow, E. 2019a. "The (Ancient Greek) Subject Supposed to Believe". *Numen: International Review for the History of Religions* 66.1, 56-88.
Eidinow, E. 2019b. "'They Blow One Way, Now Another' (Hesiod *Theogony* 875): Winds in the Ancient Greek Imaginary", in: Scheer, T.S. (ed.) 2019. *Natur – Mythos-Religion im antiken Griechenland*. Stuttgart: Franz Steiner Verlag, 113-133.
Hall, E. 2008. "Navigating the Realms of Gold: Translation as Access Route to the Classics", in: Lianeri, A. & Zajko, V. (eds) 2008. *Translation and the Classic: Identity as Change in the History of Culture*. Oxford: Oxford University Press, 315-340.
Hall, E. & Macintosh, F. 2005. *Greek Tragedy and the British Theatre 1660-1914*. Oxford: Oxford University Press.
Hardwick, L. 2011. "Fuzzy Connections: Classical Texts and Modern Poetry in English", in: Parker, J. & Mathews, T. (eds) 2011. *Tradition, Translation, Trauma*. Oxford: Oxford University Press, 39-60.
Hardwick, L. 2013. "Against the 'Democratic Turn': Counter-texts; Counter-contexts; Counter-arguments", in: Hardwick & Harrison 2013, 15-32.
Hardwick, L. 2015a. "Radicalism and Gradualism Enmeshed: Classics from the Grass Roots in the Cultural Politics of Nineteenth-century Britain", in: Hall, E. & Stead, H. 2020. *A People's History of Classics*. London: Routledge, 20-36.
Hardwick, L. 2015b. "Thucydidean Concepts", in: Lee & Morley 2015, 493-511.
Hardwick, L. 2018a. "Epilogue. Voices, Bodies, Silences and Media: Heightened Receptivities in Epic in Performance", in: Macintosh, F., McConnell, J., Harrison, S. & Kenward, C. 2018. *Epic Performances: From the Middle Ages into the Twenty-First Century*. Oxford: Oxford University Press, 558-572.
Hardwick, L. 2018b. "The Poetics of Cultural Memory: World War 1 Refractions of Ancient Peace", in: Pender, E. (ed.), *Classical Receptions Journal Special Issue: Classics and Classicists in World War 1*. Classical Receptions Journal 10.4, 393-414.

Hardwick, L. 2019. "Classics in Extremis: the Edges of Classical Reception", in: Richardson, E. (ed.), *Classics in Extremis*. London: Bloomsbury, 13-24.

Hardwick, L. 2020. "Aspirations and Mantras in Classical Reception Research: Can there Really be Dialogue between Ancient and Modern?", in: De Pourcq et al. 2020, 15-32.

Hardwick, L. 2021a. "Translation and/as Adaptation", in: Liapis, V. & Sidiropoulou, A. (eds) 2021. *Adapting Greek Tragedy: Contemporary Contexts for Ancient Texts*. Cambridge: Cambridge University Press, 110-130.

Hardwick, L. 2021b. "Tracking Classical Scholarship: Myth, Evidence and Epistemology", in: Harrison, S.J. & Pelling, C. (eds) 2021. *Classical Scholarship and Its History: Essays in Honour of Christopher Stray*. Trends in Classics: Scholarship in the Making. Berlin & Boston: De Gruyter, 9-31.

Hardwick, L. 2022. "Heightened Receptivities: When Ancient and Modern meet in Greek Tragedy", in: Karamanou, I. (ed.) 2022. *Ancient Theatre: Proceedings of the Nafplion Conference on Otherness*, University of the Peloponnese, 283-295. online: ts.uop.gr

Hardwick, L. 2024a. "Cultural Hegemonies: Subaltern Agency through Greek and Roman Texts", in: Cimino, A-M., Saldati. V., and Zuchetti, E., eds., *Class and Classics: Historiography, Reception, Challenges; Towards a Democratization of Classical Studies*. Gramsci Network, Trends in Classics Supp. Vol. Berlin & Boston: De Gruyter.

Hardwick, L. d 2024b, *Reception Studies*, 2nd edition. Classical Association: New Surveys in the Classics. Cambridge: Cambridge University Press.

Hardwick, L. 2025 (forthcoming). "Seamus Heaney's Religious Palette: Catholic, Roman, Greek", in: Murray, C. (ed.). *Cambridge Themes in Irish Literature and Culture: Religion*. Cambridge: Cambridge University Press.

Hardwick, L. & Harrison, S.J. (eds) 2013. *Classics in the Modern World: A 'Democratic Turn?'*. Oxford: Oxford University Press.

Hardwick, L., Harrison, S.J. & Vandiver, E. 2024a. *Greek and Roman Antiquity in First World War Poetry: Making Connections*. Oxford: Oxford University Press.

Hardwick, L., Harrison, S.J., and Vandiver, E. 2024b. *Rupert Brooke, Charles Sorley, Isaac Rosenberg and Wilfred Owen: Classical Connections,* Oxford: Oxford University Press.

Harloe, K. 2013. "Questioning the Democratic and Democratic Questioning", in: Hardwick & Harrison 2013, 3-13.

Harrasser, K. 2020. "The Fable of Arachne: Underweavings of Tactile Mediality", in: Michelakis 2020, 176-186.

Harrison, S.J., Macintosh, F. & Eastman, H. (eds) 2019. *Seamus Heaney and the Classics. Bann Valley Muses*. Oxford, New York: Oxford University Press.

Heaney, S. 1984. *Station Island*. London: Faber.

Hinds, S. 1998. *Allusion and Intertext*. Cambridge: Cambridge University Press.

Holmes, B. 2016. "*Cosmopoiesis* in the Field of 'The Classical'", in: Butler 2016, 269-289.

Klooster, J. & Kuin, N.N.I. (eds) 2020. *After the Crisis: Remembrance, Re-anchoring and Recovery in Ancient Greece and Rome*. London: Bloomsbury.

Kosellek, R. 2004. *Futures Past: On the Semantics of Historical Time*, tr. & intr. K. Tribe. New York: Columbia University Press.

Lee, C. & Morley, N. (eds) 2015. *A Handbook to the Reception of Thucydides*. Malden, MA & Oxford: Wiley-Blackwell.

Logue, C. 2015. *War Music: An Account of Homer's Iliad*. London: Faber.

Matzner, S. & Trimble, G. (eds) 2020. *Metalepsis: Ancient Texts, New Perspectives*. Oxford: Oxford University Press.

Mee, E.B. & Foley, H.P. (eds) 2011. *Antigone on the Contemporary World Stage*. Oxford. Oxford University Press.

Michelakis, P. 2013. *Greek Tragedy on the Screen*. Oxford: Oxford University Press.

Michelakis, P. (ed.) 2020. *Classics and Media Theory*. Oxford: Oxford University Press.

Nelis, J. 2011. *From Ancient to Modern: The Myth of Romanità during the ventennio fascista: The Written Imprint of Mussolini's Cult of the 'Third Rome'*. Brussels: Brepols.

Ngugi, wa Thiong'o 2012. *Globalectics: Theory and the Politics of Knowing*. Welleck Lectures 2010. New York: Columbia University Press.

Noakes, V. (ed.) 2008. *Isaac Rosenberg*. Oxford Authors Series. Oxford: Oxford University Press.

O'Driscoll, D. 2008. *Stepping Stones: Interviews with Seamus Heaney*. London: Faber.

Oswald, A. 2011. *Memorial*. London: Faber.

Porter, J.I. 2006. "Introduction: What is Classical about Classical Antiquity?", in: Porter, J.I. (ed.) 2006. *Classical Pasts: The Classical Tradition of Greece and Rome*. Princeton: Princeton University Press, 1-65.

Paul, J. 2013. *Film and the Classical Epic Tradition*. Oxford: Oxford University Press.

Richardson, E. (ed.) 2019. *Classics in Extremis: The Edges of Classical Reception*. London: Bloomsbury.

Roche, H. 2021. *The Third Reich's Elite Schools: A History of the Napolas*. Oxford: Oxford University Press.

Rogers, B.M. & Stevens, B.E. (eds) 2015. *Classical Traditions in Science Fiction*. Oxford: Oxford University Press.

Pharos: Doing Justice to the Classics, (https://pharos.vassarspace.net, last accessed 20 July 2022).

Postclassicisms Collective, The, 2020. *Postclassicisms*. Chicago & London: University of Chicago Press.

Stead, H. 2022. "Fire, Fennel and the Future of Socialism: Tony Harrison's *Prometheus*", in: Byrne 2022, 202-221.

Stead, H. & Hall, E. (eds) 2015. *Greek and Roman Classics in the British Struggle for Social Reform*. London: Bloomsbury.

Torrance, I. 2020. "Post-Ceasefire Antigones and Northern Ireland", in: Torrance, I. & O'Rourke, D. (eds) 2020. *Classics and Irish Politics 1916-2016*. Oxford: Oxford University Press, 326-345.

Vandiver, E. 2010. *Stand in the Trench, Achilles: Classical Receptions in British Poetry of the Great War*. Oxford: Oxford University Press.

Vandiver, E. 2022. "Controversies and Pitfalls of Translation: Herodotus in Contentious Times". *Herodotus Helpline* 16 March 2022, https://herodotushelpline.org/seminar-schedule/, last accessed 20 July 2022.

Van Steen, G. 2015. *States of Emergency: Theater and Public Performance under the Greek Military Dictatorship of 1967-1974*. Oxford: Oxford University Press.

Wrigley, A. 2015. *Engagements with Ancient Greece on BBC Radio*. Oxford: Oxford University Press.

Wyke, M. 1997. *Projecting the Past: Ancient Rome, Cinema and History*. London: Routledge.

Wyke, M. & Michelakis, P. (eds) 2013. *Antiquity in Silent Cinema*. Cambridge: Cambridge University Press.

3

ORALITY, LITERACY, AND AUTHORITY IN EUDOCIA'S *MARTYRDOM OF SAINTS CYPRIAN AND JUSTINA*

ANDREW FAULKNER

In her discussion of the performance of mime and pantomime in antiquity, Ruth Webb disentangles the coding of mime as popular from the charge that it was low art, due to its everyday subject matter and its rushed and disordered performative movement: the "coding of mime as 'popular' does not mean ... that it had no appeal to the elite ... certain qualities of mime were praised by teachers of rhetoric, who recommended mime as a model to their students".[1] Attempts to impose a rigid dichotomy between categories of 'elite' and 'popular' reception quickly break down in any period, with multifarious literary and musical genres engaging diverse audiences.[2] The reception of late antique Christian poetry of the fourth and fifth centuries was no exception.[3] The ornate classicizing language and complex allusivity of this metrical poetry in both Greek and Latin was no doubt fully accessible only to a select, highly educated group, including both Christians and pagans,[4] but it could also have been appreciated by wider audiences

---

1   Webb 2009, 97.
2   For a summary of modern attempts to define popular culture, see Grindstaff 2008, 207-210, who underscores the cultural and political dimensions of defining what is popular: "different approaches are not mutually exclusive; nor do they map neatly onto specific disciplinary traditions or methodologies; rather, they represent different—and often historically specific—ways of conceptualizing the relationship between popular cultural forms and the society that they both shape and reflect".
3   See Agosti 2012, 378-380 with further bibliography.
4   Gregory of Nazianzus (II. 1. 39 = *PG* 37. 1312-1313) famously styles his poetry a "pleasant drug of persuasion" (τερπνὸν φάρμακον πειθοῦς) for young, educated Christians, but also a means to surpass pagans and heretics (τοὺς ξένους). *Met. Ps. Protheoria* 32 (ἵνα γνώωσι καὶ ἄλλοι) also points to pagans and heretics as an intended audience.

with varying degrees of knowledge.[5] Such poetry may even have had some place in devotional prayer and liturgical worship. The fifth-century church historian Sozomen (*h.e.* 6. 25. 4-5) reports that acolytes of Apollinaris of Laodicea performed his metrical poems (ἔμμετρά τινα μελύδρια ψάλλοντες) alongside traditional holy songs and that his melodies (μέλη) were sung during daily tasks.[6] In the case of Latin poetry, the sixth-century Arator performed his poem on the Acts of the Apostles before a public audience for Pope Vigilius.[7] One might imagine in late antiquity a variety of performance contexts and levels on which such poetry was digested and appreciated by audiences.

Early Christian poetic paraphrases of scripture, a prominent genre in the Christian poetic tradition of late antiquity, are in one sense intermediaries between more recherché and popular literatures, in that they transform widely known, read, and performed scriptural texts into a register that is, in its finer points at least, accessible to a smaller audience. To take the case of the late antique metrical paraphrase of the Psalms, possibly attributed to Apollinaris of Laodicea,[8] it is significant that the Septuagint Psalms were perhaps the most widely known and popular texts in Christian communities of the period. The Psalms are frequently quoted in the New Testament, often discussed by the Church Fathers, and had an important place in early Christian worship, especially from the fourth century onward, including in less educated circles.[9] Greek- and Latin-speaking audiences listening to an elevated poetic paraphrase of the Psalms, or of other well-known scriptural texts, will have had a common reference point in their minds for understanding these elevated poetic versions. In its appeal to a more select, highly educated group, steeped in both classical learning and Judeo-Christian scripture, late antique scriptural paraphrase thus stands at an intermediary point, useful for exploring the categories of 'popular' and 'elite' as scaled rather than absolute. This is reception in a liminal space: not so much popular reception, but the conscious appropriation and re-working of the popular for a more select audience, albeit in the service of a global evangelizing project.

---

5   On the different levels of education and teaching in the Graeco-Roman world, see e.g. Kaster 1988; Cribiore 1996; Cavero 2008, 214-218. Late antique poetry is itself not uniformly erudite. The fourth-century poems of the Bodmer papyrus include examples of *ethopoieia*, which are much less allusively and theologically complex than the poetry of authors such as Gregory of Nazianzus, Nonnus, Juvencus, or Prudentius; see Hurst & Rudhardt 1999, with discussion of Agosti-Gonnelli 1995, 301-308; Agosti 2001a, 71-74; 2001b; 2002.

6   Gregory Nazianzus implies in his letter to the priest Cledonius (*Ep.* 101. 73, a tract against the theological views of Apollinaris and his followers) that Apollinaris composed a poetic paraphrase of the Septuagint Psalms and describes this as ἀντίφθογγα (τὰ νέα Ψαλτήρια καὶ ἀντίφθογγα τῷ Δαυὶδ), which in its more technical sense could imply liturgical performance of the Apollinarian metrical psalter in antiphonal response to the Septuagint text. See Faulkner 2020, 4.

7   See Green 2006, 251-252. For more on performance of poetry in late antiquity, see Agosti 2006; Cameron 2016, 178-179.

8   See Faulkner 2020. For further discussion of early Christian poetic paraphrases in both Greek and Latin, see Roberts 1985, 61-106; Green 2006; Agosti 2012, 371-372; McGill 2012, 344-345.

9   See Gillingham 2008, 13-42; Daley 2015, 11-12; Dunkle 2016, 21-24. On psalmody in fourth-and fifth-century monastic circles, see McKinnon 1994.

In this essay, I will look in more detail at the treatment of oral performance and bookish learning in one instance of early Christian paraphrastic poetry, the hexameter version of the hagiographical *Acts* of Saints Cyprian and Justina by the fifth-century empress Aelia Eudocia, wife of the emperor Theodosius II. This poem is the earliest known poetic hagiography in Greek.[10] Eudocia's paraphrase originally consisted of three books,[11] corresponding to independent prose accounts of the conversion, confession, and martyrdom.[12] The sequence of events and language of the prose are often precisely reflected in Eudocia's verse, although her paraphrase does not correspond entirely to any of the surviving recensions and displays poetic creativity.[13] The story recounts how Justina (initially named Justa) is first converted to Christianity by the preaching of a deacon named Praulius. A villain named Aglaidas falls in love with her and asks a pagan magician, Cyprian, to seduce her. Cyprian agrees and sends three demons to deceive Justina, but she defeats all three, in the process converting Cyprian himself to Christianity. Cyprian, a version of the magician-convert figure Simon Magus (Acts of the Apostles 8: 9-24), confesses in lurid detail to the Antiochenes his previous devotion to demonic powers. Ultimately, both he and Justina are martyred for their faith.

This story, a late-antique archetype for the Faust legend,[14] enjoyed popularity in the fourth century. The narrative of love, magic, conversion, and martyrdom draws upon common literary motifs found also in the Apocryphal Acts, martyrologies, and classical works, including the Greek novels and ancient biographies.[15] Hagiography circulated widely in late antiquity, both orally and by means of writing,[16] and Gregory Nazianzus attests to the appeal of the Cyprian narrative to his audience. In an oration dedicated to Saint Cyprian (*or.* 24), in which he conflates Cyprian of Antioch and Cyprian of Carthage, Gregory refers to his audience's eagerness to hear about the magician Cyprian

---

10   Photius attests a lost paraphrase of the *Acts of Thecla* by Basil of Seleucia (d. ca. 468), but this would probably have been later than Eudocia's poem. In Latin poetry, martyrs are celebrated from the fourth century by authors such as Damasus, Paulinus, and Prudentius.

11   The first two books of this poem have survived in a single manuscript in Florence (Laurentianus Plut. 7. 10). The folio containing the first 99 lines of the poem was removed to Leiden in the seventeenth century and rediscovered by Karel Adriaan de Meyier in 1965 (Leiden BPG 95; Meyier 1965). The Leiden folio has been edited by Bevegni 1982 and the remainder by Ludwich 1897, with notes and translation by Salvaneschi 1982. The third book of Eudocia's poem is not extant but is summarized by Photius *Bib. Cod.* 184.

12   The Greek *Acts* have been edited recently by Bailey 2017, who provides a text of recension C of the *Conversion*. For recensions A and B of the *Conversion*, see Radermacher 1927.

13   See Bevegni 2006, 29-30, who assumes that Eudocia based her paraphrase on a prose recension no longer extant. It is equally possible that she was familiar with and drew consciously from multiple versions to craft her own narrative. For an example of Eudocia's creativity, see Faulkner 2021.

14   See Wilson 2006.

15   Detailed discussion in Bailey 2017, 20-27, 55-64, 95-96; Sowers 2020, chapters 3-4.

16   Cf. Efthymiadis 2014, 7: "The popularity of these stories is borne out by their widespread oral transmission and accounts for the attribution of identical or similar stories and sayings to different solitaries in different collections".

(*or.* 24. 7 τοῦ πόθου τῶν ἀκουόντων).[17] Moreover, he exhorts his listeners not to give themselves over to the pleasures of the tale of Cyprian's beginnings, but rather to learn prudence from his martyr's end (*or.* 24. 9 καὶ μὴ πρὸς τὰ πρῶτά τις ὁρῶν Κυπριανοῦ, ταῖς ἡδοναῖς ἐφιέτω· τοῖς δὲ τελευταίοις σωφρονιζέσθω) – advice suggesting that it was precisely the more salacious elements of the story that audiences might have enjoyed most. Gregory's oration, which he delivered in Constantinople on the feast of Saint Cyprian (2 October 379), also bears witness to the oral transmission of the Cyprian legend, which operated alongside and in relation to written texts.[18]

Eudocia's poem itself problematizes categories of written and oral consumption of Christian scripture and holy narratives. At the outset of the poem, the virgin Justina is converted to Christianity by listening to the preaching of the gospel by a deacon named Praulius (15-25 Bevegni):[19]

> Χριστοφόρος τις ἀνὴρ Πραΰλιος ἦεν ἐκεῖσε   15
> σεπτὸς ἄγαν πινυτός τε διάκτορος οὐρανίωνος,
> ὅστις ἐϋφροσύνῃ κεκορυθμένος ἠδέ τε πίστει
> βίβλους θεσπεσίας μετεκίαθεν αἰὲν ἀείδων
> πίστιν τ' ἠγαθέην ὀμφὴν δ' ἁγίην ὑποφητῶν.
> τοῦ δὲ διηνεκέως ἀγανὴ κούρη ἀΐουσα –   20
> φωτοφόρος γὰρ ἔην ἀγχοῦ θυρίς – ἐκ θαλάμοιο
> ἐς μέγαρον ὁρόωσα διακτόρου αἰσίμου ἀνδρός,
> ἔργα θεοῖο πέλωρα, βροτοῦ δ' ὅπερ εἵλετο σῶμα
> ἀθάνατος, μεγάλων τε φάτιν ἐσθλῶν ὑποφητῶν
> παρθενικῆς δ' ὠδῖνα κλυτῆς γεραρῆς Μαρίης γε …   25

There was a man of Christ there named Praulius,
Very august and a wise deacon of heavenly God,
Who, armed with gladness and faith,
Went about constantly singing the books inspired by God,
The divine faith and the holy voice of the prophets.
The gentle girl listened to him all the time –
For her light-bearing window was close by – from her chamber
Looking upon the house of the godly deacon.
She heard of the marvellous deeds of God, and the mortal body that he chose,
He immortal, and the word of the great and good prophets,
The birth pangs of the renowned and venerable Virgin Mary …

---

17 See Bailey 2017, 4-20, who argues that Gregory intentionally conflated the two Cyprians for rhetorical effect to appeal to his audience. For McGuckin 2001, 251 the conflation is an error resulting from rushed, extempore composition after Gregory hurriedly returned from the countryside.
18 See McGuckin 2001, 251.
19 The texts here and below are those of Bevegni 1982 and Ludwich 1897. The translations are adapted from Sowers 2020.

Praulius is here depicted as a preacher communicating the Christian scriptures orally, which Justina hears from her bedroom window, a *topos* of the genre paralleled in the *Acts of Paul and Thecla* (7).[20] I have argued elsewhere that Eudocia's portrayal of Praulius here as a "singer", in combination with careful choice of vocabulary bearing metapoetic weight, strongly associates him with the classical figure of the hexameter poet, and thus with Eudocia herself, a versifier of Christian narratives.[21] This identification implies that, just as Praulius' singing attracts the young Justina, Eudocia's poetry is able to lead the young to faith (or to a deeper faith).

By associating herself in this way with Praulius, Eudocia explicitly ties her seemingly exclusive poetic project to more accessible forms of Christian preaching and the Christian evangelizing mission.[22] At the same time, Praulius is depicted by Eudocia as a more bookish figure than he is in the prose hagiography, who communicates orally scriptural narratives that are simultaneously inscribed in books. In Eudocia's poem Praulius sings the "books inspired by God" (βίβλους θεσπεσίας, 18), whereas in the prose versions there is no mention of books.[23] One imagines the deacon reading aloud from a text, or performing orally a text committed to memory, reflecting the overlap of the oral and written transmission of scripture in the first centuries of Christianity.[24] The "living" didactic voice of Praulius, commonly associated with authoritative teaching in antiquity,[25] is in the foreground, but Eudocia nonetheless reminds her audience of the role of writing in Christian teaching.[26]

---

20 See Bailey 2017, 20 comparing Thecla listening to Paul in *Acts Paul Thec.* 7 ἐπὶ τῆς σύνεγγυς θύριδος and *Conv.* 1. 3 ἀπὸ τῆς σύνεγγυς θύριδος (Eud. *Mart.* φωτοφόρος γὰρ ἔην ἀγχοῦ θυρίς).

21 Faulkner 2021. Praulius sings the gospels like an epic bard (18 βίβλους θεσπεσίας μετεκίαθεν αἰὲν ἀείδων). Eudocia elsewhere versifies scripture in her centos, for which see Rey 1998; Schembra 2006; Usher 1999, with the studies of Usher 1998; Schembra 2007a; 2007b.

22 The occasion of Eudocia's paraphrase is not certain, but it was probably composed for the Antiochenes in connection with her pilgrimage to Jerusalem in 438-439, as suggested by Livrea 1998. The Cyprian narrative would have held a lot of local appeal for Antiochian communities. Cf. Agosti 2001, 85; 2012, 202-203.

23 *Conv.* 1. 1 (Bailey) αὕτη ἤκουε Πραϋλίου τινὸς διακόνου λαλοῦντος "She heard a deacon named Praulius speaking".

24 The literature on orality and literacy in the New Testament tradition is vast. Foundational is Kelber 1983. Recent work emphasizes the complex interplay of orality and textuality; see Botha 2012; Dewey 2013; Keith 2020. On the interplay of the two in the Hellenic tradition, see Thomas 1992.

25 See Botha 2012, 21-38. Eusebius (*h.e.* 3. 39. 4) quotes Papias saying that Christian education is better delivered by the "living and abiding voice" (παρὰ ζώσης φωνῆς καὶ μενούσης) than books (ἐκ βιβλίων), a classical trope, e.g. Plato *Phaed.* 276a5-9 "living and ensouled word" (λόγον … ζῶντα καὶ ἔμψυχον).

26 At the outset of his *Stromateis* (1. 11), Clement defends the written word as a didactic medium without rejecting the authority of oral teaching, in dialogue with Plato's influential rejection of writing as inferior in the *Phaedrus*. See Wyrwa 1983, 30-46 and Hunter (forthcoming).

The experience of Justina, the idealized female convert, is in contrast a markedly oral one. In the remainder of the first book of the poem, Cyprian is enlisted by the villain Aglaidas to seduce Justina. He sends a series of demons to tempt her, but each time Justina repels the demons by praying to God. Justina's prayers, although personal confessions, themselves recount before God and the audience a summary of scriptural narratives. She rejects the second demon with the following prayer (1.115-125 Ludwich):

> ὦ κρατέων γενετῶν, ἐλεητύος ἄφθονε δωτήρ,   115
> αἰθερίων νομοδῶτα καὶ οὐρανίων ἐπίκουρε,
> ὃν γαίη τρομέει· καὶ ἀντιθέου ὀλοοῖο
> ὃς μένος αἰσχίστως ὀλέσας, γενέτου Ἀβραὰμ δὲ
> δεξάμενος θυσίην ὡσεὶ μεγάλην ἑκατόμβην·
> ὃς Βῆλον κατέριψας ἐπί τε δράκοντα κατέκτας   120
> καὶ διὰ σοῦ θεράποντος εὐσεβέος Δανιήλου
> Περσῶν ἔθνεα πάντα τεὴν θεότητα δίδαξας·
> ὃς διὰ τηλυγέτου Χριστοῦ, σέο παιδός, ἅπαντα
> εὖ διακοσμήσας καὶ ἐν χθονὶ φέγγος ἀνάψας·
> ὃς νέκυας μετὰ πότμον ὑπότροπον ἐς φάος ἦξας.   125

> O ruler of creation, bounteous bestower of mercy,
> Lawgiver and protector of aethereal and heavenly beings,
> Before whom the earth trembles; who overthrows
> And shames the strength of the nefarious enemy, accepting
> Father Abraham's sacrifice as a splendid hecatomb;
> You who threw down Baal and slew the dragon,
> And through your pious servant, Daniel,
> Taught the whole Persian race your divinity;
> You who through your only-begotten son, Christ,
> Set everything right and established light on earth;
> Who, after his death, led the dead back into the light.

Justina here evokes Old Testament narratives and figures – Abraham, Isaac, and Daniel – as well as the deeds of Christ in the New Testament, while placing emphasis on the revelatory teaching of God through scripture (Περσῶν ἔθνεα πάντα τεὴν θεότητα δίδαξας, 122). Her prayer in this sense echoes the oral performance of Praulius at the outset of the poem, from whom she learned the teachings of Christ, which are critical not simply for her conversion but also for her ability to remain a faithful Christian in the face of demonic temptation. For the audience of the poem, Eudocia's prayer is an oral performance of scripture, albeit in the more intimate context of Christian devotion and the ascetic struggle against temptation, and Eudocia introduces no textual element into the prayer. Justina's markedly aural/oral experience of scripture and holy narratives must have been the norm especially for early Christian women, and Eudocia's own literary acumen and female authorship of a classicizing poem exceptional.[27] In the preface to her cento, Eudocia points self-consciously to her identity as a female poet taking over the project of her male predecessor Patricius as something unusual: "Nevertheless, this is a work shared by us both, Patricius and me, despite the fact that I am a woman" (ἀλλ' ἔμπης ξυνὸς μὲν ἔφυ πόνος ἀμφοτέροισι, | Πατρικίῳ κἀμοί, καὶ θηλυτέρη περ ἐοῦσῃ, 34-35).[28] In this preface, Eudocia also underscores her own textual editorial activity, taking the pages of Patricius' book in her hand and revising them (9-15, using the vocabulary of pages (σελίδας), book (βίβλος), and writing (γράψα)), alongside discussion of the oral/aural experience of centonic poetry.[29]

If Justina's conversion and defence against the demons is enacted through hearing and speaking scripture, Eudocia subsequently portrays the conversion of Cyprian from his demonic and pagan beliefs in a manner that stresses Cyprian's markedly literate conception of conversion. When his demons are not successful, Cyprian recognizes the power of Christ and rejects Satan. He then makes his way to the Christian bishop Anthimus to confess and convert to Christianity (1. 219-225 Ludwich):

Κυπριανὸς δὲ λαβὼν βίβλους μαγικὰς κατέθηκεν
ὤμοισι στιβαροῖσι νέων ἀγέμεν ποτὶ οἶκον
ἀχράντοιο θεοῦ, καὶ δ' αὐτὸς ἐφέσπετο ταῖσδε.
πὰρ ποσὶ δὲ προπάροιθε πεσὼν θείου ἱερῆος,
Ἀνθίμου, ἀντίων τάδε οἱ φάτο· 'ἀθανάτοιο
οὐρανίου θεράπων στρατιῇ Χριστοῦ προβέβουλα
βύβλῳ [τ'] ἐγκαταλέξαι ἐμὸν κέαρ.'

Cyprian gathered his magical books and placed them
On the strong shoulders of his novices to carry to the house of
The undefiled God, and he followed behind the books.
Falling at the feet of the godly priest,
Anthimus, Cyprian supplicated him, saying,
'Servant of the celestial God, I want
To enlist my heart in Christ's army and his book.'

---

27   See Dewey 2013, 134: "while early Christianity was an oral phenomenon in which women could participate relatively fully, the writing of Christian texts and their selection for inclusion in the canon was the work of the small minority of literates who were mostly men".

28   On the preface generally, see e.g. Usher 1997; Agosti 2001, 74-85; Whitby 2007; Sowers 2020, 41-53.

29   On Eudocia's contrast of the oral and written aspects of cento poetry in the preface, see Agosti 2006, 59 and Sowers 2020, 44-48, "Eudocia's references to singing centos and their positive (or negative) aural effects on listeners should be balanced with her visual and material language (seeing, book, pages) as evidence for multiple, complementary reading events …centos were likely read/composed in private and performed in public …from large gatherings to more intimate audiences of trusted friends". We can imagine something similar for her paraphrastic poetry. Photius *Bib. Cod.* 183-184 reports that Eudocia also produced paraphrases of the Octateuch, Zechariah, and Daniel, all now lost.

Cyprian takes up his pagan books and delivers them to bishop Anthimus. He then beseeches him to receive and burn the books, through which he performed so many evils (δέχνυσο ... | βίβλους, ἔνθεν ἐγὼ κακὰ μυρία τεῦχον ἀλιτρός | καὶ πυρὶ τάσδ' ἀμάθυνον, 1. 237-239 Ludwich), a request which Anthimus grants (πεισθεὶς δ' ἀρητὴρ βίβλους λάβε, φλέξε δὲ πάσας, | κεῖνον δ' εὐλογέων ἀγανοῖς μύθοις ἀπέπεμπε, 1. 240-241 Ludwich). The burning of Cyprian's books marks the moment of his conversion and the triumph of Christianity over pagan sorcery. For Eudocia's Cyprian, the abandonment of his pagan books involves enlistment of his heart in another set of texts, the book of Christ (Χριστοῦ ... | βύβλῳ), an expression that points again to inscribed Christian scripture.[30] Eudocia here seems to have in mind the variant of recension A of the prose *Conversion*, εἰς τὴν βίβλον τῶν ζώντων "into the book of the living", where recensions B and C have εἰς τὴν μάτρικα τῆς στρατιᾶς αὐτοῦ "into the registry of his army".[31] However, when Cyprian first goes to the church as a catechumen, his experience of written Christian scripture is also markedly aural. He prays to God to let him hear the word of God contained in written scripture (δός με ... μῦθον ἀκοῦσαι | ἐκ γραφικῶν βίβλων, 1. 257-258 Ludwich).[32] As he enters the church, the prophets David, Hosea, and Isaiah, as well as the apostle Paul, "speak" to him (ἔννεπε 259, ἔειπεν 262 and 372, ἀγόρευε 264 and 270), indicating that Cyprian is hearing scripture read aloud or chanted. The proliferation of verbs of speaking, absent in the prose,[33] bring into relief the importance of hearing Christian truth.[34]

Speaking Christian books also play an important role in Cyprian's path to ordination following his baptism, when he first becomes a reader of the books of Christ (1. 295-299 Ludwich):

καὶ τότε δὴ θείοισι λοετροῖς ἁγνὸν ἔτευξεν.
ἠοῖ δ' ὀγδοάτῃ γέντ' αἰπυβόης πολυσέπτων
βίβλων Χριστοφάτων. ἀτὰρ εἰκάδι πεμπταίῃ τε
μείων τυτθότερός τε διακτορίῃ τετέλεστο
καὶ θυρεῶνας ἔχεν σεπτῆς ἅμα μυστιπολείης.

And then he purified him in divine waters.
On the eighth day, Cyprian became loud-crier of the revered
Books that speak of Christ. And on the twenty-fifth day,

---

30 Mat. 1: 1 βίβλος γενέσεως Ἰησοῦ Χριστοῦ. Cf. Greg. Naz. *Ep.* 32. 3-4 καὶ γὰρ πολλ' ἐμόγησας ... | ...ἃ καὶ Χριστοῦ βίβλος ἔχει μεγάλη.
31 *Pace* Bailey 2017, 133, who suggests that Eudocia's text reflects the variant of B and C.
32 Eudocia's ἐκ γραφικῶν βίβλων renders the prose ἐκ τῶν θείων γραφῶν, thus stressing the contrast between scripture as physical text and Cyprian's aural reception of the word of the God.
33 Where the initial verb ἔλεγεν of David speaking is not repeated but inferred for the subsequent scriptural voices.
34 The motif is also the subject of Psalm 105 (106): 2 paraphrased in the passage, τίς λαλήσει τὰς δυναστείας τοῦ κυρίου, ἀκουστὰς ποιήσει πάσας τὰς αἰνέσεις αὐτοῦ.

He became a lesser deacon
And guarded the doors of the holy mystery.

We come full circle back to the deacon Praulius, who first converted Justina, with Christian teaching again associated with books, but rooted in oral performance. Eudocia employs two striking *hapax legomena* of Cyprian's oral performance, αἰπυβόης and Χριστόφατος: his new status as "herald and interpreter of the divine mysteries" (*Conv.* ἱεροκῆρυξ καὶ ἐξηγητὴς τῶν θείων μυστηρίων) is rendered "loud-crier of the revered books that speak of Christ" (αἰπυβόης πολυσέπτων | βίβλων Χριστοφάτων). Not only does Eudocia introduce βιβλίων for the prose μυστηρίων, but the unique adjective Χριστοφάτων blurs the boundaries between the written text and the spoken word. The physical books of Christian scripture come alive and speak to the Christian community.

In other respects, textuality and the writing of books is explicitly tied in the poem to pagan learning and impiety. The second book of Eudocia's *Martyrdom* consists of Cyprian's confession of his past sins before the Antiochenes, an account rich in detail which, as we saw above, must have attracted the attention of ancient audiences: we hear of Cyprian's education and initiation into various cults, travels to the far ends of the earth, curses written on stones, cosmic symbols, human trafficking, human sacrifice, and every impious deed. In the midst of his litany of demonic transgressions of virtue and wisdom, Cyprian checks the flow of his narrative to say that it is not lawful for him to fill many books with such stories (2. 176-178 Ludwich):

ἀλλ' οὐ θέμις ἐστί μοι αὐτῷ
τεύχειν ἄσπετα βύβλα· πολέων [δ'] ἀπὸ τύτθ' ἀγορεύσας
δυσσεβίην κεν ἐμὴν ὕμμιν μετὰ πᾶσιν ἔειπον.

But it is not right for me
To fashion endless books. By describing a few of my many deeds,
I have related to all of you my impiety.

Eudocia here precisely follows her prose model, in which Cyprian says he should not write many books about such things (καὶ ἵνα μὴ τὰ πάντα λέγων πολλὰς βίβλους καταγράψωμαι), but elsewhere in the second book Eudocia's paraphrastic choices seem once again to highlight the association of Cyprian's earlier paganism with inscribed books. In his eventual rebuke of the devil, Cyprian says (2. 428-430 Ludwich):

ἤλιτον ἐκπάγλως φρένας ἐκ σέο ἠπεροπευθείς.
ἄφρων καὶ δυσεβὴς γενόμην, σοὶ πάνθ' ὑποείξας.
μαψιδίως σοφίην δὲ μάθον, προτέρων δέ τε βύβλους.

Because you deceived my mind, I have sinned.
I have become senseless and impious and yielded everything to you.
I fruitlessly learned wisdom and the books of the ancients.

Eudocia's phrase "books of the ancients" (προτέρων...βύβλους)[35] renders the less marked γράμματα of the prose versions, a term used of the written text but also more generally of letters and learning. The difference is subtle, but βύβλος here recalls more powerfully the integral role of physical sorcery books in Cyprian's conversion, the now destroyed source of his impiety and demonic actions. This evocation of his burned pagan books is particularly striking in the second chapter of Eudocia's poem, within the performative frame of Cyprian's confession: in contrast to the bookish source of his pagan magic, Cyprian is confessing before the people of Antioch in a public oral performance that is a spoken source of his redemption.

Eudocia's paraphrase does not depict a wholesale rejection of written learning. Her poetic activity of course assumes a deep investment in the classical poetry still taught in the education system, in both the Greek East and the Latin West, now harnessed in service of the Christian evangelizing mission. Written books are not foreign to Cyprian and Justina's experiences of conversion. They lie behind the oral recitation of the deacon Praulius at the outset of the poem, which leads Justina to Christian faith, and it is through the exchange of one set of books for another that Cyprian is transformed from demonic sorcerer to holy bishop. Like the preface to her Homeric cento, the paraphrase depicts a Christian world in which inscribed texts interact with and lie behind oral recitation and transmission of Christian narratives. At the same time, through careful adaptation of her prose models, Eudocia imbues oral performance with particular authority to deliver Christian truth and to persuade, in contrast to the static books of pagan learning that are the source of Cyprian's demonic magic. The same dynamic is found in Nonnus' *Paraphrase* of St John's Gospel a few decades later, where truth and authority are more characteristic of speech than written books, and the theme of vocal witness is stressed.[36] The treatment of orality and literacy in Eudocia's poem takes its lead from the prose hypotext(s), but we have seen that Eudocia makes paraphrastic choices which make these underlying themes more prominent. Her alignment with the figure of the oral preacher Praulius, who is portrayed as a hexameter poet engaged in the universal Christian evangelizing mission of Christianity, itself suggests self-conscious reflection on her poetic undertaking as performed, and awareness of different categories and experiences of audiences in late antiquity – categories which are problematized by the very project of recasting the popular genre of hagiography into an antiquated and less accessible register.

---

35 Contrast Cyprian's silent books of the ancient pagans with the speaking books of Old Testament prophecy described in similar language in Nonnus' *Paraphrase* 6. 218 καὶ προτέρων δεδαῶτες ἀσιγήτων ἀπὸ βιβλίων, with the commentary of Agosti 2006, 55-56.

36 See Lightfoot 2020, esp. 321-323 and 326-327: "Scripture is written when subjected to scrutiny as a source, but shifts into auditory mode when the desired emphasis is on its authority and inspired nature". She notes that oral performance is also particularly associated with God's inspiration and veracity in the Sibylline Oracles.

Bibliography

Agosti, G. 2001a. "L'epica biblica nella tarda antichità greca. Autori e lettori nel IV e V secolo", in: Stella, F. (ed.), *La scrittura infinita. Bibbia e poesia in età medievale e umanistica (Atti del Convegno di Firenze, 26-28 giugno 1997)*. Firenze: SISMEL, 67-104.

Agnosti, G. 2001b. "Considerazioni preliminari sui generi letterari dei poemi del Codice Bodmer". *Aegyptus* 81, 185-217.

Agnosti, G. 2002. "I poemetti del *Codice Bodmer* e il loro ruolo nella storica della poesia tardoantica", in: Hurst, A. & Rudhardt, J. (eds). *Le Codex des Visions*. Geneva: Droz, 73-114.

Agnosti, G. 2006. "La voce dei libri: dimensioni performative dell' epica greca tardoantica", in: E. Amato (ed.), *Approches de la Troisiéme Sophistique*. Brussels: Latomus, 35-62.

Agnosti, G. 2012. "Greek Poetry", in: Johnson, S. (ed.), *The Oxford Handbook of Late Antiquity*. Oxford: Oxford University Press, 361-404.

Bailey, R. 2017. *The Acts of Saint Cyprian of Antioch: Critical Editions, Translations, and Commentary*. PhD thesis, McGill University.

Bevegni, C. 1982. "Eudociae Augustae Martyrium S. Cypriani I, 1-99". *Prometheus* 8, 249-262.

Bevegni, C. 2006. *Eudocia Augusta. Storia di San Cipriano*. Milan: Adelphi.

Botha, P.J.J. 2012. *Orality and Literacy in Early Christianity*. Eugene: Cascade Books.

Cameron, A. 2016. *Wandering Poets and Other Essays on Late Greek Literature and Philosophy*. Oxford: Oxford University Press.

Cribiore, R. 1996. *Writing, Teachers and Students in Graeco-Roman Egypt*. Atlanta: Scholars Press.

Daley, B.E. 2015. "Finding the Right Key: The Aims and Strategies of Early Christian Interpretation of the Psalms", in: Daley, B.E. & Kolbet, P.R. (eds), *The Harp of Prophecy: Early Christian Interpretation of the Psalms*. Notre Dame: University of Notre Dame Press.

Dewey, J. 2013. *The Oral Ethos of the Early Church: Speaking, Writing, and the Gospel of Mark*. Eugene: Cascade Books.

Dunkle, B.P. 2016. *Enchantment and Creed in the Hymns of Ambrose of Milan*. Oxford: Oxford University Press.

Efthymiadis, S. 2014. *The Ashgate Research Companion to Byzantine Hagiography*. Farnham: Ashgate.

Faulkner, A. 2021. "Eudocia's Singing Deacon: Another Programmatic Passage in Late Antique Christian Verse". *Journal of Hellenic Studies* 141, 216-223.

Faulkner, A. 2020. *Apollinaris of Laodicea: Metaphrasis Psalmorum*. Oxford: Oxford University Press.

Gillingham, S. 2008. *Psalms Through the Centuries: Volume 1*. Malden: Blackwell.

Green, R.P.H. 2006. *Latin Epics of the New Testament*. Oxford: Oxford University Press.

Grindstaff, L. 2008. "Culture and Popular Culture: A Case for Sociology". *The Annals of the American Academy of Political and Social Science* 619, 206-222.

Hunter, R. (forthcoming). "Allusion or Citation? Clement of Alexandria and Classical Literature" (paper delivered in Toronto, 17 September, 2022).

Hurst, A. & Rudhardt, J. (eds) 1999. *Papyri Bodmer XXX–XXXVI: "Codex des Vision", Poèmes divers*. Geneva: Bibliotheca Bodmeriana.

Kaster, R.A. 1988. *Guardians of Language: The Grammarians and Society in Late Antiquity*. Berkeley: University of California Press.

Keith, C. 2020. *The Gospel as Manuscript: An Early History of the Jesus Tradition as Material Artefact*. Oxford: Oxford University Press.

Kelber, W.H. 1983. *The Oral and the Written Gospel: The Hermeneutics of Speaking and Writing in the Synoptic Tradition, Mark, Paul, and Q*. Philadelphia: Fortress Press.

Lightfoot, J.L. 2020. "Nonnus and the Book", in: Doroszewski, F. & Jażdżewska, K. (eds), *Nonnus of Panopolis in Context III*. Leiden: Peeters, 317-331.

Livrea, E. 1998. "L'imperatrice Eudocia e Roma. Per una datazione del de S. Cypr.". *Byzantinische Zeitschrift* 91, 70-91.

Ludwich, A. 1897. *Eudociae Augustae, Procli Lycii, Claudiani carminum Graecorum reliquiae*. Leipzig: Teubner.

McGill, S. 2012. "Latin Poetry", in: Johnson, S. (ed.). *The Oxford Handbook of Late Antiquity*. Oxford: Oxford University Press, 335-360.

McGuckin, J. 2001. *St Gregory of Nazianzus: An Intellectual Biography*. New York: St Vladimir's Seminary Press.

McKinnon, J.W. 1994. "Desert Monasticism and the Later Fourth-Century Psalmodic Movement". *Music and Letters* 75, 505-521.

Meyier, K.A. de 1965. *Codices Bibliothecae Publicae Graeci*, adiuvante E. Hulshoff Pol. Leiden: Brill.

Miguélez Cavero, L. 2008. *Poems in Context: Greek Poetry in the Egyptian Thebaid 200-600 AD*. Berlin: De Gruyter.

Radermacher, L. 1927. *Griechische Quellen zur Faustsage. Der Zauberer Cyprianus. Die Erzählung des Helladius. Theophilus*. Wien: Hölder-Pichler-Tempsky.

Rey, A.-L. 1998. *Patricius, Eudocia, Côme de Jérusalem: Centons Homériques*. Paris: Editions du Cerf.

Roberts, M. 1985. *Biblical Epic and Rhetorical Paraphrase in Late Antiquity*. Liverpool: F. Cairns.

Salvaneschi, E. 1982. "De Sancto Cypriano", in: Angelino, C. & Salvaneschi, E. (eds) 1982. *Syncrisis A: Testi e studi di storia e filosofia del inguaggio religioso*. Genoa: Il Melangolo, 11-80.

Schembra, R. 2006. *La prima redazione dei centoni omerici: Traduzione e commento*. Alessandria: Edizioni dell'Orso.

Schembra, R. 2007a. *Homerocentones*. Turnhout: Brepols.

Schembra, R. 2007b. *La seconda redazione dei centoni omerici: Traduzione e commento*. Alessandria: Edizioni dell'Orso.

Sowers, B. 2020. *In Her Own Words: The Life and Poetry of Aelia Eudocia*. Cambridge, MA: Harvard University Press.

Thomas, R. 1992. *Literacy and Orality in Ancient Greece*. Cambridge: Cambridge University Press.

Usher, M.D. 1998. *Homeric Stitchings: The Homeric Centos of the Empress Eudocia* Lanham: Rowman & Littlefield.

Usher, M.D. 1999. *Eudociae Homerocentones*. Stuttgart: Teubner.

Wilson, N. 2006. "L'archetipo tardoantico di Faust", in: Bevegni 2006, 173-202.

Webb, R. 2009. *Demons and Dancers: Performance in Late Antiquity*. Cambridge, MA: Harvard University Press.

Whitby, M. 2007. 'The Bible Hellenized: Nonnus' *Paraphrase* of St John's Gospel and "Eudocia's" Homeric Centos', in: Scourfield, J.H.D. (ed.), *Texts and Culture in Late Antiquity*, Swansea, 195-231.

Wyrwa, D. 1983. *Die christliche Platonaneignung in den Stromateis des Clemens Alexandrinus*. Berlin: De Gruyter.

4

THE VERNACULAR ALEXANDER*

MARIANNE PADE

The Lombard humanist Pier Candido Decembrio (1399-1477) was the secretary of Filippo Maria Visconti, Duke of Milan, from 1417 until the latter's death in 1447.[1] From the life of the duke, compiled by Decembrio himself, it appears that Visconti's literary taste was not of the refined humanist variety. He was mainly interested in French books containing fanciful stories of famous personalities – i.e. the *chansons des gestes* – and he liked to listen to histories relating the deeds of famous men, either already in the vernacular or in translations commissioned by him.[2] Decembrio's account is confirmed by the many translations of classical historians made by the humanists employed at his court, and by the luxury copies of already existing translations, such as Boccaccio's Livy, which Visconti had made for his library.[3]

It was probably Decembrio, the most influential humanist at the court, who was responsible for collecting a vernacular library of historical texts for Visconti. He also produced a number of translations for the duke: apart from the *Istoria d'Alexandro Magno*, we possess vernacular versions by him of the first three books of Polybius, made from the Latin version of Leonardo Bruni,[4] of the *Commentarii* of Caesar,[5] of Columella and some excerpts from Apuleius,[6] and of Appianus (for which see below on Decembrio's *Istoria*).

In this article I shall argue that Decembrio's *Istoria* constitutes a popularization of primarily Curtius' *Historia Alexandri*. I am well aware that in the fifteenth century most people were illiterate and did not have the economic means to possess books, so I here

---

* This article is largely based on material collected in Pade 1998 but my research questions are different.
1. Zaggia 1993a, 161-219, 321-382. On Decembrio especially, see 199-219 and 321-342, with previous bibliography. Older treatments include Borsa 1893 and Ditt 1931.
2. Decembrio 2019, 124, cap. LXII: *Delectatus est et Gallorum libris mira vanitate referentibus illustrium vita. Historias etiam ab antiquis editas vulgari eloquio aut a doctis traductas e latino, continentes gesta clarorum virorum, cupidissime audivit.* On the life of Filippo Maria, see Ianziti 2016.
3. Cp. Pellegrin 1955; 1969.
4. On the translation of Polybius, see his letter to Francesco Pizolpasso in Zaggia 1993a, 333 and 336.
5. On this see Schadee 2015; Donato 2018; and the edition in Decembrio 2017.
6. Borsa 1904, 520.

Pisanello, Medal of Pier Candido Decembrio, 1448. The inscription reads: CANDIDVS STVDIORVM HVMANITATIS DECVS (Candidus, an ornament of Latin letters). Photo: Wikimedia Commons

use the word 'popular' of the vernacular literary culture as opposed to the elitist humanist Latin one. I will demonstrate how Decembrio operated with different standards for his works in the vernacular from those he used for his Latin works, with regard to method of translation and compilation, as well as in the physical presentation of the *Istoria*. He aimed at readability and accessibility, rather that philological accuracy and the severe aesthetic standards of the humanist book; apparently the strategy worked, for the *Istoria* enjoyed a wide dissemination, not only in its original Lombard environment, but also in several other vernacular cultures. I know of more than 40 manuscripts of the original version in Lombard and of translations into Tuscan, Spanish, Portuguese, and French, and 12 printed editions.

Translation – Latin vs vernacular

In order to see Decembrio's *Istoria d'Alexandro Magno* in a larger context, it will be useful to look at his career as a translator and what we know about his views on translation. It is well known how he learned Greek alone, without a teacher, from Emmanuel Chrysoloras' primer, *Erotemata*. He then studied Plutarch's *Vitae parallelae* in an eleventh-

Pisanello, Medal of Filippo Maria Visconti. Photo: Wikimedia Commons

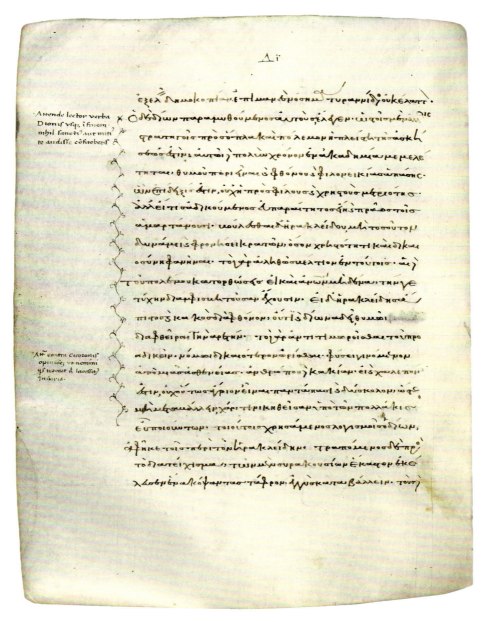

We find numerous traces of Decembrio's reading of Plutarch in the margins of the venerable Palatine manuscript. In the upper part of the left margin of this folium, opposite *Vita Dionis* 47.4, he wrote: *Attende, lector, verba Dionis usque in finem; nihil sanctius aut mitius te audisse confiteberis* (Reader, pay close attention to the words of Dion. You will acknowledge that you have never heard anything more just or mild). The moralizing gloss is typical of Decembrio's style of annotation, cp. Pade 2005. Heidelberg, Universitätsbibliothek, Pal. gr. 168-169 f.114v. Photo: Heidelberg, Universitätsbibliothek.

Fig. 3.

century Greek manuscript in the ducal library of Pavia – today MS Pal. NS. 168-169 in Heidelberg – copying the lives of Sertorius, Cato, Phocion, and Flamininus into what is now MS R 88 sup. of the Biblioteca Ambrosiana in Milan over some months in 1437.[7]

Decembrio used the existing Latin translations of Plutarch's lives to improve his mastery of the Greek originals. We get interesting glimpses both of the progress he made and of his views on translation in marginal notes in manuscripts annotated by him and in letters to friends. He repeatedly criticized inaccuracies and omissions in these translations and showed himself an adherent of the faithful, literal translation.[8] Some years ago, James Hankins summarized Decembrio's statements about translation as follows: following Jerome, sacred texts should be translated *ad verbum*, literally, even observing the word order of the original; for poetic and rhetorical texts one could translate more freely and take into account the style of the original. For historical and philosophical texts he advocated a strategy in between: the translation should be fairly literal, it should not necessarily render the word order of the original, but omissions and transpositions are to be avoided. He also discussed the rendering of technical terms in philosophical texts with Leonardo Bruni. Whereas Bruni insisted on finding Latin equivalents, Decembrio transcribed them, using terms such as *democracy* and *oligarchy*.[9]

Decembrio never said explicitly that these principles should not be respected in translation into the vernacular, but we do get the clear impression that he did not value his works written in the vernacular as highly as he did his Latin works. In a letter to Archbishop Francesco Pizolpasso he complains about not finding the time to devote himself to humanist studies, *studia humanitatis*, as he had to produce works in the vernacular for Visconti, in this case a commentary on Petrarch's sonnets and the translations of Polybius, Caesar, and Curtius.[10] In another letter he complains that his vernacular works did not really interest him,[11] but even so he was proud of the vernacular Curtius, which he proclaimed to be "worthy of a duke".[12]

Mixed signals?

The physical appearance of some of the surviving manuscripts is certainly worthy of a duke. The oldest surviving copy, Turin, Biblioteca già reale, MS Varia 131, *a*. 1438, is a luxury manuscript illuminated by the so-called *Magister vitae imperatorum* and with corrections by Decembrio himself. It is among the first examples of a text in the

---

7   For Pier Candido's work on the Heidelberg MS, see Ziegler 1934, 11-20, and Pade 2007, I, 251-254. For Plutarch in the Italian Renaissance, see Pade 2007 and 2023.
8   For his criticism of Leonardo Bruni, see Resta 1962, 27-28 and Pade 1993, 204-205; for his discussions of some translations by Iacopo Angeli da Scarperia, see Resta 1962, 25-27. See also Pade 1994, 190-194; 2005.
9   Hankins 1990, I, 120-123 references to the texts discussed in volume II; 1994, 158. For Decembrio's discussion with Bruni, see also Zaggia 1993b.
10 Zaggia 1993a, 333; on Decembio's letters, see Zaccaria 1952.
11 Zaggia 1993a, 202.
12 Zaggia 1993a, 321.

vernacular to be copied in humanistic writing.[13] The arrangement of the text on the page, the lines, the use of catchwords, and so on all follow the norms of Latin humanist manuscripts. Such a book was intended to indicate to readers that they were holding in their hands a work belonging to Latin humanist culture — even if the text copied in the book was not in Latin. On the other hand, in at least two manuscripts we find miniatures, which act as illustrations of the text and not just ornamental friezes or the owner's coat of arms. Illustrations of the text are rare in classical manuscripts, and in fact Ross – who has examined the medieval tradition of illustrations in books on Alexander – does not know of a single illustrated Curtius.[14] In vernacular books, on the other hand, illustrations are frequent.[15]

From Curtius' *Alexander* to Decembrio's *Istoria d'Alexandro Magno*

The book Decembrio presented to Visconti in 1438 was not a straightforward translation of Curtius' text; he had filled two of the great internal *lacunae*, partly with passages taken from Plutarch's *Alexander*, and compiled a *Comparison of Caesar and Alexander*, modelled on the *synkriseis* that follow almost all Plutarch's *Vitae parallelae*, but not the pair Alexander and Caesar. It was these texts – the translation of Curtius with some of the lost passaged substituted with texts from other sources and the *Comparatio* – which Decembrio referred to as his *Istoria d'Alexandro Magno*, the *History of Alexander the Great*.

The lacuna in book five

To fill the lacuna at the end of book five, where the description of Darius' death is missing today, Decembrio used the corresponding passage from Plutarch's *Alexander* (ch. 43). In the rubric he explains:

> *E perche lystoria dela morte didario era imperfecta P. Candido, ricerchata quela in le lettere grece e ritrouata inli libri di Plutarcho magistro di Traiano imperatore, fidelmente la transferita in lingua latina in questa forma*

> And because the story of Darius' death was not finished, P. Candido sought after in the Greek literature and found it in the books of Plutarch, the teacher of the Emperor Trajan, faithfully translating it into Latin.[16]

---

13   Ferrari 1988, 21, 27, and 29; see also Zaggia 1993a, 211-212. The Turin manuscript is meticulously described in Donato 2019.
14   Ross 1963, 5-65; 1967, 383-388.
15   Cp. Mitchell 1961, 9.
16   All quotes from the *Istoria* are from Pade 1998, where I mostly followed the readings of the Turin manuscript. I retained the orthography, but normalized the use of capitals. In this passage we see that Decembrio, like most of his contemporaries, believed the medieval fabrication that Trajan had been the pupil of Plutarch; for this see Pade 2007, I, 62-66.

Decembrio did actually translate the passage into Latin: we find a *Descriptio mortis Darii* which may be dated to the summer of 1437 in the Ambrosiana manuscript in which he copied the Greek texts of some of Plutarch's lives (see above).

Decembrio claimed to have rendered the passage from Plutarch's *Alexander* "faithfully" in Latin, but his vernacular versions do not follow the precepts he formulated for translations into Latin. Among other things, he modifies the beginning of the description of Darius' death, to adapt it to the last words of Curtius' text *semivivi hominis* (5,13,25).

Plutarch tells how Darius, dying, would like to thank Polistratus, because he had given him a drink, while he can only lament the fate that made him unable to repay a benefit received: ὦ ἄνθρωπε, τοῦτό μοι πέρας γέγονε δυστυχίας ἁπάσης, εὖ παθεῖν ἀμείψασθαι μὴ δυνάμενον (*Alexander* 43,4). Decembrio evidently did not understand Plutarch's Greek well, and in his versions, in Latin as well as in the vernacular, poor Darius expresses a much less regal sentiment: *'Bone vir', inquit, 'hic mihi calamitatis omnis finem statuit, ex quo fortunam in melius transferre negatum est',*[17] and in the vernacular *'o nobile homo,' dixe, 'questo mi sera fine dogni infelicitate, poi che la mia sorte in megliore stato cambiare non mi lice'.*

In most manuscripts of the *Istoria d'Alexandro*, the lacuna at the beginning of the sixth book is indicated by a rubric, which offers the reader a brief summary of the events preceding the battle with which this book currently begins:

Qui mancha el principio del sexto libro como e dito, sequita una bataglia senza el principio etiandio data dalo re Antipatro prefeto dalexandro in Macedonia contra li lacedemonii nela quale Agis re di Lacedemonia famosissimo capitanio infatti darme uirilmente combattendo fu ucciso, essendo Alexandro nele parte doriente.

Here, as was said, the beginning of the sixth book is missing; there follows a battle without the beginning between King Antipater, prefect of Alexander in Macedonia, and the Lacedaemonians in which King Agis of Lacedaemon, a renowned general, died fighting valiantly, while Alexander was in the East.

However, in one manuscript, the Barberinus latinus 4044 now in the Vatican Library, but of Lombard origin, we find a different rubric, followed by a supplement to the text that fills the gap:

Finisse el quinto libro de lystoria dalexandro magno Re di Macedonia. Incomincia el sexto scripto da Quintus Curcio Ruffo historico eloquentissimo e traduto in uulgare da P. Candido felicemente. [Inc.]: Fratanto che Alexandro Dario seguiua, li Lacedemonii per gliantique inimicicie con li Macedoni haute per instigatione dantipatro che absente Alexandro alchuna gran facenda per se adoprare desideraua, ala bataglia con queli uenero. In laquale essendo luna e laltra parte longamente affatichata, ala fine li Lacedemonii parueno douere esser superiore e certo la uictoria ottenuta hariano,

---

17   Ditt 1931, 72.

se non che Antipatro ueduti li suoi gia dela schiera partire, prise li megliori in la prima parte ad Agis soppose. Alora queli che luy circundaueno per timore del suo Re abandonata la pugna ali Macedoni dedero locho e riuolta la fortuna de li Macedoni, li Lacedemonii priseno a caciare, si chel timore del suo Re [Inc. Curtius]: (6,1) questo pericolo de la bataglia induxe…

End of Book Five of the history of Alexander, king of Macedonia. Beginning of Book Six written by Quintus Curcius Rufus, most eloquent historian, and translated successfully into the vernacular by Pier Candido [Inc.]: While Alexander was following Darius, the Lacedaemonians, for long foes of the Macedonians, were persuaded by Antipater, who hoped to be able to profit materially from the absence of Alexander, to go into battle. When after a while both parts were exhausted, the Lacedaemonians seem to be winning and would have been victorius, if not Antipater, seeing his men already withdraw, took his best men and confronted Agis. Then, fearing for the safety of their king, the Lacedaemonians abandoned the battle and left the field to the Macedonians. With this change of fortune, the Macedonians began to chase the Lacedaemonians, so that the king, fearful of [Inc. Curtius]: (6,1) the danger presented by the battle, was lead to…

The Barberini manuscript is one of only four copies of the *Istoria d'Alexandro* in which the missing chapters at the beginning of Curtius' text are substituted by a translation of Plutarch's *Alexander* 2-17; it seems possible that the description of the battle was drafted by Decembrio as part of his plan to produce a more complete account of Alexander's deeds than the one provided by Curtius' mutilated work. I have not been able to identify the source for the supplement. Apart from Curtius, I know of two descriptions of the battle between Agide and Antipater, Justinus (12,1,4-11) and Diodorus Siculus (17,62,6-63,4), but in the Barberini MS there are details that are not found in any of the two writers, namely the role played by Antipater and his meeting with Agis.[18]

The lacuna in book 10

Curtius' text has a lacuna after 10.4, which Decembrio filled by using Plutarch's account of Alexander's illness and death. Plutarch's version of the story does not agree completely with Curtius' narrative, but Decembrio warns us about it after the supplement:

Seguita el resto del duodecimo libro di Quintus Curcio Ruffo nel quale pare alchuna differentia dale parole di Plutarcho suprascripte, per che inante che Alexandro la uoce perdesse, dice luy con le sue gente darme dinante la morte parlato hauere come segue nel texto

---

18 In Smits 1987 there is an edition of some anonymous supplements to Curtius, but they were not Decembrio's source.

Here follows the the rest of Book 12 by Quintus Curtius Rufus in which there are some discrepancies from what I just quoted from Plutarch: Curtius says that before Alexander lost his voice, he talked to his comrades before dying as described in what follows.[19]

The *Comparatio* of Caesar and Alexander

Even though the *Comparatio* is always copied together with the translation of Curtius, Decembrio wrote it as a work in its own right. In the letter of dedication to Filippo Maria Visconti, he states that he completed the work shortly after his translations of Caesar and Curtius. It is modelled on Plutarch's *synkrisis*, and Decembrio used material from the two Plutarchan lives, and from Suetonius, Gellius, Livy, and Petrarch. He compares the virtues and exploits of the two heroes, demonstrating, for the most part, the superiority of Caesar over Alexander. This should not surprise us, because Visconti's predilection for the Roman hero was marked. Furthermore, there is no doubt that Decembrio was prompted to write the *Comparatio* by the so-called controversy on Scipio and Caesar, a controversy that had been going on since the mid-thirties between supporters of the republican constitution and the monarchy.[20] The Comparison does not constitute a direct contribution to this controversy, but Decembrio underlines the inevitability of Caesar's policy, referring to Aristotle's *Politics*, according to which certain men are by nature destined to reign. This passage demonstrates the self-assurance, not always justified, with which Decembrio handled Greek sources. In Aristotle's text we read the words ὥσπερ ῥήτορα (1255a), which Decembrio translates as *uno philosopho appellato Rhetora*. He could have used Bruni's translation, which has *tanquam oratorem*,[21] but obviously chose not to.

The intial supplement

Around 1450, some 12 years after he finished the the original version of his *Istoria*, Decembrio added an initial supplement to Curtius' text to substitute the missing chapters, that is, his translation of Plutarch, *Alexander* 2-17.[22] It is dedicated to the Spaniard Nuño de Guzmán, of whom there is a *Vita* by Vespasiano da Bisticci.[23] According to Vespasiano, Guzmán was a great traveller and participated in the Council of Florence in

---

19   Decembrio's copy of Curtius apparently had the text divided into 12 books, as we find it in some manuscripts.
20   Cp. Brown 1981; Pade 1990, 80-88; 2021.
21   I quote Bruni's translation from Aristoteles 1562, III, 228v.
22   Probably due to the size of the supplement, some scholars have mistakenly maintained that Decembrio translated the entire *Vita Alexandri*, for example Resta 1962, 35, n. 2. Likewise, in his introduction to Manetti's *Vita Socratis et Senecae*, De Petris maintained that Decembrio dedicated a translation of the Plutarchan pair, *Alexander & Caesar*, to Guzmán, cp. Manetti 1979, 7 n. 8.
23   For Guzmán, see di Camillo 1976, 126.

1438. There he met Gianozzo Manetti, who dedicated his *Vita Socratis et Senecae* to him. Back in Spain he remained in contact with Italy, and commissioned various manuscripts in Florence. Along with the chapters from Plutarch, Decembrio dedicated a vernacular version of Seneca's *Apocolocynthosis* to Guzmán. The initial supplement from Plutarch's *Alexander* is found in only four manuscripts, and it was not printed together with the translation of Curtius and the *Comparatio*.[24]

Decembrio based his vernacular version of *Alexander* 2-17 on Guarino Veronese's 1408 Latin translation. Though elsewhere Decembrio wrote disparagingly about his own vernacular translations (see above), in the dedication to Guzmán he took care to present his work as learned and serious: since he was compiling a *Istoria d'Alessandro* he did not translate the first chapter of the *Vita Alexandri*, where Plutarch discusses his biographical method. Instead Decembrio added his own declaration of method:

> *De lorigine antiqua dalexandro Magno, si come neglialtre uetustate sole euenire, piu a lautoritate cha ad altra ragione credere ne bisognia, poi che da letate e notitia nostra sono molto distante.*

> Regarding the origins of Alexander, as with other ancient events, one must rely on authoritative sources rather than applying other criteria, since these events are so far removed from our times.[25]

The appeal to *auctoritates* is frequent in humanist writings. The word is used either about the most authoritative witnesses for the readings of a text, or, as here, about reliable sources for an event from the past. For Decembrio this appeal no doubt served to signal his attitude as an up-to-date, humanist historian, despite the fact that he wrote in the vernacular.

Decembrio's *Istoria* – a popularization?

I mentioned earlier that with regard to translation of historical texts, Decembrio recommended a very close rendering of the original. However, he was referring to translation from Greek into Latin; his attitude is very different when it comes to translation into the vernacular. When he added the various supplements to Curtius' text, he clearly prioritized a continuous narrative over philological *acribia*, and in his rendering of Plutarch, he often modifies the original, skipping entire passages or adding material.

Translating a Latin historian into Italian with the addition of material from various sources, Decembrio produced a work that resembles other compilations in the vernacular from the same period. One example is the *Lives of the Roman emperors* which

---

24 Zaggia 1993a, 215; Pade 1998, 107-110.
25 Quotes from *Alexander* 2-17 and the introduction follow the Barberini manuscript mentioned above. For the combination *autoritate … ragione* in humanist philology, I refer to the discussion in Rizzo 1973, 293-295.

Fig. 4.

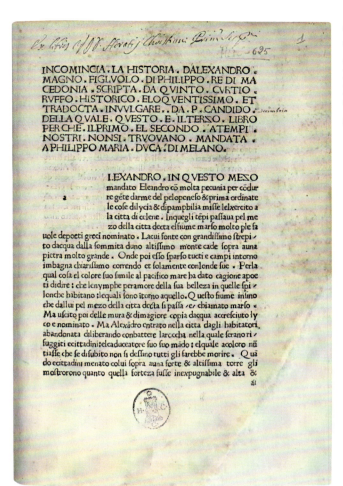

Editio princeps of the *Istoria d'Alexandro*. Florentiae: Apud Sanctum Jacobum de Ripoli, 1478. Decembrio's Lombard is translated into Tuscan. Photo: Wikimedia Commons.

includes the 12 lives of Suetonius, followed by those of subsequent emperors, taken from the *Historia Augusta*, Eutropius, Orosius, and others. The work was compiled and translated into Italian by Antonio da Rho, and the presentation copy, today MS Ital. 131 of the Bibliothèque Nationale in Paris, was copied by Angelo Decembrio, the younger brother of Pier Candido.[26] He himself made a similar compilation a few years later: in Rome he had translated Appianus (1450-1454) into Latin for Pope Nicholas V, for whom he worked as a *brevium magister*. After 1466 he moved to Ferrara, where he made a vernacular version of the Appianus for Ercole d'Este, to which he added more than 30 chapters from Plutarch's *Vita Marci Antonii* in book five.[27]

26 For the illuminator of the presentation copy, see Stefani 1985, 823-881 and 875-881.
27 A similar procedure can also be found in the context of Latin humanism, for example in Leonardo Bruni's *Cicero novus*, which is based on Plutarch's *Vita Ciceronis*, but with added material from various Latin sources, cp. Pade 2007, I, 154-165; 2019.

Conclusion

Though Decembrio prided himself on his historical method in the dedication to Guzmán, the vernacular compilations he produced for his princely patrons, Filippo Maria Visconti and Ercole d'Este, undoubtedly aimed at readability and producing a continuous narrative rather than the close rendering of the original. And in that he succeeded, to judge by the material fortune of the work. As mentioned above, I know of more than 40 manuscripts of the original version in Lombard and of translations into Tuscan, Spanish, Portuguese, and French, and 12 printed editions. The success of the *Istoria d'Alexandro* may, in my opinion, be explained by the fact that Decembrio chose a popular and traditional subject – the life and deeds of Alexander – but treated it with modern methods, thus replacing the medieval Alexander novels for readers influenced by the new humanist culture. The 'modern' aspect of the *Istoria* was emphasized by the physical appearance of some the early manuscripts, which were copied in humanistic writing and had the *mise en page* of a book belonging to Latin humanist culture. Thus the way these early copies of Decembrio's *Istoria d'Alexandro* presented themselves materially went hand in hand with the content, to produce a work with elements from both humanist avantgarde and more traditional vernacular culture: the result was a new popular history of Alexander.

Bibliography

Aristoteles 1562. *Aristotelis ... libri ...*. Venetiis apud Iunctas MDLXII, repr. Frankfurt am Main 1962.
Borsa, M. 1893. "Pier Candido Decembrio e l'Umanesimo in Lombardia". *Archivio Storico Lombardo* 20.
Borsa, M. 1904. "The Correspondence of Humphrey, Duke of Gloucester, and Pier Candido Decembrio". *English Historical Review* 19, 502-526.
Brown, V. 1981. "Portraits of Julius Caesar in the Latin Manuscripts of the Commentaries". *Viator* 12, 319-354.
Decembrio, P.C. 2017. *Volgarizzamento del Corpus Caesarianum*. Edizione critica, a cura di P. Ponzú Donato. Florence: Firenze University Press.
Decembrio, P.C. 2019. *Lives of the Milanese Tyrants*, ed. M. Zaggia, tr. G. Ianziti. The I Tatti Renaissance Library 88. Harvard: Harvard University Press.
di Camillo, O. 1976. *El Humanismo Castellano del siglo XV*. Valencia: Fernando Torres.
Ditt, E. 1931. *Pier Candido Decembrio. Contributo alla storia dell'Umanesimo Italiano*. Memorie R. Istituto Lombardo di Scienze Lettere e Arti 24. Milan: Hoepli.
Donato, P. Ponzú 2018. "Pier Candido Decembrio editore di Cesare". *Italia Medioevale e Umanistica* 59, 165191 and ill. IIV.
Donato, P.P. 2019. "MS Varia 131 of the Biblioteca Reale di Torino and Decembrio's Translation of Curtius Rufus". *Translat Library* 1.4, 1-15.
Ferrari, M. 1998. "La 'littera antiqua' à Milan, 14171439", in: Autenrieth, J. & Eigler, U. (eds), *Renaissance und Humanistenhandschriften*. Munich: Oldenbourg, 1329.
Hankins, J. 1990. *Plato in the Italian Renaissance*. Columbia Studies in the Classical Tradition 17, 1-2. Leiden & New York: Brill.
Hankins, J. 1994. "Translation Practice in the Renaissance: the Case of Leonardo Bruni", in: Ternes, C.M. (ed.), *Actes du colloque Méthodologie de la traduction: de l'Antiquité à la Renaissance*. Etudes classiques IV. Luxembourg: Centre universitaire de Luxembourg, 154-175.
Ianziti, G. 2016. "Pier Candido Decembrio and the Suetonian Path to Princely Biography", in: Baker, P. et al. (eds), *Portraying the Prince in the Renaissance: The Humanist Depiction of Rulers in Historiographical and Biographical Texts*. Berlin: De Gruyter, 237-270.
Manetti, G. 1979. *Vita Socratis et Senecae*, a c. di A. De Petris. Florence: Olschki.

Mitchell, C. 1961. *A Fifteenth Century Italian Plutarch (B.M. Add. 22318)*. London: Faber and Faber.

Pade, M. 1990. "Guarino and Caesar at the Court of the Este", in: Pade, M. et al. (eds), *La corte di Ferrara e il suo mecenatismo 1441-1598*. Copenhagen/Modena: Panini, 71-91.

Pade, M. 1993. "Il Vaticano Latino 1877. Un testimone della tradizione umanistica degli studi plutarchei". *Studi Umanistici Piceni* 13, 197-207.

Pade, M. 1994. "Revisions of Translations, Corrections and Criticisms; some Examples from the Fifteenth-Century Latin Translations of Plutarch's Lives", in: Ternes, C.M. (ed.), *Actes du colloque Méthodologie de la traduction: de l'Antiquité à la Renaissance*. Etudes classiques IV. Luxembourg: Centre universitaire de Luxembourg, 177-198.

Pade, M. 1998. "Curzio e Plutarco nell'Istoria d'Alexandro Magno: volgarizzamento e compilazione in un testo di Pier Candido Decembrio". *Studi umanistici Piceni* 18, 101-113.

Pade, M. 2005. "Le glosse nel cod. V G 14 della Biblioteca Nazionale di Napoli e il Plutarco di Pier Candiddo Decembrio," in: Abbamonte, G. et al. (eds), *Parrhasiana III. "Tocchi di uomini dotti", Codici e stampati con postille di umanisti*. AION XXVII. Rome: Istituti editoriali e poligrafici internazionali, 118-128.

Pade, M. 2007. *The Reception of Plutarch's Lives in Fifteenth-Century Italy I–II*. Renæssancestudier 14. Copenhagen: Museum Tusculanum.

Pade, M. 2019. "Leonardo Bruni and Plutarch", in: Xenofontos, S. & Oikonomopoulou, K. (eds), *Brill's Companion to the Reception of Plutarch*. Leiden & Boston: Brill, 388-403.

Pade, M. 2021. "Should They Rot in Hell? Fifteenth-century Discussions of Brutus and Cassius – and Caesar's Murder", in: Hass, T.A. & Raja, R. (eds), *Caesar's Past and Posterity's Caesar*. Turnhout: Brepols Publishers, 137-150.

Pade, M. 2023. "Plutarch in the Italian Renaissance", in: Titchener, F.B. & Zadorojny, A. (eds.), *The Cambridge Companion to Plutarch*, Cambridge: Cambridge University Press, 323-339.

Pascal Argente, C. & Porto, R.M. Rodríguez 2018. "*Ad Hispaniae fines*: The Iberian Translations of Quintus Curtius Rufus and Fifteenth-century Vernacular Humanism", in: Gaullier Bougassas, C. (ed.), *Postérités européennes de QuinteCurce: De l'humanisme aux Lumières* (xive-xviiie siècle). Turnhout: Brepols, 189-211.

Pellegrin, E. 1955-1969. *La bibliothèque des Visconti et des Sforza Ducs de Milan au XVe siècle*. Paris: Service des publ. du C.N.R.S and *Supplément*. Florence: Olschki.-Paris: De Nobele.

Resta, G. 1962. *Le epitomi di Plutarco nel Quattrocento*. Padova: Antenore.

Rizzo, S. 1973. *Il lessico filologico degli umanisti*. Roma: Storia e Letteratura.

Ross, D.J.A. 1963. *Alexander Historiatus. A Guide to Medieval Illustrated Alexander Literature*. Warburg Institute Surveys. London: The Warburg Institute.

Ross, D.J.A. 1967. "Alexander Historiatus, a Supplement". *Journal of the Warburg and Courtauld Institutes* 30, 383-388.

Schadee, H. 2015. "The First Vernacular Caesar: Pier Candido Decembrio's Translation for Inigo d'Avalos. With Editions and Translations of Both Prologues". *Viator* 46, 277-304.

Smits, E.R. 1987. "A Medieval Supplement to the Beginning of Curtius Rufus' 'Historia Alexandri': An Edition with Introduction". *Viator* 18, 91-124.

Stefani, L. 1985. "Per una storia della miniatura lombarda da Giovannino de' Grassi alla scuola cremonese della II metà del quattrocento: Appunti bibliografici". *La miniatura italiana tra gotico e rinascimento* 2. Florence: Olschki, 823-881.

Zaccaria, V. 1952. "L'epistolario di Pier Candido Decembrio". *Rinascimento* 3, 85-118.

Zaggia, M. 1993a. "Appunti sulla cultura letteraria in volgare a Milano nell'età di Filippo Maria Visconti". *Giornale storico della letteratura italiana* 170, 550-551.

Zaggia, M. 1993b. "La versione latina di Pier Candido Decembrio dalla 'Repubblica' di Platone: per la storia della tradizione". *Interpres* 13, 7-55.

Ziegler, K. 1934. "Plutarchstudien: Geschichte der Heidelberger Plutarchhandschrift 168/9". *Rheinisches Museum* 83, 11-20.

5

FINDING PERICLES LOST

INDICATORS OF THE MEANING OF DANISH TRAVEL ACCOUNTS AND NOSTALGIC ENCOUNTERS WITH NINETEENTH-CENTURY GREECE IN TRANSITION

JENS KRASILNIKOFF

In recent decades, several studies have explored various aspects of the Danish reception and appropriation of the classical Greek past. In several respects, Leo Hjortsø started this trend in 1964, with the publication of *Græske Billeder. Med danske Forfattere og Kunstnere i Grækenland*.[1] In this collection of excerpts of travel accounts with an introduction, Hjortsø offered a diachronic perspective on Danish authors' and artists' encounters with modern Greece in the making.[2] Hjortsø surmised that these Danes expected to find reminders of the classical Greek Man in his contemporary (male) nineteenth-century Greek descendants. Ostensibly, this did not happen, and as we shall see the ensuing disillusionment is apparent in harsh comments regarding the failure of the new Greece to be cast in the image of its glorious past.

Modern research perspectives on these accounts focus on the archaeological and architectonic expeditions, and thus chart the history of Danish contributions to the reconstruction of nineteenth-century Europe's rediscovery of past and contemporary Greece's material culture.[3] Although some of these approaches revealed elements of Danish national and cultural interest in these enterprises, the impact of these discoveries on contemporary Danish cultural and pedagogic developments in the school system is unclear. Recently, however, researchers from Aarhus – Lærke Maria Andersen, Troels Myrup Kristensen, and Vinnie Nørskov – presented a convincing review of how the reception of the classical heritage of Greece evolved and resonated with nineteenth- and twentieth-century Danish society in a range of different guises.[4] These studies

---

1 English translation of the Danish: "Greek Images. With Danish Authors and Artists in Greece".
2 Hjortsø 1964.
3 Ditlevsen 1978; Rathje & Lund 1991; Christiansen 2000.
4 Andersen Funder, Kristensen & Nørskov 2019.

are highly rewarding, but from a cultural historian's perspective, it is not yet clear how and why the ever-changing and diverse nineteenth-century Danish narratives about modern Greece in the making came to be, and what they mean for our understanding of nineteenth-century Europe's uses of the classical Greek past.

At the beginning of the nineteenth century, and most clearly expressed in the narratives of early travellers to Greece including P.O. Brøndsted, contemporary Greeks were measured against nineteenth-century perceptions of the classical Greeks, and this trend continued in various guises throughout the century. However, no later than 1830, elements of European history from the end of the classical period to the final decades of Ottoman rule in the European territory of its empire were also used to explain the negative developments of Greece in transition. Moreover, over the course of the nineteenth century, Greece was evaluated through the lens of growing northern and central European nationalist awareness, which suggests that Danish travellers sought Greece not merely to connect with its classical past and to appropriate it to the notions advocated by the international philhellenist movement, but also to confirm their Danish identity and its dependence on a classical heritage.[5]

This chapter explores the meaning of the above-mentioned accounts and their "uses of history" from a diachronic perspective, and asks how and when the past was incorporated into and exploited by the discourses of Danish meetings with nineteenth-century Greece.[6] Evidently, given the number of extant travel accounts, a full study of these exceeds the scope of this chapter. Instead, and echoing Hjortsø's approach, some selected examples must suffice to illustrate my points and conclusions.[7]

Peter Oluf Brøndsted (1780-1842)

Travel accounts and dissertation, 1810 and 1812
The accounts of the Danish archaeologist P.O. Brøndsted cover a number of journeys and excavations that he undertook between 1810 and 1813 in the eastern part of the Mediterranean region (Fig. 1). The first and oldest account is from 1810, when Brøndsted responded to meeting Greeks on Corfu and in Athens.[8] His first impressions were not flattering. He declared that the Turks, and before them, the Romans, were able to conquer the Greeks because of the latter's inherited decay, degeneration, and failure to cooperate as one people to counter external threats. According to Brøndsted, the Greeks

---

[5] E.g. Angelomatis-Tsougarakis 1990 on British travellers' accounts of nineteenth-century Greece; Tsigakou 2008 and Greenhalgh 2019 on the acquisition of antiquities from the Ottoman Empire.

[6] Regarding the meaning of "uses of history", see Aronsson 2004 and Nielsen 2010. There are good clarifications of the adjacent fields of uses of history and memory studies in Warring 2011 (in Danish).

[7] In this chapter, I have chosen to work with some of Hjortsø's examples, but also found it necessary to include new ones.

[8] Brøndsted 1844, I, 27. See also Schou-Rode 2008, especially 43-44 on the passages of Brøndsted's diaries concerning Athens.

C.A. Jensen, Portrait of P.O. Brøndsted, 1827, Ny Carlsberg Glyptotek. Photo: Ny Carlsberg Glyptotek, Copenhagen.

Fig. 1.

of his day were jealous, self-indulgent, and suffered from "childish inconsequence" – and had been so ever since the classical period. Brøndsted's first impression led him to declare classical antiquity the yardstick against which Greece of his day must be evaluated; he thus introduced to his Danish audience the narrative of Greek history from antiquity to the beginning of the nineteenth century as a long series of defeats, degeneration, and corruption.

Two years later, in 1812, Brøndsted presented a more nuanced version of the Greece of his day in his detailed account of the excavation of the Apollo sanctuary at Phigaleia in the Peloponnese. In the summer of 1812, Brøndsted and a consortium of British, German (Bavarian), and Estonian "philhellenes" entered the Arcadian highlands with the purpose of discovering new "treasures of art" from the classical past.[9] In their own words, this international group of philhellenes engaged in yet another enterprise to meet the growing interest in Greek antiquity amongst the educated citizens of urban Europe. Recent studies of the emergence and nature of European philhellenism also identify its self-indulgent and naïve nature – trends clearly reflected in Brøndsted's narratives.[10] However, as we shall see, the prospect of financial gain also contributed to the companions' enthusiasm.

The challenges faced by the consortium included raising funds for travel and the excavation, as well as the ongoing quarrels with the Ottoman authorities, with whom

9   Brøndsted 1861 (reprinted in Hjortsø 1964, 59-75).
10 See the contributions in Vöhler et al. 2021, especially the editors' introduction and Moyseos's and Matalas's papers.

5 • Finding Pericles lost   63

Fig. 2. Thomas Cole, *Dream of Arcadia*, about 1838. Gift of Mrs. Lindsey Gentry, 1954.71. Photography courtesy Denver Art Museum.

they clashed several times. Initially, the Pacha – the local Turkish governor – insisted on having his part of the profits from the excavation, and instructed one of his officials, a Greek – Vasilachi – to join the consortium as his agent. This Vasilachi was instructed to oversee the expedition's financial transactions, including surveying salary payments to local hired labourers at the excavation. In Brøndsted's account, Vasilachi represented the negative version of an 1812 degenerate servant of the Ottomans ("the dog of the Pacha"), in contrast to the local community of unspoiled, honest, and authentic shepherds of the Arcadian highlands.

Clearly, Brøndsted contrasted the urbanized Greeks in the service of the Turks with the population of the unspoiled and remote mountainous regions of Greece. The explanation of the differences between the two groups of Greeks encountered by Brøndsted was distance: the shepherds existed in an enclave apart from Ottoman influence, and thus may have retained unique and original characteristics not unlike those that the philhellenes sought in the first place. Apparently, Brøndsted confirmed this point in a new and refined guise when he interviewed Ali Pacha, the Turkish governor of Ioannina, later that year.[11] What Brøndsted found in Ali Pacha was an intelligent usurper *in spe*, who later unsuccessfully rebelled against the Ottoman rule. Alternatively, this could be a parallel drawn between the noble qualities of the shepherds and the calculating qualities of Ali Pacha and his subjects.

Earlier in 1812, *en route* to Phigaleia, Brøndsted was in his true element. On entering Arcadia, he compared his impressions to earlier, sixteenth- through eighteenth-century

---

11   Brøndsted 1999, with Isager's introduction, 11-23.

Martinus Rørbye, *Arcadian shepherd*, 1835. National Gallery of Denmark.

Fig. 3.

fantasies of the (lost or happy) Arcadia, a lush and fertile landscape where the locals thrived in pastoral settings – an imaginary, idyllic mountainous landscape of the past (Fig. 2).[12] With a touch of irony, Brøndsted remarked at first, as he travelled through Arcadia *en route* to Phigaleia, that the landscape should correctly be called "stony Arcadia", but later, when he approached Phigaleia, "happy Arcadia" emerged, with its lush woods, rivers, and pleasant atmosphere.

Throughout his expedition, Brøndsted repeatedly returned to the theme of Arcadia, and at the end of the day, when excavations were nearly concluded, the philhellenes of the consortium celebrated with a dance with the local shepherd community in the cellar of the newly cleared temple. In his imagination, Brøndsted actually found reminders of happy Arcadia, its idyll and undisturbed originality represented by the local shepherds (Fig. 3); he flattered himself and his companions with visions of how this revelation,

12 Brøndsted 1861 (in Hjortsø 1964, 62). Barthélémy 1788 and Sonnini 1801 continued to address this theme when others actually visited Greece. Rackham 1990 and Grove & Rackham 2003, 8-17 discuss the seventeenth- and eighteenth-century constructions of the lost Arcadia, along with the emergence of the theory of ruined landscapes and desertification, and how they contradict the evidence of historical landscape development.

and the acquisition of the marble reliefs of the temple, would be a notable contribution to the growing awareness of Greece's classical heritage.

Brøndsted's rationale for the expedition was to save Greece's classical heritage from Ottoman neglect and local Greek ignorance, and to demonstrate that the population of the mountains was a reservoir of ancient and original inherited human traits that could be re-activated by the right influence (read: by the likes of Brøndsted and his compatriots). The moral excuse for this expedition of philhellenes was that they were acting as agents for the preservation and revitalization of the classical heritage; their organization saw itself as the vital link between antiquity and the European cultural dominance of the early nineteenth century.[13] Thus, Brøndsted observed a disruption and discontinuity between classical antiquity and his present, and he presented an existential use of history with a clear pedagogic purpose. Classical Greece was (still) a school of cultural and political enlightenment, which remained attractive and controllable only if it was supervised by apt statesmen such as Pericles, and his peers and heirs, the philhellenes. Brøndsted's use of history remained relevant only if he was able to convince his audience of his contention that classical heritage really was the yardstick against which all European cultures should be measured. His use of Greek orthography and words in his narrative of the Phigaleia expedition demonstrates that the readership he addressed was exclusively the segment of the early nineteenth-century Danish population that was able to read ancient and contemporary Greek. Hence, Brøndsted's historical awareness materialized in a setting where the inherent qualities of the classical past were about to re-emerge. Concurrently, and because of this, his stance as a "philhellene" became a missionary quest and a claim of control over the re-discovery of Europe's Greek origins. However, in his later years, Brøndsted developed a more nuanced approach to Europe's emerging "revolutionary" drives towards national independence.[14]

Brøndsted's classical Greece was the Athens of Pericles, and presumably because of this, the precise political and cultural context of the Phigaleia sanctuary remained obscure to his readers. However, Brøndsted juxtaposed Arcadia and Athens to shed light on the contemporary state, including both the drawbacks and potential of Turkish-dominated Greece undergoing transformation.

Johannes Ferdinand Fenger (1805-1861)

Travel account, 1832
In the aftermath of the Greek War of Independence, Johannes Ferdinand Fenger – priest, theologian, and chairman of the Danish Missionary society – travelled Greece and Turkey (Fig. 4).[15] In his account of his 1832 travels – "based on his diary and his memory" – Fenger observed that the enthusiastic support for the Greek cause at the beginning of the war had almost died out, to be replaced by harsh comments on the

---

13 Brøndsted 1861.
14 See Isager 2008 for a discussion of this subject.
15 Lund 2019, 12.

Johannes Ferdinand Fenger (1805-1861), copperplate engraving. The Royal Danish Library.

Fig. 4.

nature of the Greeks, who utterly failed to take advantage of their newly won freedom.[16] Clearly, Fenger contributed to the ongoing debate on the meaning of the classical past for the future of modern Greece, but his theological background and involvement in the "outer" mission to non-Christian parts of the world undoubtedly inspired him to identify Christianity's potential to help to build newly established Greece.

Fenger, still an optimist when it came to the new Greece, pondered how its classical heritage combined with its Christian legacy would eventually overcome all difficulties ("If only the leaven of Christianity would enter the masses, then a pleasing spectacle would unfold in Greece").[17] According to him, Greece's hope rested on its ability to combine its classical heritage with Christianity, which in time would lead it onto the promising path to becoming a distinct European nation.

Like Brøndsted in about 1830, Fenger was interested in the Paris revolution and the liberal projects that emerged in various European nations, and yet on one particular question, his views diverged considerably. This question concerned the role of religion in the modern nation-state. According to Fenger, what united European nations and Greece in cultural communality was Christianity in its broadest sense. From a historical perspective, Rome's reception of classical antiquity and its derivate, Christianity, seem to be central to this historical thinking. Fenger envisioned a European future that rested on the combined foundations of Europe's classical heritage and Christianity, but without attributing much importance to the fundamental differences of Protestant, Catholic, and Orthodox churches and their implications for societal development. Instead, he found

---

16 Fenger 1832, 76.
17 Fenger 1832, 76. In Danish: "Gid blot Christendommenss Suurdeig maatte gjennemtrænge dens Masse, saa skulde vi nok faae et Syn at see i Grækenland, som skulde være underligt for vore Øjne".

hope for Greece in its long, ongoing, and shared European history from antiquity to his day, and he added Christianity and its distinct European context to the dominant Danish narrative of Greece's past and present states.[18]

Fenger clearly acknowledged that the course of history from antiquity to his present was one of discontinuity and occupation.[19] But he regarded the development of Christian Europe from the later Roman period to his day as an advantage. He thus presents a combination of political and ideological forms of the uses of history, and finds hope in Christianity's potential for future state-building in Greece and Europe. Fenger's historical consciousness was modelled over a solid scholarly background, as he was a theologian with extensive knowledge of classical languages. As a child of his time, and like many of his educated contemporaries, Fenger travelled for educational purposes (*dannelsesrejse* in Danish), which took him across the eastern Mediterranean region including the Near East. He juxtaposed the dominant theme of Greece's classical past with what he saw as one of the more culturally potent outcomes of antiquity: Christianity.

Apparently, however, Fenger ignored the declining importance of the church initiated by the first French revolution of 1789 and its subsequent life in France and other parts of Europe, around 1830. Clearly, Fenger, who lived in the absolute monarchy of Denmark with its close connections between state and church, presumed that the innate force of Christianity, and not the rise of a modern type of nation-state, would form the Greece of the future. We are still very far from the type of state that Eric Hobsbawm, Benedict Anderson, and others envisioned as emerging in post-revolution Europe, constructing and inventing (secular) traditions to support the development of collective memory that commemorates the anniversaries of the nation-state and its many forms of nationalism.[20] In fact, one might note that the development of the modern nation-state over the course of the nineteenth century took many forms; Fenger's vision of Greece depended on continuity, rather than a break with the past.

Fenger's travel account of 1832 was a notable success, and copies of it found their way to educated middle-class readers, who were curious about news from the new Greece. The account balances observations of local folklore and remarks on linguistic questions, but was not distancing in its use of Greek orthography, as Brøndsted's was. Fenger made an effort to present his book to a broader audience, and thus managed to produce the first generally popular Danish travel account of his day.

Michael Gottlieb Bindesbøll and Martinus Rørbye, travel companions to Athens, central Greece, and Euboea, 1836

In the spring of 1836, the architect Michael Gottlieb Bindesbøll and the painter Martinus Rørbye travelled Greece (Fig. 5). Various parts of their travels are described in Bindesbøll's *Rejsebrev fra Grækenland* (1836), notably the journey from Athens, via Delphi, to

---

18   Fenger 1832, 13-16.
19   Fenger 1832, 9-10.
20   Hobsbawm 1992; Anderson 1991.

Portraits by Constantin Hansen of Michael Gottlieb Bindesbøll (1849), Thorvaldsens' Museum, and Martinus Rørbye (1837), National Gallery of Denmark.

Fig 5.

Chalcis, on Euboea.[21] Bindesbøll occasionally supplemented his account with Rørbye's comments, so it contains the various impressions of both companions. Rørbye's diary has survived, and is now accessible via the New Carlsberg Foundation's sources for Danish art history website.[22]

Before reaching Euboea, Bindesbøll was captivated by the picturesque landscape, its mountain-dwellers, the lush "wine-mountains" – wine fields in mountainous regions – and gardens, and glimpses of classical ruins. However, when they finally reached Chalcis, the two companions were captivated by a city "still entirely Turkish in costume and manner of living". In his diaries, Rørbye expressed his fascination with this still-intact urban Turkish culture, and notes how even contemporary Constantinople paled in comparison. Rørbye could not conceal his fascination with everything, from the ancient "Janissary-style" (more correctly, "Ottoman-style") coffee bars to the inhabitants' child-like reactions to their artwork (Fig. 6).

Rørbye complained that he was constantly stopped in the streets or approached in cafés by people wanting to see his artwork; everyone looked for portraits of someone they knew. However, everything was done honestly, a hallmark of the Turks – not at all like the "sly and calculating" Greeks. This statement contradicts their earlier fascination with the hearty mountain-dwellers and shepherds, or when the two companions previously praised the colourful costumes at a dance on Aegina. But not all urban Greeks failed to impress the two travellers. For instance, they were impressed with one of their earlier

21 Bindesbøll 1836.
22 https://roerbye.ktdk.dk/

Fig. 6.   *Det indre af en tyrkisk café* (Interior of a Turkish café), Martinus Rørbye, 1836. National Gallery of Denmark.

acquaintances, Nikétas Stamatelopoulos, the "Turk-butcher", or, as Rørbye calls him in his diary, the "Turk-eater".[23] Nikétas Stamatelopoulos, a war hero, spoke modestly of his own achievements in the War but praised those of others; he now wore a Bavarian colonel's uniform, which, Bindesbøll noted, did not do him justice when compared to the "noble and colourful" Albanian costume.[24]

Like others before them, Bindesbøll and Rørbye came to Greece for its classical heritage, but they found something else that spoke to them as artists: a colourful and picturesque landscape, and two distinct cultures, they claimed (Fig. 7). They added an important but not always consistent proto-anthropological element to the study of Greece, which nonetheless originated in an orientalism that clearly depicted both "cynical Greeks" and "childish Turks" as the "other": the antithesis of "European honesty and rationality". Yet elements of classical Greek virtues are mentioned frequently, and the two travel companions subscribed to a not-altogether-consistent continuity between antiquity and the present.

As Fenger did before them, Bindesbøll and Rørbye provided a travel account aimed at the educated reader with a basic knowledge of Greece's classical heritage, and who was interested in the encounter between the region's two dominant cultures of that time: Greek and Ottoman Turk. Hence, Bindesbøll described his encounters with one

---

23   https://roerbye.ktdk.dk/n/Q8rCwhVB https://roerbye.ktdk.dk/n/Q8rCwhVB
24   Bindesbøll 1836 (Hjortshøj 1964, 80).

M. Rørbye, *Udsigt fra Athenatemplet på Akropolis* (View from the temple of Athena on the Acropolis), 1844. National Gallery of Denmark.

Fig 7.

culture in its remaking and one in its decline, together with popular references to Greece's classical past.

Henrik Scharling (1836-1920)

Travel account from 1860, published in 1866
Based on his diaries of a journey to Greece in 1860, another theologian, Henrik Scharling, considered the Greek character, and, like Brøndsted, saw a challenged people, suspicious of any form of authority.[25] Scharling observed that the philhellenes had flocked around the Greek independence project in the expectation of finding contemporary Greeks identical to the Greeks of antiquity. But this was not at all the case, Scharling concluded. Although he agreed with Brøndsted's analysis of 1810 (that all Greeks were depraved), he added the important point that the Greeks of the classical period also lapsed into moral decay and corruption when proper leadership was absent.[26] The Greeks of antiquity had Pericles to lead them, so they succeeded where their descendants,

---

25   Scharling 1866, 94 (excerpts reprinted in Hjortsø 1964, 33-36, who incorrectly believes that Scharling's travels took place ca. 1865).
26   Scharling 1866, 96.

owing to a lack of proper leadership, had so utterly failed.[27] It is hardly a coincidence that Scharling wrote this account shortly after the Danish Prince William's succession to the Greek throne as King George I. Scharling addressed one of the major questions of his day, which was how the Greek city-state had failed to counter the Macedonian onslaught, and how smaller states were unified by monarchs. Clearly, the unification of Germany under Prussian leadership was on everyone's mind in the years leading up to 1871, and this development had an impact on contemporary studies of state-building in Greco-Roman antiquity, which saw a parallel between the achievements of Philip of Macedonia and Kaiser Wilhelm's German Reich of 1871.[28] Scharling consequently identified one of the more important aspects of early studies of the Greek polis, but because of his theological approach to cultural development, he noted the religious and thus the moral development of societies too. For him, ancient Greece remained the point of departure, but a systemic criticism now appeared, which merged with arguments that went beyond mere politics – what if the Greeks of antiquity had a proper religious framework as their societal foundation? Moreover, Scharling was troubled by the younger generation of intellectual Greeks, who favoured Voltaire over Christianity, but he remained confident that the newly founded academic milieu would manage to combine knowledge and faith to the benefit of the new nation.[29]

Scharling combined the moral and political uses of history. Essentially, although he did not oppose the conventional approach to classical antiquity in its entirety, he nonetheless supplemented it with a theologian's strong sense of morality. He suggested that classical antiquity could not stand alone, but when it was combined with Christianity, Greece would prosper. In his view, history was a process where the stiffened and incomplete "antiquity" was infused with a positive catalyst, such as Christianity. His account is a political statement, popular in the sense that it presents a contemporary political question in both a historical and a contemporary Danish context.

Professor Johan Louis Ussing (1820-1905)

Travel accounts, 1847, and 1882 visit to Sparta
Professor Johan Louis Ussing visited Greece several times – first as a recently graduated philologist in 1847, and later, in the 1880s, as an accomplished academic now explicitly more interested in the material culture and heritage of ancient Greece.[30]

In Ussing's first account, from 1847, he focused on the challenges of travelling in Greece, and on whether or not the landscape of contemporary Greece agreed with de-

---

27 Scharling 1866, 94-96, 156-157.
28 The theme of the failing Greek poleis and the rise of monarchy in the fourth century BCE reverberated throughout modern studies. E.g. McKechnie 1989, 6-15; Hansen 1992.
29 Scharling 1866, 134-136. In the broader European context, the interest in Greek antiquity and Athenian democracy became still more interconnected with the development of individual nations; see Hansen 1992.
30 Andersen Funder, Kristensen & Nørskov 2019, 79-81.

scriptions of the past. At one point, when approaching Attica and Athens, Ussing offered an ethnic or racial explanation for Greece's decline since antiquity. He declared that the most severe mischief done to Greece was the uncontrolled immigration of Romans, Albanians, and so on, which had diluted the "blood" of the original population and led it to depravity. This development benefited the immigrants, who succeeded in being assimilated into the Greek culture. However, the general outcome of these amalgamations was a general degeneration of the Greek population, and diminished prospects for building a sound state with a future.[31] Along these same lines, Ussing argued that the Greeks "defended the faith of their fathers", but he was by no means convinced that they were genuinely "religious in nature". Instead, he surmised, the Greeks had a strong urge to debate and quarrel, essentially preventing the true development of religious feeling.[32]

In 1882 Ussing visited Sparta. By this time his interest in Greece had changed profoundly. This travelogue was more focused on antiquity, and when his present entered the narrative, Ussing was concerned about historical geography – especially how to identify ancient sites in the landscapes of his day, and their history. In fact, Ussing created (his own) *lieux de mémoire* in order to establish connections between the classical past and his present. Modern Greece was somewhat of a nuisance to Ussing, and he complained about the new laws that prohibited the sale and restricted the excavation of antiquities, which led to the unfortunate practice of decapitating marble statues and other mutilations of ancient artwork that fueled the clandestine and illegal sale of Greece's cultural heritage.

Ussing confined his observations of modern Greece to remarks on the poor food and shabby circumstances of the mountain-dwellers he met *en route* through Arcadia to Sparta. When he finally approached Sparta, he concentrated on recognizing the past in the present, and found academic satisfaction in making himself acquainted with the place in ways inaccessible to the local population. This is the full-blown, self-confident but arrogant and self-indulgent modern academic. The reader is not introduced to the debate on Greek decline, but is instead presented with the prospect of being educated about the might and splendour of ancient Sparta, with – let us not forget – glimpses of the Spartan myth including the selection of infants, the Agogé, blood broth, and the return of the Heraclides. Again, this interest in the historical dynamics of migration and race emerges through an otherwise orthodox walk through Sparta's archaic and classical history. Ussing offers his reader an ongoing comparison between history and country, and he reconnects the Sparta of the glorious past with the withered remnants of it in the present. Most importantly, and in contrast with previous Danish travellers to Greece, to Ussing the Greek populace of his day is no longer a link between past and present. Instead, his and his peers' appropriation of the Greek past transformed contemporary Greece into an uncharted landscape only waiting to be re-opened by academia. With Ussing, the Danish popular interest in classical Greece took a new direction, claiming this field as a research-based encounter with, and narrative about, the Greece of the past.

---

31   Ussing 1847, 21-22.
32   Ussing 1847, 27-29.

Fig 8.

Photography by S. Junker-Jensen of Henrik Cavling, 1896. The Royal Danish Library.

Henrik Cavling (1858-1933)

War correspondent for the first Greco-Turkish War, 1897
As a young reporter and war correspondent, Henrik Cavling covered the three-month war of 1897 between Greece and the Ottoman Empire over Crete (Fig. 8). Previously, the Ottoman Empire had agreed to grant the island extended autonomy, but uprisings on the island prompted Greek initiatives to claim the island for Greece. Prior to the outbreak of hostilities, Cavling had arrived in Athens to follow the rising tension between the two adversaries. With his talent for capturing the atmosphere, he wired several articles to *Politiken*, a recently founded Danish newspaper in whose early history Cavling played an important role.[33]

Subsequently, war broke out when a Greek expeditionary force under the command of Colonel Vassos landed near Chania, and the subsequent battle was won by the Greeks. After covering the initial stages of the conflict in Athens, Cavling was bound for Crete to cover the merits of the Greek garrison under siege, and he was soon involved in the conflict as a dispatch courier from the Greek foreign office to Colonel Vassos.

Before departing for Crete, Cavling cabled several articles to *Politiken*, including one published on 16 March 1897 stating that, to the educated classes of Greece, the unity of the country pointed to the nation's resurrection as a historical people, and a renewal

33   Kaarsted 1960, 9-13.

Photograph of Timoleon Vassos and his son at the headquarters of the Greek Army, Crete, 1897. Library of Congress.

Fig. 9.

of the time when Pericles ruled, Sophocles and Euripides composed their dramas, and Phidias adorned the Parthenon.[34]

On his arrival in Crete, Cavling was immediately taken to Vassos, who introduced him to his staff, including his son, a young artillery officer (Fig. 9). Vassos made a favourable impression on Cavling, with his blue eyes and noble appearance, not unlike the heroes of the Greek past – and it seems as though our Danish reporter had finally found the lost Pericles! Vassos and his officers made a great impression on Cavling, who noted their good manners and fluent French, as well as the fact that some of them had visited Denmark. In Copenhagen, some of them were entertained by the celebrated Madam Halkier and other upper-class women of Denmark's capital. Here in contested and remote Crete, not yet formally a part of Greece, Cavling encountered good breeding, education, and sophistication among the officers of the regular army, which he contrasted with the insurgents – local Cretan forces that teamed up with the regular Greek Army to counter the troops of Sultan Abdul Hamid II. In Cavling's words, these insurgents dressed in yellow skin boots, baggy blue trousers and shirt, a blue headscarf arranged as a turban, and a red sash around the waist, along with a large knife and a pistol in the belt. He states that these "natural-born warriors" (and shepherds!) "conducted themselves in a chivalrous manner", and resembled the heroes of the War of Independence, clad

---

34   *Politiken* March 16, 1897. Reprinted in Kaarsted 1960, 40.

in the Albanian costume, and key figures in Brøndsted's and Bindesbøll's travelogues of 70 or 80 years before.

Compared to the former Danish travellers to Greece, Cavling was not as direct in his use of Greek antiquity. Instead, to express his hopes for contemporary Crete, he noted the "rightful Greek claim to Crete, and hope that the great powers (England and France) will acknowledge the historical Greek claim to the island" – this must be a reference to then-recent archaeological investigations on the island that proved that Crete's past was indeed Greek (including at Knossos and the discovery of the Law Code of Gortyn). The Greeks in Cavling's account are cast in the role of heroes, examples to be followed, but first and foremost as a combination of sophisticated Europeans and admirable, "intact" representatives of something originally "Greek". The "reservoir" was activated in times of crisis – when Greece stepped up and did what was necessary on the battlefield. Greece won wars, but observers before Cavling noted that Greeks were poor at winning the peace.

Concluding remarks

P.O. Brøndsted and his fellow philhellenes were committed to presenting the cultural heritage of classical Greece to the citizens of Europe's capitals; Brøndsted actually succeeded in extracting "art treasures" from the excavation at Phigaleia. Moreover, in his account of the excavation, Brøndsted connects the Renaissance and Enlightenment imaginings of Greece (the theme of Arcadia) with his own discoveries, and writes of the potential of those "uncorrupted" Greeks who allegedly survived in geographically remote enclaves, uninfluenced by the Ottomans. By connecting the classical with the present in this manner, he redefined the role of the exclusive international community of philhellenes as that of providing a new vision for the future, which could include the uncorrupted and remote, but nonetheless accessible, human reservoir of mountainous Greece. However, most Europeans in Greece in the early nineteenth century, including Lord Byron, and especially those concentrated in Athens, participated in what recent studies have called "regular plundering expeditions", to appropriate showpieces of Greece's material culture of the classical period. It is difficult not to evaluate Brøndsted's achievements in this light, too.

In the wake of the Greek war of independence (1821-1830), Danish authors, academics, and artists travelled to Greece to study how the descendants of Pericles met the expectations of the European philhellenes, that is, in establishing a new Greece of freedom and prosperity. This did not happen; disappointment with the achievements of modern Greece overshadowed the first accounts.

In the mid-nineteenth century, discourses on the significance of the extended lack of Greek independence for its future development tended to predominate. Disputes about the importance of the European past and Christianity were formulated in the search for a new paradigm for Greece's future, whereas academia took over in the latter part of the nineteenth century, and once again, the focus was on the accomplishments of the classical Greeks. In developing this idea, several commentators contended that classical and contemporary Greeks possessed the same negative characteristics, and that modern Greece would need a Pericles to lead Greece's positive development. Then (Danish) hopes were invigorated by the coronation of the Danish Prince William as King George I of Greece in 1863.

From Brøndsted in 1812 to Ussing in the 1880s, classical Greece was overtly perceived and evaluated as a nation, not as separate city-states with individual characteristics. Ussing's change of perspective was due to historians' growing interest in the history of classical Greece, based on the historians Herodotus, Thucydides, and Xenophon. Thus, from the mid-nineteenth century, the focus shifted from Sparta to Athens as the model polis of the classical period. Historians such as George Grote and others promoted this new paradigm, and from then on, university historians and philologists such as Ussing concentrated on reconstructing the classical Greek past (essentially a scientific approach to the uses of history), and left to others the discussion of Greece's fate from the death of Alexander the Great to 1821.

From Bindesbøll's and Rørbye's travels in the 1830s and onwards, Danish observers interested themselves in the attractions of the contemporary Greece they encountered. Now, one could travel Greece to study its people and cultures in their current state. This "other" had a strong appeal, and spoke readily to travelling artists, only to be reinforced in the twentieth century, when alternatives to classical Greece and their *mirabilia* became even more significant. One important point may be that these travellers always reached this new and other Greece through an initial interest in Greece's classical heritage.

At the end of the nineteenth century, in the diaries of Henrik Cavling, Greece emerged as a European nation; Cavling actually managed to identify a Greek hero in the person of Colonel Vassos, not unlike the Pericles type so sought after by previous authors. Vassos and his staff were the positive outcome of the Greek elitist's encounters with European (French), and especially Danish, cultural refinement. And in his preliminary thoughts about the outcome of the conflict, Cavling identified the strongest argument for Greece's rightful claim to Crete in its classical Greek heritage.

Throughout the nineteenth century, from Brøndsted to Cavling, it became increasingly important for Danish travellers to make a popular impact and to disseminate their experiences to a Danish audience. Brøndsted's texts are littered with quotations in Greek, suggesting his audience was to be found among his peers. The "popular" element in Brøndsted's accounts is not easy to find because of its strong academic and elitist tone. Instead, Brøndsted's achievement was the pioneering of a genre in the Greek context, to which succeeding travellers and authors committed themselves later in the nineteenth century. The later accounts by Fenger, Bindesbøll, and Scharling were more "popular" regarding both their dissemination and their content. This development emerged because it became fashionable to demonstrate (educated) interest in the classical past among the emerging self-confident Danish upper bourgeoisie.

To Brøndsted, and in particular Fenger and Scharling, Pericles remained lost, but their disappointment at not finding Pericles' descendants ready for the restoration of Greece was mitigated by two new strands: on the one hand, Ussing insisted that the attraction of Greece lay in its past, studied and presented from an academic standpoint;

on the other, Cavling managed to find Pericles reborn, and even to make his narrative accessible to the broadest audience through newspaper reports. Thus, Cavling brought Greece's classical past to the attention of newspaper readers now witnessing on a daily basis the dramas being acted out by the reborn heroes of Greece.

Bibliography

Andersen Funder, L.M., Kristensen, T.M. & Nørskov, V. 2019. *Classical Heritage and European Identities. The Imagined Geographies of Danish Classicism*. London: Routledge.
Anderson, B.R.O.G. 1991. *Imagined Communities: Reflections on the Origin and Spread of Nationalism*, 2nd edition. London & New York: Verso.
Angelomatis-Tsougarakis, H. 1990. *The Eve of the Greek Revival. British Travellers' Perception of Early Nineteenth-Century Greece*. London: Routledge.
Aronsson, P. 2004. *Historiebruk – att använda det förflutna*. Lund: Studentlitteratur.
Barthélémy, J.J. 1788. *Voyage du jeune Anacharsis en Grèce*. Paris: Chez De Bure l'aîné.
Bindesbøll, M.G. 1836. "Breve fra Grækenland", *Dansk Kunstblad* 14, 93-99.
Brøndsted, P.O. 1844. *P.O. Brøndsteds Reise i Grækenland i Aarene 1810-1813, I–II. Tillige indeholdende Forfatterens Biographie ved J.P. Mynster*. Copenhagen: N.V. Dorph.
Brøndsted, P.O. 1861. "Udgravningen af templet ved Phigalia", unpublished dissertation, published by M. Hammerich, Copenhagen in *Nordisk Universitets Tidsskrift*, VII.i, 64-86. Repr. in: Hjortsø (ed.) 1964, 59-75.
Brøndsted, P.O. 1999. *Interviews with Ali Pacha of Joanina in the Autumn of 1812; with some Particulars of Epirus, and the Albanians of the Present Day*. Edited with an introduction by Jacob Isager. Athens: The Danish Institute at Athens.
Bundgaard Rasmussen, B.B., Jensen, J.S., Lund, J. & Märcher, M. (eds) 2008. *Peter Oluf Brøndsted (1780-1842). A Danish Classicist in his European Context. Acts of the Conference at the Royal Danish Academy of Sciences and Letters, Copenhagen, 5-6 October 2006*. Historiske-filosofiske skrifter 31. Copenhagen: Det Kongelige Danske Videnskabernes Selskab.
Campbell, J.K. 1973. *Honour, Family and Patronage: A Study of Institutions and Moral Values in a Greek Mountain Community*. Oxford: Oxford University Press.
Christiansen, J. 2000. *I lyset fra Akropolis. Danmark og Grækenland i 1800-tallet*. Copenhagen: Ny Carlsberg Glyptotek.
Ditlevsen, K.H. 1978. *Rejsen til Athen – Danske i Grækenland i 1800-tallet*. Copenhagen: Gad.
Fenger, J.F. 1832. *Om det Nygræske Sprog og Folk. Erindringer fra en Reise i Grækenland aaret 1831*. Copenhagen: C. Græbe & søn.
Greenhalgh, M. 2019. *Plundered Empire: Acquiring Antiquities from Ottoman Lands*. Heritage and Identity 6. Leiden: Brill.
Grove, A.T. & Rackham, O. 2003. *The Nature of Mediterranean Europe. An Ecological History* (second printing with corrections). New Haven & London: Yale University Press.
Grote, G. 2010. *A History of Greece*, 1-12 (1st edition 1846-1856, London). Cambridge: Cambridge University Press.
Hansen, M.H. 1992. "The Tradition of the Athenian Democracy A.D. 1750 – 1990". *Greece and Rome* 39, 14-30.
Hjortsø, L. 1964. *Græske Billeder. Med danske Forfattere og Kunstnere i Grækenland*. Copenhagen: Gyldendal.
Hobsbawm, E. 1992. "Introduction. Inventing Traditions", in: Hobsbawm, E. & Ranger, T. (eds), *The Invention of Traditions*. Cambridge: Cambridge University Press, 1-14.
Isager, J. 2008. "P.O. Brøndsted, a Revolutionary?", in: Bundgaard Rasmussen, Jensen, Lund & Märcher 2008, 117-127.
Kaarsted, T. (ed.) 1960. *Henrik Cavling som krigskorrespondent. Artikler og breve fra den græsk-tyrkiske krig 1897*. Aarhus: Universitetsforlaget.
Lund, J. 2019. "Christian Tuxen Falbe: Danish Consul-General and Antiquarian in Greece", *Proceedings of the Danish Institute at Athens* 9, 11-34.
Matalas, P. 2021. "Europeans in the Greek Landscape: Idealization, Appropriation, Disillusionment", in: Vöhler, Alekou & Pechlivanos 2021, 195-209.
McKechnie, P. 1989. *Outsiders in the Greek Cities in the Fourth Century BC*. London & New York: Routledge.

Moyseos, D. 2021. "Philhellenism as an Exploration of Identity and Alterity in the Literary Tradition of Travels to the East in the Nineteenth Century", in: Vöhler, Alekou & Pechlivanos 2021, 155-176.

Nielsen, N.K. 2010. *Historiens forvandlinger. Historiebrug fra monumenter til oplevelsesøkonomi*. Aarhus: Aarhus University Press.

Rackham, O. 1990. "Ancient Landscapes", in: Murray, O. & Price, S. (eds), *The Greek City. From Homer to Alexander*. Oxford: Clarendon Press, 85-111.

Rathje, A. & Lund, J. 1991. "Danes Overseas: A Short History of Danish Classical Archaeological Fieldwork", in: Fischer-Hansen, T. Guldager, P. Lund, J., Nielsen, M. & Rathje, A. (eds), *Recent Danish Research in Classical Archaeology: Tradition and Renewal*. Copenhagen: Museum Tusculanum Press, 11-56.

Scharling, H. 1866. *Grækenland. En Rejsebeskrivelse. Med to lithographier og tolv træsnit*. Copenhagen: Forlagt af den Gyldendalske boghandel.

Schou-Rode, G. 2008. "Under the Cover of P.O. Brøndsted's Diaries. Some Remarks on the Content and Style of P.O. Bøndsted's Diaries from his Grand Tour through Germany, France, Italy, Greece and Turkey in the Years 1806-1811", in: Bundgaard Rasmussen, Jensen, Lund & Märcher 2008, 35-46.

Sonnini, C.S. 1801. *Voyage en Grèce et en Turquie fait par ordre de Louis XVI*. Paris, An IX.

Tsigakou, F.-M. 2008. "Foreign Travellers to Pre-Revolutionary Athens: Antiquarians and Treasure Hunters", in: Bundgaard Rasmussen, Jensen, Lund & Märcher 2008, 54-61.

Ussing, J.L. 1847. *Reisebilleder fra Syden. Bind 2*. Copenhagen: C.A. Reitzel.

Ussing, J.L. 1883. *Fra Hellas og Lilleasien i foraaret 1882*. Copenhagen: Gyldendalske Boghandels forlag (F. Hegel & Søn).

Vöhler, M., Alekou, S. & Pechlivanos, M. (eds) 2021. *Concepts and Functions of Philhellenism: Aspects of a Transcultural Movement*. Trends in Classics – Pathways of Reception 7. Berlin and Boston: De Gruyter.

Warring, A. 2011. "Erindring og historiebrug. Introduktion til et forskningsfelt". *Temp – tidsskrift for Historie* 1.2, 6-35.

6

ÓR NA GRÉIGE IS STÓR NA HÉIGIPT

CLASSICAL ANTIQUITY IN IRISH-LANGUAGE POPULAR POETRY OF THE EIGHTEENTH AND NINETEENTH CENTURIES

GREGORY R. DARWIN

Introduction

During the eighteenth and early nineteenth centuries the public visibility and prestige of the Irish language were at their lowest point.[1] The sixteenth and seventeenth centuries had seen the expansion of English power in Ireland under Tudor and Stuart monarchs. This expansion and consolidation of power was accompanied by the large-scale transfer of land ownership, and with it political power, from the Gaelic aristocracy to a predominantly Anglophone, Anglican, and Loyalist minority (Covington, Carey & McGowan-Doyle 2018b, 1). This political dominance was maintained, in part, by anti-Catholic legislation widely known as the Penal Laws, which restricted access to land, military training, education, and political representation, as well as limiting the activities of Catholic clergy (O'Connor 2018, 259-264).[2] One consequence of this sustained dominance of Anglophone élites and institutions was a language shift from Irish to English throughout much of the country: the 1851 census reports that less than a quarter of the population could speak Irish.[3] Despite the "invisibility" of the Irish language in official sources, there is nonetheless a substantial and largely understudied

---

[1] "After 1700, speakers of Irish were excluded from the centres of power and education which would have facilitated participation in the kind of intellectual activity found in other linguistic communities at the time. For this reason, they became, as it were, inaudible to outsiders, even if those outsiders lived in geographical proximity to them" (Doyle 2015, 83).
This research was conducted when the author was employed as a postdoctoral researcher at Aarhus University, as part of the ongoing project "Classical Influences and Irish Culture (CLIC)", funded by the European Research Council (Horizon 2020 grant no. 818366).

[2] The impact of these laws on education is discussed by O'Higgins 2017, 100-113.

[3] Traditional narratives claim that the use of Irish declined dramatically in the first half of the nineteenth century, and that the establishment of the National Schools in 1831 and the potato blight of the 1840s played a major role in language shift. More recent work by Aidan Doyle (2018)

Irish-language literary corpus, especially verse, dating to the period.[4] While Daniel Corkery's thesis of the "Hidden Ireland" (1967) is often overstated, it is fair to say that there was a wealth of economic, artistic, and intellectual activity which occurred in these centuries through the medium of the Irish language, and which was effectively invisible to English-speaking élites, as well as to contemporary historians and critics with no knowledge of the Irish language.[5]

Despite social marginalization and restricted access to formal education among the Irish-speaking population, knowledge of the past, including knowledge of classical antiquity, formed part of their intellectual and cultural life. One channel through which such knowledge was accessed was the remains of the older poetic and scribal classes who were previously patronized by the native aristocracy: patterns of patronage persisted among minor Gaelic gentry, although poets often had to sustain themselves through other means, such as manual labour, and copying manuscripts for Anglophone antiquarians who had begun to develop an interest in the so-called 'reliques' of Gaelic tradition.[6] Another channel by which such knowledge was accessed were the so-called "hedge schools" which loom so large in Irish popular historical memory: informal, and indeed illegal, rural private schools which provided an education for the children of the landed gentry and large farmers, along with the lower classes to some extent, where arithmetic and literacy in English formed a major part of the curriculum (O'Higgins 2017, 1-9). While such informal schools were not unique to Ireland prior to the widespread adaptation of universal education throughout Europe, one striking feature of Irish hedge schools was the teaching of classical languages; motivated, in part, by the necessity of preparing children for study in seminaries abroad. As Laurie O'Higgins notes in her recent monograph *The Irish Classical Self*, while memory of the hedge school has been subject to romantic distortion, "nonetheless, eighteenth and early nineteenth century Ireland *was* unique in Europe for significant popular study of Classics, as varied evidence shows. By 'significant' I do not mean large numbers overall, but sufficient to constitute a pattern, to make a mark, and create a memory in the wider culture" (2017, 6).

One nineteenth-century song, known as *Amhrán na Leabhar* (The Song of the Books), offers a hint about the mental world of these schools in Ireland.[7] The song was composed by the Kerry poet and schoolmaster Tomás Ruadh Ó Súilleabháin around 1822, on the occasion of the loss of the poet's personal library when the ship that was transporting it from Derrynane to Portmagee hit a rock and sank. Presumably the crew survived,

---

      has suggested that language shift was a more prolonged process, beginning in the early eighteenth or later seventeenth century, with multiple complex and interacting causes.

4   On the "invisibility" of the language, see Doyle 2018. A broad overview of the existing literary corpus in Irish is given by Buttimer 2006.

5   Cf. Doyle 2015, 83. On contemporary attitudes to and debates regarding the Irish language among historians, see Kane 2018, 81-85.

6   On patronage of poetry, see Buttimer 2006, 353-360 et passim; on other forms of employment for scribes and poets, see Denvir 2006, 560-564.

7   The most recent edition and commentary is Sharpe & Hoyne 2020, xv–xxiv.

as the song makes no mention of any human victims, but the ship's cargo could not be recovered. Many Irish songs composed in the period commemorate local tragedies, including shipwrecks and drownings, and it is noteworthy that Ó Súilleabháin felt that the loss of a library was an event worthy of commemoration in such a way.[8] Five of the song's eleven stanzas, normally omitted in contemporary performances, offer a catalogue of the books lost. Many of these are books that we would expect a schoolteacher to possess: works on mathematics, the natural sciences, history, and grammar; we also find books of the Bible and vernacular religious works in Irish and other languages, a late eighteenth-century manual of divination, and numerous works of Irish narrative literature. The poet furthermore lists some classical works as part of his library, including the *Distichs* of Cato, Euclid's *Elements*, and *Ár na Trae* or 'the destruction of Troy'. The latter work is, almost certainly, pseudo-Dares Phrygius' *De Excidio Troiae Historia* (History of the Destruction of Troy), a late antique prose re-telling of the Trojan war, which had been translated into Middle Irish some centuries previously.[9]

This is, of course, a song rather than a shelf-list, and it would be difficult to reconstruct Ó Súilleabháin's library on the basis of it. It seems unlikely that every book that was lost would be mentioned – and indeed, the poet makes such no claims to exhaustiveness. On the other hand, the poet undoubtedly exaggerates, such as when he claims to have had a copy of the Psalter of Cashel, a high medieval devotional manuscript which is believed to have been lost during the latter half of the seventeenth century (Ó Riain 1989). Although we cannot, therefore, assume that Ó Súilleabháin owned a copy of – or had even read – every book that he mentions, the presence of titles and authors in this catalogue nonetheless indicates an awareness of these works and authors, and a sense of their cultural value and prestige. The loss of such works, including classical authorities, was seen as an event worthy of commemoration by the poet as well as by his audience(s).

References to classical authorities and classical tradition are not infrequent in Irish-language poetry and songs composed in the eighteenth and nineteenth centuries: Irish-language poets became familiar with classical tradition and languages through study at hedge schools and seminaries, while scribal training also provided some familiarity with Latin as well as earlier forms of the Irish language, and thus with high medieval vernacular adaptations of classical and late antique literary works.[10] While such highly

---

8   For example, Antaine Ó Reachtairí's song *Eanach Dhúin* was composed on the occasion of 20 people drowning during an attempt to cross the Corrib by boat in 1828. A version of the song can be found in Hyde 1933, 69-73; an English translation is given in Ó Tuama & Kinsella 1981, 248-253.

9   The standard edition of *De Excidio Troiae Historia* is Meister 1873. The Middle Irish translation, *Togail Troí*, exists in no fewer than four recensions; for bibliographical information about editions and translations of these adaptations, as well as a discussion about their relationship with medieval Irish literature more generally, see O'Connor 2014, especially 13-17. For discussions on the impact of these adaptations on Early Modern Irish literature, see Ó Háinle 2015; Darwin 2021, 225-228.

10 In addition to *Togail Troí*, an adaptation of pseudo-Dares Phrygius' account of the fall of Troy mentioned above, other medieval adaptations of classical and post-classical works include Virgil's

educated literati were, no doubt, a small minority in the Irish-speaking world, their poems had a much broader audience: in the absence of any significant print culture in Irish, poetry was typically performed publicly, often set to music, and transmitted both via manuscript culture and orally.[11] *Amhrán na Leabhar* is something of an extreme case, as roughly 70 years elapsed between the song's composition and the earliest known written witness for it, but there are numerous other examples of authored poems with robust oral traditions along with, and in some cases prior to, manuscript and published transmission.[12] These poems and songs, including their classical elements, were therefore relevant and intelligible for a broader audience. Additionally, we find anonymous works composed in the same period which include references to classical antiquity. We can safely assume that not all – and perhaps not even most – of these songs were authored by individuals who had received an education in the classics. The foregoing indicates an engagement with classical antiquity which extended beyond direct engagement with classical texts and languages among Irish-speakers in the eighteenth and nineteenth centuries; in other words, a widespread popular reception. The remainder of this discussion will consist of an overview of the most commonly encountered forms of classical allusion and reference within this poetry, followed by some tentative conclusions regarding the significance of such references for contemporary audiences.[13]

Greece

References to Greece are relatively common in the poems surveyed: most rely on the idea of Greece as a distant land of great wealth or sophistication, and betray little direct familiarity with its geography. Thus, in the lament for Pádraig Mac an tSaoi by Peadar

---

Aeneid, Lucan's *Bellum civile*, Statius' *Thebaid*, a summary of Achilles' boyhood deeds based on Statius' *Achilleid*, and various works whose immediate sources are more difficult to determine. See O'Connor 2014.

11   For a survey of the relationship between metrical form and musical practice in the Irish-language song tradition, see Blankenhorn 2003.

12   For example, Seán Ó Tuama's edition of *Caoineadh Airt Uí Laoghaire*, the lament by Eibhlín Dhubh Ní Chonaill for her husband Art Ó Laoghaire, murdered in 1773, was mainly based on a transcription of an oral performance made by Nóra Ní Shindile in 1800, with variant readings from a version recorded from the same performer later in life, and a seemingly independent manuscript version. In the appendix, Ó Tuama gives an account of several other manuscript and oral versions of the lament (1961, 45-50).

13   The present study is based on published editions of Irish poetry, many of which were published around the turn of the twentieth century as part of the Gaelic Revival in Ireland. Several of these editions are now out of print, but are thankfully digitized as part of the Royal Irish Academy's *Corpas Stairiúil na Gaeilge / Historical Irish Corpus 1600-1926* (http://corpas.ria.ie/, accessed at various points between August 2021 and February 2022). Since many of these editions lack information on the musical and performative context of these poems, the present study is, out of necessity, primarily focused on their textual content, although it is noted at various points that these poems were publicly performed rather than privately read. See Blankenhorn 2003, 345-346. All translations are the author's, unless noted otherwise.

Mac Ualgairg, the women who lament Pádraig's death are clad in silk cloaks of Greek manufacture: "gach bantracht óg na sról-bhrat **gréagach**" (Ó Muirgheasa 1934, 127), and in a poem attributed to Toirdhealbhach Ó Cearbhalláin (1670-1738), the poet imagines himself drinking Greek wine with his beloved at the fair: "is nach deas an gléas a bheith ag siubhal chun aonaigh, is **fíon na Gréige** bheith dhá ól ann" (Ó Tiománaidhe 1906, 14). These ideas of distance and wealth lend themselves well to hyperbole: thus, the anonymous poet of *D'aithneoinn mo ghrá* (I Would Recognize my Love) would follow her beloved to Greece or even England to be with him (Ó Buachalla 1978, 44), and the poet of *Brighid Bhéasach* (Well-mannered Bríd) would bestow all of his wealth to his beloved, even if he were king of Greece (Hyde 1893, 126). In Art Mac Cumhaigh's lament for the ruined ancestral castle of the O'Neills at Glasdrumman Lake, the poet contrasts the wealth of the Mediterranean with the thought of being buried in his ancestral territory. Addressing the bird that had been singing to him from the ruins, he states:

Ó bhreoidh tú mé le glór do bhéil
is nach bhfóir le leigheas ón mbás mé,
is go cóige Laighean is cóir dúinn gléas
go Dún Uí Néill ar máirseáil;
ór na Gréige is stór na hÉigipt,
is seinm dá dtéad ar chláirisgh,
ní fhóirfeadh an méid sin – is foghaim go léir é –
a stór, muna n-éagfainn láimh leat.

You have wounded me sore with the sound of your words,
For no cure will now save me from death,
To the Province of Leinster we aught now to go
And march to Ó Néill's strong fort;
The gold of Greece or the wealth of all Egypt,
And music of strings played on harp,
All this cannot ease me, and I gain it all,
My love, if we die apart.

(Ní Uallacháin 2003, 259-264, tr. Ní Uallacháin)

Occasionally, these poems contain references to the anonymous "King of Greece", or to his son or daughter. Like the references to the country itself, these rely on the conceit of Greece as a distant and fantastic or wealthy land, and betray little familiarity with its geography or political structure, in either antiquity or the present day.[14] The immediate

---

14 E.g. *An Bhanab ón gCarraig Léith* (The Abbess of Carriglea; de Brún, Ó Buachalla & Ó Con Cheanainn 1971, 14); *Dónall Óg* (Young Dónall; de Brún, Ó Buachalla & Ó Con Cheanainn 1971, 73-74); *Páidín Bán Ua Cormaic* (Fair-haired Páidín Ó Cormaic; Ó Tiománaidhe 1906, 25); *Brighid bhéasach* (Well-mannered Bríd; Hyde 1893, 126).

source for many of these allusions would seem to be the Irish oral storytelling tradition, rather than any particular classical narrative: perhaps inspired by medieval romance, Greece often functions as a distant land where fantastic and magical events can occur, and the children of monarchs often play the role of protagonists in Irish wonder-tales (Bruford 1966, 21-29).[15]

Greece has a similar function in the conceit that the Gaels – or certain families with aristocratic pedigrees, such as the FitzGeralds – are Greek in origin. While this idea is quite rare in poems dating to the eighteenth and nineteenth centuries, it is much more frequently found in professional bardic poetry of the sixteenth and seventeenth centuries.[16] Undoubtedly some of the popularity of this idea in bardic poetry, with its strict metrical requirements, was due to the possibility of alliteration between the words *Gaedheal* (Gael) and *Gréag* (Greece). Ultimately, this idea has its origins in the medieval Irish historiographic tradition, where an origin in Greece was one of several narratives offered for the ethnogenesis of the Irish (Jaski 2003). The infrequency of this motif in later popular poetry is not terribly surprising: with the downfall of the Gaelic aristocracy in the later seventeenth century, the mythologies which supported élite social institutions, including such origin myths, became increasingly irrelevant.

As noted above, these references rely upon vague notions of Greece as a distant land of wealth and wonder, which were in wide circulation within the native learned and popular tradition, and betray very little direct familiarity with classical narratives. While it is possible to dismiss these allusions as not a form of classical reception at all, it is hard to divorce them entirely from the more specific allusions to classical heroes and deities which occur more broadly within this repertoire, and in some cases alongside these vague invocations of Greece. The discussion now turns to references to specific figures from classical tradition.

Heroism

A common rhetorical device in bardic poetry of the sixteenth and seventeenth centuries is a simile directly comparing the subject of the poem with a hero or otherwise famous man from classical tradition, usually on the grounds of their strength, military prowess,

---

15   See also "The Adventure of the Men from Sorcha" (MacNeill 1908, 61-75) and *Créd so ag buaidhreadh ban nGaoidheal* (What is this Perturbing the Women of the Gael?; Mac Airt 1944, 226-232). On the "non-geographic" use of Greece as a space in medieval Irish literature, see McCoy 2017, 210-211.

16   Examples of this conceit in post-bardic poetry include *Peigí Ní Nuinsion* (Ó Tiománaidhe 1906, 37), *Cuirim séad suirghe* (I Send a Love Token, by Pádraigín Haicéad; Ní Cheallacháin 1962, 8-9), *Is bocht mo bheatha* (My Life is Wretched, by Dáibhí Ó Bruadair; Mac Erlean 1910, 56-57), and three poems by Aogán Ó Rathaille: the lament for Gerald son of the Knight of Glin (Dinneen & O'Donoghue 1911, 146), a poem in praise of Lucy Fitzgerald (Dinneen & O'Donoghue 1911, 170), and the lament for Eoghan son of Cormac Riabhach Mac Carthy by Aogán Ó Rathaille (Dinneen & O'Donoghue 1911, 216). On this conceit in bardic poetry, see Knott 1922, lix; Darwin 2021, 204, 225-226.

beauty, generosity, or other masculine virtues (Darwin 2021, 226; McManus 2009). This same practice can be found in elegies dating to the eighteenth centuries: the deceased is compared, perhaps somewhat hyperbolically, to the great martial heroes of the past. For example, in a lament for Eoghan Mac an Álta of Tír Eala, County Meath, composed by Uilliam Ó Maoil Chiaráin in the middle of the eighteenth century, the poet likens Eoghan to the heroes of the Trojan war:

> *Ó d'imthigh uainn Eoghan an leomhan ba tréine,*
> *Mar Achilles eolach ag seoladh Gréagaigh,*
> *Nó mar Hector na Traoi ag claoidh Mermidhdons,*
> *Nó mar Pháris mhac Phrí ar thaoibh cnuic sléibhe,*
> *Nó Alasdrán uaibhreach 'raibh na slóighte dhó 'géilleadh.*

> Since Eoghan left us, the mightiest lion,
> Like wise Achilles guiding the Greeks,
> Or Hector of Troy, conquering the Myrmidons,
> Or Paris son of Priam on the mountainside,
> Or proud Alexander, whom hosts gave homage.

> (Ó Muirgheasa 1934, 79)

The poet apparently saw no contradiction in invoking figures from both sides of the conflict, offering instead a non-partisan appreciation of heroic virtue. Similarly, the poet of the elegy for Pádraig Mac an tSaoi mentioned earlier states that:

> *Bá é súd crann seasta ar thoiseach na gcéadthaí,*
> *Mar Gholl nó Osgar bhéirfeadh osadh i ngéibhionn,*
> *Nó mar Hector go dian ag claoidh na nGréagach,*
> *Nó mar Pháris éachtach chuaidh le bainríoghan na sgéimhe,*

> He was the steadfast tree at the head of hundreds
> Like Goll or Oscar who brought respite to captives
> Or Hector, subduing the Greeks with vigour
> Or death-dealing Paris who eloped with the queen of beauty.

> (Ó Muirgheasa 1934, 129)

Goll and Oscar are figures known from the so-called Fenian Cycle (in Irish, *Fiannaíocht*), a body of Irish and Scottish tales and ballads centred around the figure of Fionn Mac Cumhaill and his band of warriors known as the Fianna.[17] Like the Trojans, the Fianna are associated with the distant pre-Christian past, although their exploits are typically

---

17   For an accessible introduction to this body of literature, see Nagy 2010 and references.

situated within the familiar landscapes of the Gaelic world as opposed to those of the Mediterranean. Such juxtapositions of native and classical literary tradition are fairly frequent in the poems surveyed; the implications of this will be explored later.

A similar juxtaposition of classical and native tradition appears in the Jacobite song *Bím-se buan ar buaidhirt gach ló* (Every Day I Am Afflicted by Sorrow) by Seaghán Clárach mac Domhnaill (Dinneen 1908, 1-3).[18] Mac Domhnaill likens Charles Edward Stuart, the Young Pretender, to a range of figures from native Irish tradition: Aonghus Óg, Lughaidh Mac Céin, Cú Raoi Mac Dáire, Conall Cearnach, Fearghus Mac Róigh, and Conchobhar Mac Neassa. The deities Mars and Cupid are both made manifest in his body, indicating his martial prowess and beauty: "Tá Mars is Cúipid dlúith i gcóir / i bpearsain úir 's i ngnúis mo stóir" ("Mars and Cupid are [bound] close together in the young body and countenance of my beloved"), and the refrain of the song repeatedly states "S é mo laoch, mo ghile mear, 's é mo Shaesar, gile mear" ("He is my hero, my gallant darling, he is my Caesar, gallant darling"). In general, metaphorical comparisons to Caesar are quite common in the poems surveyed – so much so that it is not always clear whether the poet intended to invoke any particular Roman emperor, or whether the word *Saosar* or *Caesar* functions as a common noun meaning 'hero, warrior'.

While comparisons between contemporary men and martial heroes from classical antiquity abound in both panegyric and elegiac bardic poetry of the sixteenth and seventeenth centuries, in the eighteenth century such comparisons are largely restricted to elegies for the dead. A notable exception is Jacobite verse, although these poems are composed for a distant saviour, rather than a present and living patron. This absence is, perhaps, not particularly surprising: praise poems were a form of political propaganda for the Gaelic and Old English military aristocracy of the later middle ages, and functioned within a later medieval and early modern political context. Poems extolling the martial skill and wealth of a patron were, at best, an expensive anachronism in a period when most of the Irish-speaking gentry lived on greatly diminished estates and had no access to military training.

Women

While some of the anonymous poems, especially those written in a female lyric voice, may have been written by women, none of the poetry consulted can be securely attributed to a female poet. This absence is not surprising, as poetry – especially written poetry – is traditionally a masculine craft in Irish culture. Women formed a minority of Irish-language poets in the period in question, as indeed they do in the present day (Ní Shíocháin 2021; Ní Dhomhnaill 2005, 43-58). One known female poet from the eighteenth century was Máire Ní Chrualaoich; while none of her own poetry has survived, she is commemorated in elegies by three better-known male poets. Of relevance

---

18   The song is generally better known at present as *Mo ghile mear* (My Gallant Darling), from a musical setting in a collection of poems by Mac Domhnaill arranged by Dónal Ó Liatháin in the 1970s.

to the current discussion is the elegy written by the Cork poet Seán na Raithíneach Ó Murchadha (ca. 1700-1752):

An bláth is buacaighe ghluais puinn eadrainn beó i nÉirinn,
bás cé fuair sí, a huaislidheacht mairfidh go deó déidheannach;
Sápphó suadh-ghníomhach nduain-mbinn startha agus cómad Ghaedhilge.
Máire shuairc Ní Chruadhlaoich, eala agus ógh, is Phoénics.

The fairest flower that held sway here in Ireland
Was snatched by death yet lives, her fame eternal.
Wise-acting Sappho of metres, couplets, sweet songs
Dear Máire Ní Chrualaoich, phoenix, virgin, and swan.

(Bourke et al. 2002, 441-442, tr. Biddy Jenkinson)

Like the male subjects of the elegies discussed above, Ní Chrualaoich is explicitly likened to figures from classical antiquity, albeit to a poet and a mythical bird rather than to martial heroes. As Marie-Louise Coolahan (2013, 9-10) has noted, the allusion to Sappho is potentially double-edged: on the one hand, Sappho is the archetypal female poet from antiquity, while on the other, her name may have had connotations of sexual promiscuity and deviance for contemporary audiences. Ó Murchadha's description of her as an *ógh* ('virgin') and as a pure-white swan are perhaps intended to pre-empt these potential readings.

Although there are very few surviving poems *by* women from the period, references *to* women are quite common in the works surveyed. Women are the subjects of panegyrics and the object of the poet's desire in romantic verse, as well as playing the role of the *spéirbhean* ('sky-woman'): a woman who appears to lament the dead or utter prophecy in political verse, at times understood to be a personification of the sovereignty of Ireland.[19] The women in these poems, both real and imagined, are often directly likened to various women and goddesses from classical antiquity, and these comparisons are framed in the conventional terms of praise for women in the poetry of the period: sweetness of voice, brightness of skin, radiance of eye, and so on. In a lengthy poem in praise of a woman named Cáit, the Louth poet Peadar Ó Doirnín (ca. 1700-1769) states:

Is ó táid tréithre uile ardghéagaibh Pharnassus 'do lár,
is an cháíl chéanna bhí i gclár chléibhghil Phenelope an áigh,
cás Dheirdre chuaigh i ndáil Naoise fán tuile ar an tsnámh,

---

19 A particularly explicit example of this identification appears in Aogán Ó Rathaille's *Mac an Cheannuidhe* (The Merchant's Son), where the poet beholds a "gentle maiden, whose name was Erin" (Dinneen & O'Donoghue 1911, 12-13). The most in-depth study to date on such visionary poetry in the seventeenth and eighteenth century and its political and religious context is still Ó Buachalla 1996.

más lánrogha leat, go lá an éaga biaidh mise ar do scáth.
Is í mo Cháit bhéilbhinn na mball saorchumtha is gile nó an blath
a bhfuil lánéifeacht an bhánlaoige ina timpeall gan smál;
is gath gréine mo ghrá péarlach is is loinnir ar dhath
an tsnáth shaibhir ler ghnáth Hélen a hinneal gach lá.

Since all the virtues of the high-limbed women of Parnassus are present in you
and the same fame that was in the bright face of Penelope of the slaughter
Like Deirdre who pursued Naoise and swam over wave:
If it is indeed your will, until the day of my death I will be by your side.
My sweet-mouthed Cáit of the well-wrought limbs is brighter than the flower,
who is, without flaw, cloaked in the full power of womanhood.
My pearl-white beloved is a sun-beam, and a brilliant flame,
the rich thread with which Helen attired herself each day.

(Ó Buachalla 1976, 34-35)

Deirdre is a well-known character from Irish narrative tradition who was betrothed to an older king and eloped with Naoise, a much younger and more attractive man.[20] Like Helen's abduction by Paris, this was the cause of a bloody and destructive conflict; unlike Helen, Deirdre is typically portrayed as making an active decision to escape a betrothal that was made before her birth. As in the elegies and Jacobite songs discussed above, the poet clearly saw nothing inappropriate about invoking classical and native Irish narrative in the same breath.

Such explicit comparisons between contemporary women and women from classical antiquity are typically made on the grounds of beauty rather than any other qualities – the equation between Máire Ní Chrualaoich and Sappho made in her elegy being a noteworthy exception. The number of figures from classical antiquity who figure in such comparisons is quiet small, despite the frequency with which these comparisons occur.

Helen is by far the most frequent classical referent here, and poets often invoked her role in the destruction of Troy, perhaps simply as a means of identifying her, but perhaps also as an insinuation about the destructive nature of desire.[21] Other commonly

---

20   The Old Irish version of the tale is known as *Longes mac nUislenn* (The Exile of the Songs of Uisliu), and was most recently edited and translated as Hull 1949. An Early Modern Irish version also exists, *Oidheadh Chloinne hUisneach* (The violent death of the children of Uisneach), edited and translated as Mac Giolla Léith 1993. Deirdre's story became popular among Irish playwrights in the early twentieth century; see, for example, George William Russel's *Deirdre* (1902), William Butler Yeat's *Deirdre* (1907), and John Millington Synge's *Deirdre of the Sorrows* (1910).
21   For example, Fiachra Mac Brádaigh's *Aisling* (Ó Buachalla 1976, 27), Peadar Ó Doirnín's *M'uilleagán dubh ó* (O My Dark-haired Young Woman; Ó Buachalla 1976, 35), and Art Mac Cumhaigh's *Úr-chill an Chreagáin* (The Graveyard of Creggan; Ó Buachalla 1976, 41).

invoked figures include the goddesses Juno, Minerva, Pallas, and Venus; the nine Muses; Cassandra; and Constantina, daughter of the emperor Constantine.[22]

A recurring motif appears in visionary poems that feature the *spéirbhean*. After the poet sees the strange woman and is impressed by her beauty, he asks her a series of questions in order to ascertain her identity, displaying his familiarity with classical and other traditions in the process. A brief example of this motif appears in a verse sometimes sung in the Jacobite song *Cáit Ní Dhuibhir*:

Do shuigh sí ar bhinse taobh liom 's mo ghéaga do thit liom síos,
do cheapas gur phlanda ón nGréig í is gur bhaol dom í theacht im líon;
"An tú Júnó, Pallas, Vénus, nó Hélen do loisc an Traoi,
nó an bhean do chloígh na céadta, nó bhfuil gaol agat le Cáit Ní Dhuibhir?"

She sat on the ledge beside me, and my limbs fell down, weak
I thought it was a fair maiden from Greece that surely came near me
"Are you Juno, Pallas, Venus, or Helen who burned Troy?
Or the woman who subdued hundreds, or are you a relation of Cáit Ní Dhuibhir?"

(Ó Buachalla 1978, 5)

These sequences of rhetorical questions invoke the same classical referents as the similes discussed above: Helen and other women contemporary with the Trojan war, the Muses, other goddesses, and so on. Classical and native traditions are often juxtaposed, especially those of Helen and Deirdre, suggesting a popular equation of the two figures.[23]

This type of rhetoric was familiar enough that it could be parodied. In *Amhrán an Phictiúra* (Song of the Picture), the Clare Island poet Mícheál Mac Suibhne recalls coming home late one night and being terrified by a painting of a Turk which his mother had hung up. In his drunken state, the poet assumes the picture is a person and attempts to identify it. First, he lists various classical deities, then proceeds to a small catalogue of heroes, before turning to more sinister beings:

An tú Mag Ag nó Polyphemus?
Nó tabhair sgéala chugam anois gan mhoill;
Nó an tú Arson a léir, mar léightear,
Chuaidh i n-éigcéill i bhfad san gcoill?

---

22 See also Eoghan Ruadh Ó Súilleabháin's visionary poem *Tráth is mé cois leasa* (Once as I Was by the Earthen Mound; Ua Duinnín 1901, 92-94) and Uilliam Ó Maoil Chiaráin's poem in praise of Nancy Dolan (Ó Muirgheasa 1934, 50-52).
23 In addition to the poem in praise of Cáit by Ó Doirnín cited above, this juxtaposition is found in Ó Doirnín's poem *Méabha is Mánas Buí* (Maeve and Yellow Magnus; de Rís 1969, 32), Ó Maoil Chiaráin's *Géag Ráth Árlain* (Scion of Rathaldron; Ó Muirgheasa 1934, 43), and the anonymous *Ceanadus a' tSlóigh* (Kells of the Throng; de Laoide 1914, 16).

An tú Hercules fuair buaidh ar Ghréagaibh
Le neart a ghéaga is le lúth a lainn?
Nó an tú Cerberus an maistín craosach?
Cia'r chuir an ghéar-bhruid sin ar do dhruim?

Are you Magog or Polyphemus
– Tell me, without delay –
Are you Arson[24] who, as we read,
Went astray far into the woods?
Are you Hercules who overcame the Greeks
With the strength of his limbs and swiftness of his blade?
Are you Cerberus, the deep-mouthed mastiff?
Who placed that sharp goad on your back?

(Ó Tiománaidhe 1906, 66)

Divinity

In addition to figuring in the direct comparisons and rhetorical questions discussed above, the gods of Greece and Rome appear in the poems surveyed to represent spheres of human activity or the natural world. Cupid, unsurprisingly, appears in romantic poetry, and Bacchus is invoked in some poems in connection with revelry and drink.[25] As noted earlier, Seaghán Clárach Mac Domhnaill invokes Mars and Cupid in praise of the martial prowess and beauty of the Young Pretender. Phoebus is invoked as a personification of the sun and the light of day.[26] In the Jacobite song *Rosc Catha na Mumhan* (Battle Chant of Munster), by the Cork poet Piaras Mac Gearailt (1702-1795), the poet sees his anticipation of the return of the Pretender in the natural world:

D'aithnigheas féin gan bhréag ar fhuacht
'S ar anfaithe Thétis taobh le cuan,

---

24   The identity of this 'Arson', or the narrative being alluded to, is unknown to the author.
25   E.g. the poet Diarmuid Ruadh mac Muireadhaigh refers to Cupid's arrows as the source of his love-sickness in *Amhrán na Bradaíle* (Song of the Pilfering; de Brún, Ó Buachalla & Ó Con Cheanainn 1971, 44), and there are references to Cupid tormenting the poet in Uilliam Ó Maoil Chiaráin's song *Nancy Bhéasach* (Well-mannered Nancy; Ó Tiománaidhe 1906, 14) and in the anonymous *An Mhódhamhail Mhaiseach* (The Beautiful, Modest Lady; Hyde 1893, 120). In his lament for Art Óg Ó Néill, Art Mac Cumhaigh invokes Bacchus as a metaphor for the hospitality and carousing which he will no longer enjoy at the deceased's home (Ó Buachalla 1976, 45).
26   E.g. Peadar Ó Doirnín's *Cáit bhéilbhinn* (Ó Buachalla 1976, 34), Eoghan Mac Carrthaigh's *Go moch is mé im aonar gan aon im chómhair* (It Is Early and I Am Alone with No-one in My Company; Ó Foghludha 1938, 40), and Uilliam Ó Briain's song in praise of the daughter of Ó Biataigh of Moynalty (Ó Muirgheasa 1934, 59).

Ar chanadh na n-éan go séiseach suairc,
Go gcasfadh mo Shéasar glé gan ghruaim

I have seen, without a lie, from the cold
and the raging of Thetis by the bay,
from the pleasing, tuneful singing of the birds
that my bright Caesar will come without despair.

(Ó Foghludha 1905, 23)

A common device in elegiac verse is to portray the natural world in disarray, as if partaking in the poet's own performance of grief. In some poems, this upheaval is depicted through the actions of various classical deities: Phoebus for the sun, Nereus or Thetis for the sea, and so on. One example of this trope is in the *beochaoineadh* ('lament for a living person') of Seán Clárach Mac Domhnaill, written by Seán Ó Tuama (ca. 1707-1775):

Atá spéirling is stoirm ghaosmhar ar uisce
Ag réabadh 's ag briseadh slím-chranna seoil,
Is caor-thonna neimhe ag Téitis ar muire,
Ag scéithchaint faoi imeall tíortha tar neoin;
Na stéid-eacha buile ag Phoebus ag rithe,
Gan géilleadh ná urraim díreach don chóir,
Phlégon ar mire, Aetan i bhfuinneamh,
Aeolus go tuirseach fíor-lag ar neoin.

There is tempest and wild storm on the water
Tearing and breaking the thin masts of the ships
Thetis, in a frenzy, raises fiery waves
that strike the very edges of the land
Phoebus's enraged steeds run
without yielding or bending to the natural order
Phlegon enraged, Aetan incited,
Aeolus despondent and weak.

(Dinneen 1908, 57)

The Kerry poet Aogán Ó Rathaille (1670-1729) was evidently fond of this motif, as it appears in no fewer than four of his elegies.[27] The gods of classical mythology feature in Ó Rathaille's verse in other ways, such as in his hyperbolic description of the divine

---

27 The elegy for Seaghán Brún, the second of the two elegies for Donnchadh Ó Ceallacháin, and the elegies for Seon Hassiadh and Eoghan Mac Cormaic Riabhaigh Mac Carthaigh (Dinneen & O'Donoghue 1911, 50-53, 92-95, 198-201, 220-225).

manufacture of a pair of shoes which a friend had gifted him (Dinneen & O'Donoghue 1911, 100-107). In three of his elegies, the gods are described as presiding over the birth of the subject of the poem, and bestowing various gifts pertaining to their particular domains upon him.[28] Implicit in these elegies is the idea that the gods of classical Greece and Rome are present in the Irish landscape and that, as with the Homeric heroes, they take a personal interest in the lives and deeds of certain leaders and, perhaps, their people.

Other references

The majority of references to classical antiquity in the poems surveyed fit neatly into the categories discussed above: vague references to the land of Greece, direct comparisons between the subjects of poems and classical figures, and references to the gods, especially in the context of elegies. There are, however, some other forms of classical reference or comparison which are worth discussing briefly.

Some poets praised the subjects of poems for their mastery over classical and other languages. In his poem in praise of the Ó Raghallaigh of Áth Cairn, County Cork, Uilliam Ó Maoil Chiaráin describes Ó Raghallaigh's wife as "'sí is eagnaidhe a léigfeadh dán i mBéarla is i Laidin" ("the wisest of all who would read poems in English or in Latin"; Ó Muirgheasa 1934, 38). An anonymous poem on the death of Seaghán Clárach Ó Domhnaill refers to the poet as "seabhac na sáimhe, sás na scéal do scríobhadh i Laidin go breágh, i mBéarla, nó i nGréigis ghlinn" ("a tranquil hawk who would write the sense of stories in fine Latin, English, or clear Greek"; Dinneen 1908, 61). While such praise was, no doubt, sometimes hyperbolic, these references indicate that such knowledge was held in high esteem. Poets also occasionally likened other Irish poets and musicians to their counterparts: in a poem on the decline of the native aristocracy, Peadar Ó Doirnín enumerates the amusements of courtly life: hunting hares, carousing, listening to the music of the harp and to poets who are likened to Ovid – "le file faobhrach mar Ovid caomh" ("listening to a sharp-edged poet like fair Ovid") (Ó Buachalla 1976, 30). Describing the welcome he would receive in Drogheda, the Armagh poet Art Mac Cumhaigh (1738-1773) likens the music of the harp that he would hear there to the music of Orpheus: "gheobhainn siamsa de'n gcláirsigh bhí tráth ag Orphéas" (I would find diversion from the harp that Orpheus once had") (Ó Muirgheasa 1934, 16).

Two eighteenth-century poems, both by Uilliam Ó Maoil Chiaráin, draw upon late medieval and early modern ecclesiastical ideas on the imminence of death and the vanity of earthly things, ideas which were widespread in Latin, Irish, and other vernacular languages (cf. Ó Háinle 2000). In both of Ó Maoil Chiaráin's poems, as in earlier Irish explorations of this theme, classical, biblical and native narrative traditions

---

28 The first lament for Donnchadh Ó Ceallacháin, and the laments for Diarmaid Ó Laoghaire na Cillíneach and Geralt, son of the Knight of Glin (Dinneen & O'Donoghue 1911, 80-81, 128-131, 154-157). This motif appears occasionally in later elegies, such as that of Piaras Mac Gearailt for the 'Squire Geal Freeman' (Ó Foghludha 1905, 56-58).

are used as a source of moral exempla.[29] In a song on the faithlessness of women, Ó Maoil Chiaráin states:

Chualaidh mé dá léigheamh gur éaluigh a bhean ó Dháibhi,
Is arís ó Righ na Féinne gur éaluigh sí Gráinne;
Dh'imthigh Helen le n-a sgéimh, agus Déirdre le n-a háille,
'S goidé'n fáth dhúinn 'bheith 'dréim leo? acht béid ag an bhfear is áil leo.

I have heard it being read that David's wife left him
and that Gráinne left the King of the Fiann
Helen with her charm left, and Deirdre with her beauty
Why do we strive after them? They'll only belong to the man whom they desire.

(Ó Muirgheasa 1934, 24)

The "King of the Fiann" is Fionn Mac Cumhaill, mentioned earlier; his betrothal to Gráinne and her elopement with a younger man is the subject of a popular early modern Irish tale, *Tóruigheacht Dhiarmada is Ghráinne* (The Pursuit of Diarmuid and Gráinne; Ní Shéaghdha 1967). Gráinne's involvement in a love triangle with disastrous consequences would seem to motivate the implicit comparison with Deirdre and Helen, although no such explanation can be offered for David's wife (perhaps this is a misremembered version of the story of Bathsheba and Uriah). As is the case in many of the poems discussed above, events from classical and native narrative tradition seem to occupy the same mental 'space' for the poet.

Dán ar an mBás (A Poem on Death) takes the form of a long dialogue between an anonymous young man and Death. In response to the young man's boasting, Death states:

Is faobhrach mo lanna 's ní sgarann aon slán liom,
Claoidhfidh mé tusa, má's measamhail 's má's áluinn,
Má's óg, is má's másach, is má's féiceamhlach breagh thú;
Ní bhacann sin mise, is goinfead gan spás thú,
Mar rinneas le Hector, Narcissus, is Dáibhi;
Cé gur tréan agus saoghalta nó Críostaidhe chum crábhaidh,
Le mo shaighdibh gur ghoineas gach duine de'n Ádhamh-chloinn,
'S ní éistim le leithsgéal, 's béidh tú mar chách liom.

---

29 Cf. the use made of biblical, classical, and native tradition in Bonaventura Ó hEodhasa's 1611 translation of *Cur mundus militat*, a medieval Latin poem on the vanity of the world popularly attributed to Saint Bernard (Mhág Craith 1967, 55-58; 1980, 25-26). See also *Créad fa seachnainn-se suirghe* (Why Should I Avoid Courtship?), a poem attributed only to *An Parson* (The Parson) and found in the early sixteenth-century Scottish manuscript The Book of the Dean of Lismore, edited and translated as Gillies 2008.

> My blades are sharp, and no one escapes me
> I will wear you down, though you are esteemed and beautiful
> though you are young and strong, and fair of appearance
> That does not concern me, I will strike you without respite
> as I did to Hector, Narcisuss and David;
> Whether they were mighty and worldly, or pious Christians,
> With my arrows have I wounded every one of Adam's children
> I hear no excuses, you will be one and the same to me.

(Ó Muirgheasa 1934, 92)

As the poem progresses, Death lists other figures he has laid low: despite their strength and military power, Samson, Caesar, Priam, and Joshua could not escape death, nor could Hippocrates and Galen despite their intellectual achievement, nor Croesus despite his wealth. Such themes of *memento mori* are quite rare in the poems surveyed, especially in comparison to the poetry of previous centuries. This development most likely reflects changes in both devotional practices and the material circumstances of audiences: messages about the vanity of earthly aspirations are less immediately relevant when the predominant cultural narrative is one of disenfranchisement and dispossession.

Conclusions

References to classical tradition in the form of comparisons, metaphorical identifications, and brief allusive statements are fairly common in the poems surveyed. More sustained engagements, such as adaptations or retellings of classical narrative, do not occur. Such retellings may have been felt to be generically inappropriate for song – while there is an older tradition of mythological or historical narrative songs, most of the narrative songs composed in the period in question reflect the experiences of the poet and their community, or at least of the poetic ego.[30] Metaphors, similes, and brief allusions also place fewer demands, in terms of familiarity with classical tradition, on performers, singers, and audiences. As noted above, direct familiarity with classical languages and text was only available to a minority of Irish speakers, in particular those with clerical or scribal training; in most cases, it would seem that familiarity with the worlds of classical mythology came from Irish-language sources – in other words, persons such as Helen or Achilles had found a home for themselves in the Irish literary tradition.

---

[30] Narrative songs include the Fenian ballads, or "lays" as they are commonly known (following the Irish and Scottish Gaelic use of *laoithe*), mentioned above. The largest collection of lays was edited and translated as *Duanaire Finn* (Fionn's Poem-book; MacNeill 1908; Murphy 1933; 1953). In the modern period, narrative songs include songs commemorating tragedies such as *Amhrán na Leabhar* and *Eanach Dhúin*, which have been previously discussed, romantic songs, and visionary or prophetic verse.

Critics of Irish poetry, if they have offered comment on the use of classical learning in works of the period, have generally taken a negative view of it. In his edition of the works of Aogán Ó Rathaille, Patrick Dinneen refers to the catalogues of deities which appear in the poet's elegies as "the greatest blemish in these compositions" (1911, xxxv), and Cecile O'Rahilly dismisses much of the post-seventeenth-century tradition as "stereotyped and hackneyed" (1952, ix). Such assessments privilege the contemporary experience of *reading* these poems, as well as post-Romantic sensibilities which value novelty and individual genius. The repetition of classical names, whether individually or as part of a catalogue, has an impact in oral performance; moreover, these songs were composed with particular social functions of commemoration and consolation in mind, and much of what might be seen as cliché abets those functions.[31] As O'Higgins (2017, 72) notes:

> such capacious interrogation may strike modern readers as mechanical; yet it bore incantatory power. Through it, the poet laid out the cultural context in which the woman would tell her story, and the audience, hear it. She was not Helen, Medea, or Deirdre, but Ireland's history would be told in their shadow. The catalogue celebrated the fact that the poets' intellectual 'stock' includes classical literature as well as Irish—and implicitly claimed that the Irish and classical literary traditions constituted a literary and imaginative continuum, habitable by a single mind.

This juxtaposition of figures from Classic and Gaelic historical and mythological tradition is, as we have seen, a recurring feature of these poems. The idea of the commensurability of Irish with classical languages has roots in the middles ages: the eighth- or ninth-century *Auraicept na nÉces* or Scholar's Primer lists Irish alongside the Isidorean three sacred languages of Hebrew, Greek, and Latin; we find echoes of this text within the grammatical tracts which professional poets studied carefully in the sixteenth and seventeenth centuries.[32] The survival of this idea of the commensurability of these traditions in the modern period is not mere antiquarianism. Irish identities were largely conceived of in sectarian terms in the eighteenth and nineteenth centuries: an identification with Rome in antiquity might bolster an identification with contemporary Rome, and form part of a national identity that sees affinities with Catholic Europe rather than neighbouring Britain. As noted in the introduction, the period in question was one

---

31 In reference to Ó Rathaille's elegies, and Dinneen's criticism of them, Breandán Ó Buachalla (2004, 31) notes that "although their underlying 'sameness' defies modern demands for originality, the stability of the genre suggests that they were efficacious within the culture and the mourning ritual in which they were originally embedded".

32 The medieval *Auraicept* and its commentary was edited and translated by Calder 1917. An edition and translation of the 'canonical' *Auraicept*, representing the oldest stratum of its textual tradition, was prepared by Ahlqvist 1983. See Engesland 2024 for a recent discussion of this passage. An early modern retelling of the *Auraicept*'s account of the origin of the Irish language can be found at Mac Cárthaigh 2014, § 4.

when the Irish language and its speakers were excluded from many aspects of public life, and language shift was underway in much of the island because of the perceived economic advantages of English. Despite the relatively modest means of most poets, and especially their audiences, the repeated commemoration in performance of an Irish classical past offered some consolation: a sense of shared ownership of a metaphorical treasure which rivalled that of the great civilizations of antiquity.

Bibliography

Ahlqvist, A. (ed.) 1983. *The Early Irish Linguist: An Edition of the Canonical Part of the Auraicept Na n-Éces*. Helsinki: Academia Scientiarum Fennica.

Blankenhorn, V.S. 2003. *Irish Song-Craft and Metrical Practice since 1600*. Lewiston, N.Y: Edwin Mellen Press.

Bourke, A., Kilfeather, S., Luddy, M., Mac Curtain, M., Meaney, G., Ní Dhonnchadha, M., O'Dowd, M. & Wills, C. (eds) 2002. *The Field Day Anthology of Irish Writing, Volume IV: Irish Women's Writings and Traditions*. Cork: Cork University Press.

Bruford, A. 1966. "Gaelic Folk-Tales and Mediæval Romances: A Study of the Early Modern Irish 'Romantic Tales' and Their Oral Derivatives". *Béaloideas* 34, i–285.

de Brún, P., Ó Buachalla, B. & Ó Con Cheanainn, T. (eds) 1971. *Nua-Dhuanaire: Cuid I*. Baile Átha Cliath: Institiúid Ard-Léinn Bhaile Átha Cliath.

Buttimer, N. 2006. "Literature in Irish, 1690-1800: From the Williamite Wars to the Act of Union", in: Kelleher & O'Leary 2006, I, 320-371.

Calder, G. (ed.) 1917. *Auraicept Na N-Éces: The Scholars' Primer, Being the Texts of the Ogham Tract from the Book of Ballymote and the Yellow Book of Lecan, and the Text of the Trefhocul from the Book of Leinster*. Edinburgh: John Grant.

Coolahan, M.L. 2013. "Reception, Reputation, and Early Modern Women's Missing Texts". *Critical Quarterly* 55.4, 3-14.

Corkery, D. 1967. *The Hidden Ireland: A Study of Gaelic Munster in the Eighteenth Century*. Dublin: Gill and Macmillan.

Covington, S., Carey, V.P., & McGowan-Doyle, V. (eds) 2018a. *Early Modern Ireland: New Sources, Methods, and Perspectives*. London: Routledge.

Covington, S., Carey, V.P. & McGowan-Doyle, V. (eds) 2018b. "Introduction: The Past, Present, and Future of Early Modern Ireland", in: Covington, Carey & McGowan-Doyle 2018a, 1-26.

Darwin, G.R. 2021. "On Greek and Latin Names in Early Modern Irish Syllabic Verse". *Celtica* 33, 195-247.

Denvir, G. 2006. "Literature in Irish, 1800-1890: From the Act of Union to the Gaelic League", in: Kelleher & O'Leary 2006, I, 544-98.

Dinneen, P. (ed.) 1908. *Amhráin Sheagháin Chláraigh Mhic Dhomhnaill...: maille le beathaidh an fhilidh agus foclóir*. Baile Átha Cliath: Conradh na Gaeilge.

Dinneen, P. & O'Donoghue, T. (eds) 1911. *Dánta Aodhagáin Uí Rathaille – The Poems of Egan O'Rahilly*. London: Irish Texts Society.

Doyle, A. 2015. *A History of the Irish Language: From the Norman Invasion to Independence*. Oxford: Oxford University Press.

Doyle, A. 2018. "Language and Literacy in the Eighteenth and Nineteenth Centuries", in: Kelly 2018, 353-379.

Engesland, N.E. 2024. "*Auraicept na nÉces* 'The Scholars' Primer'", in Clarke, M., Poppe, E. & Torrance, I. (eds) 2024. *Classical Antiquity and Medieval Ireland*. London: Bloomsbury Academic, 293-305.

Gillies, W. 2008. "Créad Fá Seachnainn-Se Suirghe?" *Scottish Gaelic Studies* 24, 215-243.

Hyde, D. (ed.) 1893. *Abhráin Ghradha Chúige Connacht or Love Songs of Connacht*. Baile Átha Cliath: Gill and Unwin.

Hyde D. (ed.) 1933. *Abhráin Agus Dánta an Reachtabhraigh*. Baile Átha Cliath: Oifig Dhíolta Foilseachán Rialtais.

Hull, V. (ed.) 1949. *Longes Mac N-Uislenn: The Exile of the Sons of Uisliu*. New York: Modern Language Association of America.

Jaski, B. 2003. "'We Are of the Greeks in Our Origin': New Perspectives on the Irish Origin Legend". *Cambrian Medieval Celtic Studies* 46, 1-53.

Kane, B. 2018. "Making Early Modern Irish Studies Irish? Teaching, Learning, and Researching Early Modern Irish in a Digital Age", in: Covington, Carey & McGowan-Doyle 2018a, 79-95.

Kelleher, M. & O'Leary, P. (eds) 2006. *The Cambridge History of Irish Literature*. 2 vols. Cambridge: Cambridge University Press.

Kelly, J. (ed.) 2018. *The Cambridge History of Ireland: Volume 3: 1730-1880*. Cambridge: Cambridge University Press.

Knott, E. (ed.) 1922. *The Bardic Poems of Tadhg Dall Ó HUiginn (1550-1591) Vol. I: Introduction and Text*. London: Irish Texts Society.

de Laoide, S. (ed.) 1914. *Duanaire Na Midhe*. Baile Átha Cliath: Conradh na Gaeilge.

Mac Airt, S. (ed.) 1944. *Leabhar Branach – The Book of the O'Byrnes*. Dublin: Dublin Institute for Advanced Studies.

Mac Cárthaigh, E. (ed.) 2014. *The Art of Bardic Poetry: A New Edition of Irish Grammatical Tracts I*. Dublin: Dublin Institute for Advanced Studies.

Mac Erlean, J.C. (ed.) 1910. *Duanaire Dháibhidh Uí Bhruadair – The Poems of David Ó Bruadair: Part I*. London: Irish Texts Society.

Mac Giolla Léith, C. (ed.) 1993. *Oidheadh Chloinne hUisneach: The Violent Death of the Children of Uisneach*. London: Irish Texts Society.

MacNeill, E. (ed.) 1908. *Duanaire Finn: The Book of the Lays of Fionn. P. 1*. London: Irish Texts Society.

McCoy, P.R. 2017. "Sloiged Már Rucsat Gréic Hebríb Fechtas N-Aile: A Middle Irish Retelling of a Greek Battle". *Proceedings of the Harvard Celtic Colloquium* 37, 203-216.

McManus, D. 2009. "Good-Looking and Irresistable: The Hero from Early Irish Saga to Classical Poetry". *Ériu* 59, 57-109.

Meister, Ferdinand (ed.) 1873. *Daretis Phrygii de Excidio Troiae Historia*. Leipzig: De Gruyter, Inc.

Mhág Craith, C. (ed.) 1967. *Dán Na mBráthar Mionúr Cuid I – Téacs*. Baile Átha Cliath: Institiúid Ard-Léinn Bhaile Átha Cliath.

Mhág Craith, C. (ed.) 1980. *Dán Na mBráthar Mionúr Cuid II – Aistriúcháin, Nótaí, Etc*. Baile Átha Cliath: Institiúid Ard-Léinn Bhaile Átha Cliath.

Murphy, G. (ed.) 1933. *Duanaire Finn: The Book of the Lays of Fionn. P. 2*. London: Irish Texts Society.

Murphy, G. (ed.) 1953. *Duanaire Finn: The Book of the Lays of Fionn. P. 3, Introduction, Notes Appendices and Glossary by Gerard Murphy*. London: Irish Texts Society.

Nagy, J.F. 2010. "Finn and the Fenian Tradition", in: Wright, J.M. 2010. *A Companion to Irish Literature. A Companion to Irish Literature*. Malden, MA & Chichester: Wiley-Blackwell, 27-38.

Ní Cheallacháin, M. (ed.) 1962. *Filíocht Phádraigín Haicéad*. Baile Átha Cliath: An Clóchomhar Tta.

Ní Dhomhnaill, N. 2005. *Selected Essays*, ed. Oona Frawley. Dublin: New Island.

Ní Shéaghdha, N. (ed.) 1967. *Tóruigheacht Dhiarmada Agus Ghráinne: The Pursuit of Diarmaid and Gráinne*. London: Irish Texts Society.

Ní Shíocháin, T. 2021. "The Oral Tradition", in: Darcy, A. & Wheatley, D. (eds) 2021. *A History of Irish Women's Poetry*. Cambridge: Cambridge University Press, 74-88.

Ní Uallacháin, P. (ed.) 2003. *A Hidden Ulster: People, Songs and Traditions of Oriel*. Dublin: Four Courts Press.

Ó Buachalla, B. (ed.) 1976. *Nua-Dhuanaire: Cuid II*. Baile Átha Cliath: Institiúid Ard-Léinn Bhaile Átha Cliath.

Ó Buachalla, B. (ed.) 1978. *Nua-Dhuanaire: Cuid III*. Baile Átha Cliath: Institiúid Ard-Léinn Bhaile Átha Cliath.

Ó Buachalla, B. 1996. *Aisling Ghéar: Na Stíobhartaigh Agus an Taos Léinn, 1603-1788*. Baile Átha Cliath: Clóchomhar Tta.

Ó Buachalla, B. 2004. *Dánta Aodhagáin Uí Rathaille: Reassessments*. London: Irish Texts Society.

Ó Foghludha, R. (ed.) 1905. *Amhráin Phiarais Mhic Gearailt*. Baile Átha Cliath: Conradh na Gaeilge.

Ó Foghludha, R. (ed.) 1938. *Eoghan an Mhéirín Mac Carrthaigh*. Baile Átha Cliath: Oifig an tSoláthair.

Ó Háinle, C. 2000. "Congaibh Ort, a Mhacaoimh Mná (DG 103): Content and Form". *Éigse* 32, 47-58.

Ó Háinle, C. 2015. "Three Apologues and In Cath Catharda". *Ériu* 65, 87-126.

Ó Muirgheasa, É. (ed.) 1934. *Amhráin Na Midhe*. Baile Átha Cliath: Comhlacht Oideachais na hÉireann.

Ó Riain, P. 1989. "The Psalter of Cashel: A Provisional List of Contents". *Éigse* 23, 107-130.

Ó Tiománaidhe, M. (ed.) 1906. *Abhráin Ghaedhilge an Iarthair, an Chéad Chuid*. Baile Átha Cliath: Conradh na Gaeilge.

Ó Tuama, S. (ed.) 1961. *Caoineadh Airt Uí Laoghaire*. Baile Átha Cliath: An Clóchomhar Tta.

Ó Tuama, S. & Kinsella, T. (eds) 1981. *An Duanaire: 1600-1900: Poems of the Dispossessed*. Mountrath: Dolmen.

O'Connor, R. 2014. "Irish Narrative Literature and the Classical Tradition, 900-1300", in: O'Connor, R. 2014. *Classical Literature and Learning in Medieval Irish Narrative*. Cambridge: D.S. Brewer, 1-22.

O'Connor, T. 2018. "The Catholic Church and Catholics in an Era of Sanctions and Restraints, 1690-1790", in: Kelly 2018, 257-279.

O'Higgins, L. 2017. *The Irish Classical Self: Poets and Poor Scholars in the Eighteenth and Nineteenth Centuries*. Oxford: Oxford University Press.

O'Rahilly, C. (ed.) 1952. *Five Seventeenth Century Political Poems*. Dublin: Dublin Institute for Advanced Studies.

de Rís, Seán (ed.) 1969. *Peadar Ó Doirnín*. Baile Átha Cliath: Oifig an tSoláthair.

Sharpe, R. & Hoyne, M. (eds) 2020. *Clóliosta: Printing in the Irish Language 1571-1871. An Attempt at a Narrative Bibliography*. Dublin: Dublin Institute for Advanced Studies.

Ua Duinnín, P. (ed.) 1901. *Amhráin Eoghain Ruaidh Uí Shúilleabháin*. Baile Átha Cliath: Conradh na Gaeilge.

7

FROM THE RUBICON TO STEVNS AND BACK

INTERTWINED RECEPTIONS OF CAESAR IN *ELVERHØI* AND *ASTERIX* IN DANISH

TRINE ARLUND HASS

Since the 1960s, Uderzo and Goscinny's comic book series about the fictional resistance of Asterix and his fellow Gauls against Caesar's campaigns have conquered readers all over the world. Their key concept is, as will be familiar to most, a reverted perspective on the Roman action in Gaul in the 50s BCE known through the words of the conqueror Caesar in his *Commentarii De Bello Gallico*. In the comics, we see events from the point of view of the invaded – or rather the last fictional Gaulish stronghold, a small village inhabited by ordinary, recognizable people, among them the protagonists Asterix and Obelix. Comic effect is often obtained by placing the words and rationales of the conqueror in the mouths of the conquered Gauls. This makes for a refined critique of power without turning completely against Caesar. He is never made into a classic cartoon villain, although he is shown with a temper worthy of one. Caesar's position as a superhuman statesman is deflated – he is brought down to size and shown to be a person with flaws. This does not turn the reader against him but rather enables them to embrace him more. It is probably no exaggeration to say that this version of Caesar and the comic way into the world of ancient Roman culture paved by his fictional Gaulish 'nemeseis' has been a first introduction to the Roman world for many.

Although Denmark was never part of the Roman empire, the *Asterix* comics have been as successful here as anywhere else, since Denmark is just as influenced by Graeco-Roman culture as any other region of the Western world. By replacing the references to French culture of the original with similar references to Danish culture, history, geography, and so on, the Danish translator of the series for five decades, Per Då, has given the Gallo-Roman narrative of the series a Danish dimension too. This prompts the underlying assumption of this essay: that the Danish translations of *Asterix* present a Julius Caesar of a particularly Danish flavour. In the following I address one such example in the Danish version of the volume *Le bouclier Arverne* (1967; in English *Asterix and the Chieftain's Shield*, 1968; in Danish, *Asterix romernes skræk*, 1972). Here, the translator has inserted a reference to what is arguably one of the most famous uses of Caesar in Danish cultural history: a line from *Elverhøi*, a musical play by Johan Ludvig Heiberg (1791-1860), which I examine both in terms of translation strategies and as a popular Danish reception of Caesar.

In a sense, *Elverhøi*, like the *Asterix* series, deals with a conquest and presents an encounter between a great ruler and representatives of the common people. Its general nature and scope, however, is significantly different. *Elverhøi* cultivates local folklore and ballads; as such, it is characteristic of the time when it was written. During the nineteenth century, the Danes were adjusting to a new self-conception, as the period's general focus on negotiating national identities in the Danish case coincided with a severe reduction in territory and financial crises. Following the strategy summed up in a popular saying, *hvad udad tabes må indad vindes* (what is lost outwardly must be won inwardly),[33] the local past, history, and folklore became primary sources and foci of the arts. *Elverhøi* is usually found to be a classic example of this. The most famous line in the play – the one people will know, if any – is, however, a direct reference to and quotation of Julius Caesar's famous dictum *alea iacta est*.

The ideas about Danish identity developed in this period, called the Danish 'Golden Age', are still to a large extent valid today. Any Danish participation in larger football tournaments confirms that the idea of Denmark as a small yet far from insignificant nation founded in the 'Golden Age' still thrives today. One of the most popular football anthems, *Re-Sepp-ten*, originally composed for the World Cup in Mexico in 1986, compare the Danes to the little, ugly duckling of Hans Christian Andersen's famous fairytale from 1843. This national narrative enables Danish identification with the fictional Gauls in the tiny village, who repeatedly prove able to resist the mighty power of Rome against all odds.

Elverhøi

Elverhøi was the result of a commission by the Danish court for a play in celebration of the wedding between Prince Frederik (VII) and Princess Vilhelmina Marie, and was written for the Royal Theatre in Copenhagen.[34] These circumstances alone place the play in an ambitious and elitist context, but it is a comedy, and it did and

---

33   The saying was invented by the writer H.P. Holst (1811-1893), to be embossed on a medal made for the Scandinavian Industry and Art Exhibition held in Copenhagen in 1872. It is, however, often attributed to Enrico Dalgas (1828-1894), who is famed for co-founding and heading *Det Danske Hedeselskab* (the Danish Heath Society, 1866–), a high-profile, idealistic, national initiative working to develop the moor landscape of Jutland for cultivation. Nielsen 2019.

34   The wedding united two branches of the Danish royal family: Vilhelmina Marie was one of only two surviving legitimate children of the ruling King Frederik VI (r. 1808-1839), both of whom were women and thus unable to inherit the throne. The next in line after Frederik VI was his cousin, son of the brother of his father, Christian VII. He, who later became King Christian VIII (r. 1839-1848), was the father of the groom, who, after his father, became King Frederik VII

does appeal broadly; it was an immediate success when it premiered in 1828 and has been ever since. With approximately 1,000 performances at the Royal Theatre, it is the most frequently performed play in Denmark and often referred to as the Danish national play.[35] Its national character made it part of the repertoire of a national romantic cultural wave washing over Denmark during the early years especially of the Nazi occupation of 1940-1945.[36] The latest staging of *Elverhøi* by the Royal Theatre in Copenhagen was in 1996, when Copenhagen was the European Capital of Culture. This was an open-air performance in the forest park Jægersborg Dyrehave just north of the city, originally set up by King Christian V (r. 1670-1699) for *par force* hunting and today a UNESCO world heritage site. As recordings made by the Danish Broadcasting Corporation show, it was a great display with an immense line-up of participants, counting a cast of the most popular Danish actors and best dancers of the Royal Ballet, a large orchestra and choir, and many extras in costume, including quite a few on horseback.[37] Coaches brought large crowds of people to the woodlands of Dyrehaven to see the play. On arrival, people would pick up picnic baskets before taking their places in the clearing organized as a theatre space – this is seen in the recording of the play as the overture was playing. The recorded performance was furthermore attended by Princess Benedikte, sister to Queen Margrethe II of Denmark, thus bringing together crown and people, which coincides with the play in terms of both its content and the original intention of its genesis.

Heiberg and the commission

The commission for the play was won by Johan Ludvig Heiberg (1791-1860) over another leading figure of the cultural environment in Denmark at the time, Adam Oehlenschläger (1779-1850). Oehlenschläger is traditionally said to have introduced Romantic poetry to Denmark with his work *Digte* (*Poems*) of 1802; the most famous poem, 'The Golden Horns', is about how a young woman and a farmer each discover a large, golden horn made around 400 AD. Oehlenschläger's poem revolves around actual archaeological discoveries made in 1639 and 1734 respectively, but stolen and remelted in the same year as his *Digte* was published. The well-established author also wrote several dramas, of which especially the tragedies were successful. Heiberg, in contrast, was a rising star, with new views on poetry and aesthetics.[38] He had written a dissertation on Calderón

---

(1848-1863). Prince Frederik and Princess Vilhelmina Marie were separated in 1834 and divorced in 1837.
35   See e.g. Lyding and Holm [no year] and Auken 2008a.
36   Hertel 2011, 14-15.
37   The recording is available at https://www.dr.dk/bonanza/serie/492/tv-t---90erne/39476/elverhoej-– although the performance is in Danish, watching the first 5-10 minutes will give an impression of the particular staging as well as a sense of the music, which is an integral part of the play and of its success.
38   Differences in their views on aesthetics, poetry, and not least drama were exposed in polemic exchanges between the two authors in nine issues of the literary journal *Kjøbenhavns Flyvende Post*,

in 1817 and in 1825 introduced Danish plays in the tradition of vaudeville – a farce with music – which he had become familiar with in France and felt might work as a 'cure' for the crisis of his age.[39] The vaudeville's combination of dialogue and music with characters unmarked by the complications characteristic of dark Romanticism but concerned with smaller intrigues, made it a great success with Danish audiences, and Heiberg became influential both in art theory and as a practitioner.[40] In 1831, he married the popular actress Johanne Luise Pätges – for whom he wrote the role of Agnete in *Elverhøi* (Fig. 1a) – and the norms and trends of Northern taste and society were set at their home, especially during the 1830s. Literary historian Sune Auken defines the novelty of Heiberg's vaudeville dramas as follows:

> *In terms of literary history, the novelty of the Heibergian vaudeville is not just its lightness and the elegance of its completion. The novelty is that this elegance and lightness is the very point of the work. It does not pretend to be a fundamental, existential drama intent on moving and shaking its audience to their core but is characterized and must make its impression by its refinement, its delicacy, its mild yet often satirical humour, as well as its precise, eloquent, and carefully composed grace.[41]*

Heiberg's ideas of aesthetics were further influenced although not completely defined by Hegel, whom he met during a period of academic employment in Germany (1822-1825), and whose logic Heiberg introduced to Denmark in a publication from 1824. It has been found, as we shall see later, that this Hegelian influence is prominent in *Elverhøi*.[42]

---

which was founded by Heiberg. Heiberg's critical review of Oehlenschläger's tragedy *Varangians in Constantinople* (first performed 17 November 1827) in the journal in December 1827 provoked a response from Oehlenschläger, and the debate continued from there. See Stewart 2007, 290-300.

39 Nagy 2008, 358.

40 Auken 2008b, 269-274; Heiberg 1826. Heiberg's writings in the journal *Kjøbenhavns flyvende Post* or *Flyverposten*, founded and published by Heiberg, became an important forum of literary debate. Especially during January and February 1828, Heiberg formulated the aesthetic views which became so influential. Written in response to Oehlenschläger, Auken calls them "one of the most significant contributions to scholarly Danish aesthetics". Andersen and Petersen 1924, 411-439 describes his art-historical system as uniting French classicism and German idealism and thus, while clearly affected by Hegelianism, it deviates from Hegel's taste and his posthumously published lectures of aesthetics (1832).

41 Auken 2008b, 272: "Den litteraturhistoriske nyhed i den heibergske vaudeville er ikke bare den lethed og elegance, hvormed den er gennemført. Nyheden er, at denne elegance og lethed er selve pointen med værket. Det giver sig ikke ud for at være et grundlæggende, eksistentielt drama, som skal røre og gribe tilskueren i hans dybeste grund, men er karakteristisk ved og skal gøre indtryk ved sit raffinement, sin forfinelse, sin milde, men dog jævnligt satiriske humor og sin præcise, velformulerede og velkomponerede ynde". This and subsequent translations from Danish are mine unless otherwise stated.

42 Andersen and Petersen 1924, 422; Stewart 2007.

The complicated plot

Elverhøi is a romantic comedy of mistaken identities, full of all kinds of twists and turns, most of which are important for the analysis of the passage in question. It is set in Stevns, a peninsula in southeast Zealand separated from the mainland by the stream Tryggevælde Å, on an unspecified day in the seventeenth century during the reign of King Christian IV (r. 1588/1596-1648), probably the best-known of the Danish kings.[43] Heiberg specifies in his introduction to the play's print version that although it features some historical persons (notably the aforementioned king), it is not a history play.[44]

The action takes place on the wedding day of Elisabeth Munk and Master Ebbesen, the vassal of Stevns. The marriage and date of the wedding is arranged by King Christian IV, who is Elisabeth's godfather and who placed her, having lost her parents at a very young age, in the guardianship of Master Walkendorff of Højstrup in Stevns. For her christening, the king gave her a ring with a very special diamond, which later proves to be important – it has since gone missing. At the outset, the missing ring seems to explain why Walkendorff is anxious that the king might turn up for the wedding.

The problem, from the start, is that Ebbesen does not love Elisabeth but the peasant girl Agnete, daughter of the smallholder Karen, who lives by the stream Tryggevælde near Elverhøj (Elves' Hill), where a bridge connects Stevns and Zealand. Elisabeth does not love Ebbesen either; she loves Herr Flemming, a courtier. Ebbesen and Agnete are in the habit of meeting in secret at night on Elves' Hill, on which occasions Agnete has been mistaken for an elf maiden, who, according to local folklore, inhabits the hill, as does the Elf King. Agnete's mother Karen is a firm believer in the elves and transmits her knowledge about them by telling stories and singing ballads about them. She is the first person on stage, and the play opens with one of her songs. Next enters King Christian IV, but Karen does not recognize him, and he does not reveal his identity to her. From his first appearance, Christian notices something is being concealed and begins working secretly to disclose it, immediately sensing that the elf maiden must be the key. When Walkendorff enters and states his concerns, Karen believes she can appease him since she knows the Elf King will tolerate no other king to enter Stevns, his realm, and she believes the kings of Denmark to be aware of this.

The play culminates on the night of the wedding, but the central scene is set on Elves' Hill. King Christian, under the cover of going on a night-time hunt, rides towards it to face the people of the legends head on and uncover the truth about their nature. Before bringing the play to its dramatic climax by crossing the bridge over the stream

---

43 Formally the second-longest reigning monarch in Denmark after Margrethe II, Christian IV left a significant mark on the capital by erecting several iconic buildings, including Rundetårn, Børsen, and Rosenborg Slot. Gamrath 1991 and Lockhart 1992 give surveys of the general history of scholarship on Christian IV in Danish and English respectively, although both works primarily deal with the substantial number of works issued in connection with the dedication of the year 1988 to Christian IV.

44 Heiberg 1861, 45.

Fig. 1a. C.V. Bruun, engraving depicting Johanne Louise Pätges, last married to Heiberg, as Agnete in *Elves' Hill*). From *Danske Theater-Costumer tegnede og udgivne af Christian Bruun,* Copenhagen 1828.

Fig. 1b. C.V. Bruun, engraving depicting the costume of Christian IV in *Elves' Hill*. From *Danske Theater-Costumer tegnede og udgivne af Christian Bruun,* Copenhagen 1828.

Tryggevælde into the realm of the Elf King, he says the famous line: "I may not be Caesar and these waves not the Rubicon, and yet I say: IACTA EST ALEA" (III.7).[45] He then crosses the bridge accompanied by singing huntsmen.

The same evening, Agnete is devastated and confesses her love for Ebbesen to her mother (III.6). This provokes Karen to make a confession too: Karen found the child she has called Agnete on Elves' Hill, shortly after the death of her own daughter by that name, and raised her as her own. The child wore a diamond ring on a necklace, which Karen believes to be the token of the Elf King, designating the child to be his future bride. Karen buried the ring on the hill. Now she is terrified to learn that Agnete has been meeting her beloved secretly on Elves' Hill, the home of her betrothed, the Elf King. She sends Agnete there to try and make peace with the Elf King. Exhausted by

---

45 "Vel er jeg ikke Cæsar, / Og disse Bølger ikke Rubicon; / Men dog jeg siger: jacta est alea!" Heiberg 1862, 467.

the confusion, Agnete falls asleep for a minute on the hill, dreaming that the Elf King and his maidens are dancing and that he approaches her with a diamond ring – the dream is played out for the audience (IV.2). Meanwhile, a local man, excited by Karen's stories and ballads, is digging for the Elf King's alleged treasure (IV.1). He happens to find the diamond ring – but when he sees Agnete, he assumes she is the elf maiden and flees in fear (IV.3). Consequently, Agnete, as she wakes up, sees the diamond ring from her dream. She does not, however, see the Elf King, but the 'real' king, Christian IV, stands before her only a moment later.

When Christian IV sees Agnete, he is convinced that he has found the alleged elf maiden (IV.5). Agnete freely admits to being human, presenting herself as Mother Karen's daughter, but from her way of speaking Christian IV senses her nobility and he furthermore recognizes the diamond ring in her hand. He knows that the young woman is in fact not Agnete but the real Elisabeth Munk! She, in turn, senses the royalty of Christian's being, leading her to acknowledge him as the true monarch, right there on the Elf King's hill. Christian invites Agnete, the real Elisabeth Munk, to accompany him to the wedding at Højstrup. There everything is chaos, but King Christian effectively untangles all confusion in the final act. Walkendorff admits that both the young Elisabeth Munk and her diamond ring went missing, as well as to bringing up his orphaned niece, who was very conveniently called Elisabeth too, in Munk's place. Christian IV's disclosure of secrets and rejection of legends and myths enable the lovers to be united in the right order. To conclude, the royal anthem is played and the characters sing – not the original lyrics but a new text composed by Heiberg.

Christian IV and Caesar

The references to Caesar and his dictum only take up three lines of text, but their occurrence immediately before the dramatic climax of the meeting between the King and Agnete, presenting both the *peripeteia* and *anagnorisis* of the play, encourages consideration of their role in the clash between Christian IV and the world of elves and legends. Vilhelm Andersen and Carls S. Petersen give an accurate and concise analysis of the function of both King Christian and Agnete in their influential history of Danish literature published 1921-1934:

> *The play follows the deepest tendency of poetic realism and Hegelian philosophy: finding the sensible in the real by letting reality step into the place of the phantom everywhere: Christian the Fourth in the place of the Elf King, Agnete in that of the elf maiden.*[46]

Before considering how Christian IV's reference to Caesar works in *Asterix*, I will briefly consider the function of the passage as reception within the play. For this I will employ

---

46 Andersen and Petersen 1924, 422: "Den poetiske Realismes og den hegelske Filosofis dybeste Tendens: at finde det fornuftige i det virkelige følger Stykket ved overalt at lade Virkeligheden træde i Drømmebilledets Sted: Christian den Fjerde i Ellekongens, Agnete i Elverpigens".

terminology developed by the "Transformationen der Antike" project, which will also be used in the following alongside Heiberg's own ideas of dramatic character types.[47]

In saying "I may not be Caesar and these waves not the Rubicon, and yet I say: *iacta est alea*" Christian IV first rejects being Caesar, that which, in a reception context, might be termed a case of *negation*:

> *A transformative process of active and explicit exclusion. The object is rejected, but it continues to remain present though the negative relationship or rather is first constructed via this relationship. As opposed to ignorance, negation entails a demonstrative repudiation.*[48]

In this particular case, the negation indeed remains present; it is barely exclaimed before the negation is moderated. This underlines the importance of the repudiatory component described in the definition above for our case: Christian IV rejects being Caesar but insists on claiming his famous dictum, thereby inviting us to continue considering his crossing of the tiny stream in the Danish landscape in light of the Roman example he evokes. It is fair to say that the well-known passage in Act III.7 is also a favourite and if the comparison seems comic, it is not surprising. Christian IV is easy to represent on stage since his appearance, especially at a mature age, was rather characteristic (Fig. 2) – to the extent that representations of him often border on caricature (Fig. 3). It is not least his appearance that makes his rejection superfluous and comic – anyone can see who this character represents. That the whole thing is played out on stage – Christian taking Caesar's words into his mouth while moving on to cross a river, thus performing the same physical action as Caesar, confirms that the rejected Roman model is indeed that – a model – which continues to function as such although it is rejected in words.

Relying on Christian IV's physical appearance for the representation of his character on stage would seem to put him in the first of the three character types defined by Heiberg in his theoretical, Hegel-inspired writings, that of the "immediate character":

> The immediate character is that which people display in all accidental aspects; it is that which one meets with 'Hello' and 'good-bye.' Here all the external idiosyncrasies make their mark, for example, outward appearance, physical defects or ridiculousness, what is characteristic in manner of dress, etc.; then the more idio-

---

47 In a forthcoming volume, I present a fuller examination of the role of classical references in *Elverhøi* and their effect on the characterization of Christian IV in the play.
48 Bergemann et al. 2019b, 21. The "Transformationen der Antike" project prefers the term 'transformation' to 'reception' because it stresses the *change* involved in the reception process. Baker, Helmrath & Kallendorf 2019a, 3.

Fig. 2.

Karel van Mander III, *Christian IV, 1638-41*, oil on canvas, National Gallery of Denmark. Karel van Mander III (ca. 1609-1670) painted several portraits of Christian IV and may even have invented the type which this painting represents,[50] and which came to dominate from the 1630s. Reaching far beyond the king's lifetime, this type shaped the Romantic representations of Christian IV, the best-known of which is probably Wilhelm Marstrand's painting (ca. 1864) of Christian IV on the ship Trefoldigheden at the battle of Kolberger Heide (1644).

syncrasies, which, however, do not disclose the true inner person but are accidents for the soul, just as those physical idiosyncrasies are accidents for the body.[49]

The comical aspect, I would say, is an effect partly of Christian IV's superfluous rejection of being Caesar and partly of the resulting comparing of the small, domestic-scale conflict unfolded in the play with the world-changing consequences of Caesar's crossing of the Rubicon. As such, the comic lies in the situations – the act of the negation and unfolding of parallel yet significantly different actions – more than the characters.[51] As the

---

49 Stewart 2007, 307, quoting Heiberg, "Tre Maaneder efter Brylluppet – Flyttedagen", *Kjøbenhavns flyvende Post* 2.44, 2 June 1828, p. 187; *Prosaiske Skrifter* 4, 145. Translation and references from Stewart.
50 Eller [no year].
51 Cf. Nagy 2008, 371, on Heiberg's view of drama, tragedy, and comedy, as well as what is comic: "Nothing is comic with respect to its material, Heiberg argued; it is only with the action that

Fig. 3.

Drawing by Valdemar Møller, originally published in the newspaper *Politiken* 13 June 1940. Image from the digital collections, The Royal Library of Denmark. Då is not the only one to have reapplied Heiberg's comparison of Christian IV and Caesar to seemingly absurd contexts, as this witty drawing featured in one of the largest Danish newspapers shows. The accompanying text says: 'A local historian in Køge has discovered that Christian IV was the first to camp in a tent at the beach of Greve.' Dialogue originally printed with drawing: 'I may not be Caesar, and may have run out of petroleum and yet I say: the dice are cast – now let's have soup.'

plot thickens, Christian IV's quality as a dramatic character expands in the culminative act IV, when he stands before Agnete, and when he solves the chaotic knot of mistaken identities in the last act. His character, in his search to discover the secrets at Stevns, displays traits rather characteristic of Heiberg's second type, the 'reflective character':

> The reflective character is a sharp and powerful tendency, which the essential in the person assumes but which, precisely because it does not reveal itself in external trivialities but works according to plan and with reflection, is more difficult to discover and presupposes a longer and deeper knowledge of the person.[52]

In Christian's immediate sensing of the secrecy in the first act, a seed is planted for the expansion of his character, which then may seem to be somewhat overshadowed by the outburst in III.7 relying on the immediate features of the king. Nonetheless Christian does gradually reveal a significant depth, embracing but reaching beyond the characteristics of Heiberg's second type of character, which may turn him into Heiberg's third type, the "true character". This encompasses the qualities of the first two:

> The true character is the unity of the immediate and the reflected character; it is the individual itself, in its reality, both in its essential main characteristic and all

---

it becomes such. In focusing on the genre he was most fond of, vaudevilles, he developed this theory further and defined tragedy as drama where character takes the precedence, comedy where situation is the dominant element, while the most developed form, the 'summit of aesthetic sophistication,' is vaudeville, in which all these factors are united".

52   Stewart 2007, 307.

the accidental secondary traits which surround and modify the main one. The former gives the character its value and meaning, while the latter give it reality and immediate life.[53]

Christian IV gains depth as a character when he confronts legends and myths on Elves' Hill and brings Agnete as well as the rest of his people in Stevns to see and understand the truth about their identities and the order of their world. In his scene with Agnete, Christian's royalty radiates from him – it is not his physical features she recognizes but his inner qualities, the core of his being, and she concludes not that he is Christian IV, but "the monarch" (IV.5), thus signalling how his being transgresses the physical nature of his representation on stage and the particular embodiment as Christian IV. He is not only a true character in a technical sense, but the sovereign by divine right.

Christian IV's negated evocation of Caesar, I would argue, prepares what we could, with Andersen and Petersen above, call his 'confrontation' with the Elf King in the scene just mentioned. While the rejection of similarity labels the conflict of the drama as small, the following conditioning of the rejection, in which Christian applies Caesar's dictum to his world, holds on to the image of Christian as Caesar, labelling his crossing of Tryggevælde Å as a campaign with which he instates himself as ruler of the realm. As said, this is a way of holding on to the comic comparison and with it the lightness of the vaudeville. However, that it coincides with Christian's growth as a dramatic character also means it prepares the message about his true majesty.

It must be fair to expect somewhat different reactions to and associations among the audience in Heiberg's day, composed of people in a country governed by absolute monarchs for 168 years, and a more recent audience whose ideal and experience is democratic rule. It is likely that the latter would dwell on the ironic contrast between Caesar's dramatic and influential crossing of the Rubicon and the small-scale situation at the stream of Tryggevælde, appreciating Christian IV as a perfect example of the self-ironic Dane who takes pride in the recognition of the smallness of their nation in comparison to others. The royalist audience, however, might have been more receptive to the unfolding depth of Christian's character and the message this can be seen to convey. In relation to this, I would understand the 'confrontation' of Christian and Caesar as marking the starting point of the development of his depth: Heiberg's Christian may relish the lightness of comedy but at the same time proposes himself as an alternative to Caesar being on an alternative yet somewhat parallel quest. Denmark is shrinking in Heiberg's time, but by rejecting Caesar, the embodiment of Rome, Heiberg's Christian scorns the vastness of empire, asserting himself against it as the embodiment of 'Danish-ness',[54] who actively wills the small and claims profundity and intimacy as

---

53 Stewart 2007, 308. Stewart renders further reflections on the nature of the relationships between the characteristics of the defined types in building successful dramatic characters; Stewart 2007, 305-310.
54 Accordingly, Wenchel states how Heiberg "gave new legitimation to the *Royal* Theatre as a *national* institution that gathered all the Danish people under the patronage of the King". Wenchel 2008,

majestic virtues, in which the Danes excel to an extent that fully compensates for their immediate smallness. Set against the backdrop of Caesar's accomplishment, Christian IV is made to insist that his securing of the wellbeing of his people in Stevns is an accomplishment equal to crossing the Rubicon and revolutionizing the Roman republic. Christian's key quality, allowing him to perform in this regard, is his special insight into the nature and wellbeing of his people. He is not an anti-Caesar, but a smaller yet perhaps more profound double. The result is a confirmation of the special bond between the monarch and his people.

Asterix and Tryggevælde Å

The plot of *Asterix and the chieftain's shield* goes as follows: Asterix and Obelix escort their chieftain to a clinic offering hydropathic treatment in the region of Auvergne – he is suffering from stomach-aches caused by overeating. Quite contrary to how the Gauls deal with Alesia, which several people loudly reject knowing anything about several times in this volume, Auvergne is associated with pride: it was in this region, at its capital Gergovia, that Caesar suffered a considerable defeat to the Gauls under the direction of Vercingetorix in 52 BCE.

Having left the chieftain to undergo treatment, Asterix and Obelix explore the region and accidentally encounter Caesar's special envoy Tullius Fanfrelus (in English Noxius Vapus, in Danish Tullius Ambasadorus). To no-one's surprise, this almost immediately escalates violently, leaving the Romans defeated with little exertion from the Gauls. The envoy, unaware of whom he has encountered, reports back to Caesar of conflict stirring among the Gauls of Gergovia. In answer to this and in order to suppress any nascent rebellion, Caesar decides to have what he terms a Gaulish-style triumph there, at the place of symbolic importance for the Gaulish resistance. Caesar declares that he wants to be carried by Gaulish subjects on the shield of none other than the Gaulish hero and national symbol, Vercingetorix, which was surrendered to him after his victory at Alesia. It is when Caesar conceives this plan that he makes the reference to *Elverhøi* in the Danish version.

The rest of the story is a race between the Roman envoy and Asterix and Obelix to find the shield, which is not stored, it turns out, among Caesar's other spoils. After various frustrated attempts to track it down, it finally turns out that the shield has been in Gaulish possession all along: it is the very one on which Vitalstatistix (in French Abraracourix, in Danish Majestix) is usually carried. Vitalstatistix is recognized by a local Gaul when he comes to meet Asterix and Obelix, having completed his hydropathic treatment. The therapy seems to have left him a mere shadow of himself, but while hardly recognizable to Asterix and Obelix (or the reader), the local Gaul finds the chieftain to be the spitting image of the young man to whom he gave the shield many years ago.

It almost comes to a massive, violent clash between armed Roman forces lead by Noxius Vapus and a large number of Gergovians gathered by Asterix, but the Romans

---

398, original emphases.

are stopped by a mysterious stranger, who, when he lowers the hood hiding his face, turns out to be none other than Julius Caesar himself. Before the eyes of Caesar and his troops, Vitalstatistix is carried forward on the shield of Vercingetorix by Obelix and cheered on by Asterix, in a second, fictional humiliation of Caesar at Gergovia.[55] The Gauls return home, and while they visit several inns on their way back, so that Vitalstatistix recovers his usual, round figure on the way, the story ends as it always does, with a banquet.

Closing in on the particular use of *Elverhøi*, the passage of importance to the present discussion is when Caesar makes his plan to humiliate the Gauls at Gergovia. Here, I first provide the French original and the English translation, which follows the French text quite closely, then the Danish translation, accompanied by my attempt at a literal translation of the Danish into English.

French:
– C: Je vais leur montrer, à ces gaulois! Veni, vidi, vici, et eux, ils rigolent! Je vais leur montrer qui est le maitre.
– C: Je vais faire une démonstration éclatante! Un triomphe à Gergovie, haut lieu de l'orgueil gaulois!… Un triomphe à la gauloise!
– À la Gauloise?
– C: Les arvernes devront m'acclamer pendant que je défilerai devant eux, debout sur un bouclier! sur le bouclier de leur chef!… sur le bouclier de VERCINGÉ-TORIX
– Ab imo pectore bravo, ô César!

English (Bell & Hockridge, 1968):
– C: I'll show those wretched Gauls! Veni, vidi, vici and all they do is laugh, I'll show them who's boss!
– C: I shall give them a dazzling demonstration of my power! I'll have a triumph at Gergovia itself, the place that is the pride of all Gaul. A genuine Gaulish triumph!
– Genuine Gaulish triumph?
– C: Yes! I shall make the Arvernians applaud me as I am carried past them on a shield, their own chieftain's shield! The shield of VERCINGETORIX!
– Bravo, Caesar, ab imo pectore!

Danish:
– C: Jeg skal vise det latterligt lille folkefærd, hvem der er herre i landet! Jeg må sige noget historisk!
– C: Vel er jeg ikke galler, og vel er dette aldeles ikke Tryggevælde å, men dog siger jeg: Her er ikke noget at rafle om.

---

55   It has been suggested that Asterix has taken Vercingetorix' place as national hero. See Amalgor 2015a fn. 8 for further references, as well as Teitler 2002 and Amalgor 2015b, 120 on historical parallels of carrying leaders on shields.

Fig. 4. René Goscinny & Albert Uderzo 1972, *Asterix: Romernes skræk*, translated by Per Då, København: Gutenberghus-forlaget, p. 18.

– T: Det var en tolver, Cæsar!
– C: De overgivne gallere skal bære mig på selve Vercingetorix' skjold og hylde mig som ene rette herre! Cæsars sejr skal være hævet over enhver mistanke! Dixi!
– T: Det er alle tiders citat!

The Danish in English translation:
– C: I'll show that ridiculous, little tribe who's the ruler of this country! I must say something historical!
– C: I may not be a Gaul, and this is absolutely not the stream Tryggevælde, and yet I say: no dice![56]
– That's a 12, Caesar![57]
– C: The vanquished Gauls will carry me on the shield of Vercingetorix himself and celebrate me as the only rightful master! Caesar's victory will rise above any doubt! Dixi!

It is obvious that Då's Danish translation is remarkably free, compared to the English. Caesar's famous quotation *veni, vidi, vici*, which he uses to justify his rage at the lack of Gaulish recognition of his military sovereignty in Uderzo and Goscinny's text, is not rendered in the Danish, although the expression is as much a commonplace in Danish as it is in English and French. Instead, we find a pun on the equally famous *alea iacta est*, the first part of which draws on the aforementioned famous Caesarean phrase from *Elverhøj*: "I may not be Caesar, and these waves not the Rubicon, and yet I say: *iacta est alea*!"

---

56   The pun on *jacta est alea* is better in Danish: *rafle* means throwing dice and the expression *ikke noget at rafle om* means there will be no discussion of the given matter.
57   12 is the maximum points betting on (some of) the football pools.

Per Då's translation strategy and his Caesar from a reception perspective

The Danish translator Per Då (1921-2011) displays an inclusive view of Caesar, allowing the character to encompass reimaginations of himself as they have unfolded in the centuries, even millennia, after his death. This means abolishing the academic, historicist approach that locates the truth that must guide the explorer, in the historical figure and his era. Caesar's absurd, meta-awareness of his own historicity is a trait found in the French source texts of the series, though not in the passage we are studying where Då has decided to stress it. It underlines the conflict between the fictional representation and the historical figure, but Caesar must encompass both for the absurdity of the impossible representation to stand out and have a comic effect.

With Lotman, who has examined reader positions included by Susan Bassnett in her reflections on literary translation, we may say that Då's position as a reader and subsequently translator of Uderzo and Goscinny's text is one "[w]here the reader discovers elements not basic to the genesis of the text and uses the text for his own purpose".[58] Då may, as initially indicated, have identified certain similarities between the plots of *Le bouclier Arverne* and *Elverhøi*, although they are somewhat generic: both are stories about objects and people lost and found – Elisabeth Munk with her diamond ring and the chieftain and his shield – and both result in the confrontation and rejection of acclaimed, false leaders by true and rightful ones – Christian IV for the Elf King and Vitalstatistix for Caesar. Furthermore – and this is, admittedly, speculative – it might just be that Christian IV's characteristic appearance was felt to provide a further parallel. Considering the half-long hair, the very long queue, the moustache, and 'van Gogh' beard that are characteristic of the king as portrayed both in his own time (figs. 2 and 5) and later (figs. 3 and 6), his style rather resembles that of the Gaulish than Roman visual ideals, even in the case of Dieussart's portrait (Fig. 5) in which Christian is wearing a laurel wreath and Roman dress. These visual similarities may just be a welcome coincidence; the reference to *Elverhøi* does not at all depend on it, but if considered, they add the idea that the Danish 'Caesar' Christian IV is closer to the chieftain of that small village we all know and love than to an emperor of Rome, which would fit the Danish national narrative.

Per Då has not written about his translations or translation strategy, and to my knowledge there are no previous academic studies of them. As to statements about his thoughts on translation, we can rely only on interviews he has given to various Danish media. In these, it seems Då's tone is always slightly tongue in cheek. He characterizes his translation strategy as follows in an interview from 2006:

'My translations are extremely independent. Furthermore, I have often, in my capacity of editor, been at the other end of the table, saying to many a translator: "look at the image, that is what it is all about. You are writing comics, not novels!",' this he

---

58 Bassnett 2013, 89-90. Lotman's work came out in Russian in 1970 and in Italian in 1972, see Lotman 1972.

Fig. 5.

François Dieussart, bronze bust of King Christian IV as Roman emperor, modelled 1643. The Royal Danish Collection, Rosenborg. Dieussart's representation, modelled in 1643 when the king was 66 years old, illustrates how the Roman emperors were models of leadership even in regions beyond the limits of their empire. Like van Mander III's portrait, this representation is Christian IV as he himself wished to be represented.

underlines – and it has always been a hobby horse of Per Då's that Asterix should speak Danish in the Danish editions.
[…]
'How much of a difference is there between your version and the original?'
'There is an enormous difference, they are so different that I would not dream of revealing it to Uderzo, should I ever meet him again,' says Per Då.[59]

Då gives the impression that he started working on Asterix by accident. The task had originally been given to someone else, but Då was asked to take over, allegedly while

---

59 "'Mine oversættelser er overordentlig selvstændige. Desuden har jeg, som redaktør, ofte siddet på den anden side af skrivebordet, og derfra har jeg sagt til mange oversættere: "Se på billedet, det er det, som det kommer an på. Det er tegneserier og ikke romaner, I skal lave!"' understreger han, og det har hele tiden været en kæphest for Per Då, at Asterix i den danske udgave skal tale dansk … Hvor stor forskel er der på din udgave og original-udgaven? 'Enorm, så meget, at jeg aldrig vil drømme om at afsløre det for Uderzo (Asterix's tegner), hvis jeg skulle træffe ham igen,' siger Per Då". Christiansen 2006.

60 Thorvaldsen's Museum has a plaster version of the statue dating to 1840 (IN A152), after which the bronze cast was made. https://www.thorvaldsensmuseum.dk/en/collections/work/A152, last accessed 7 February 2022.

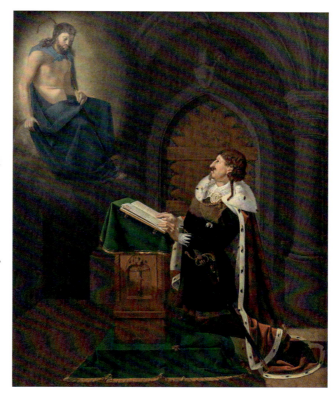

Fig. 6.

Ditlev Blunck, *Christian IV's Vision at Rothenburg Castle,* 1823, oil on canvas, National Gallery of Denmark. Christian IV supposedly had a vision of the suffering Christ in 1625 upon his entry into the Thirty Years War against the Catholic league, causing financial ruin and loss of Danish territory. Blunck's depiction, while resembling Mander's type especially in its rendering of the characteristic facial features, beard, and hair, deviates in showing perhaps a younger and surely slimmer version of Christian IV. Thorvaldsen's bronze statue in Christian IV's chapel in Roskilde Cathedral is quite similar (1845).[60] Despite the difference in his general figure, his identity is clear.

the carrier was waiting in the office to take the manuscript to the printer. He corrected, among other matters, the name of the bard, finding that the original attempt at a calque, 'Forsikringetorix' (equivalent to 'Insurance-torix') for 'Abraracourix', did not work. Gjørup, who renders this in another interview piece, uses the names of the Gauls as an example of Då's selectiveness and linguistic sensitivity. Some names Då transferred more or less directly from the French: 'Asterix' and 'Obelix', of course, but also 'Godemine' for 'Bonemine'. Others he borrowed from the German translations, such as 'Majestix' for the chieftain and 'Miraculix' for the druid. Yet others Då invented himself, such as 'Trubadurix' for the bard and 'Hørmetix' for the fishmonger (*at hørme* means 'to stink').[61] At a certain point, the licensors installed a control function; a person who "knew Danish – to some extent – and reported back to Goscinny" was charged with checking Då's translations against the French original.[62] Då proudly states that Goscinny only twice during Då's work on 24 volumes questioned translations of particular phrases and in both cases accepted Då's suggestions once they had been explained to him. It is, on the other hand, also clear from the interviews that Då had

61   Gjørup 2000/2011.
62   Gjørup 2000/2011.

regular discussions with the person checking his translations, just as Då makes it quite clear that he found this person's sense of the Danish language to be gravely lacking and their interventions unconstructive.[63]

Seen within a translations study framework, the Danish editions of *Asterix* could be described as focusing on what Nida terms "dynamic equivalence" – aiming for equivalent effect – rather than "formal equivalence", in that they remain loyal to the plot and tone of the source text while focusing less on precise rendering of its linguistic meanings.[64] Då's intention, expressed in the first of the two quotations above, to make the characters of the comics speak Danish in the Danish editions similarly clearly indicates that he is set on a translation strategy of "domestication". This concept was defined as follows by Schleiermacher in his dissertation "Über die verschiedenen Methoden des Übersetzens" (1813), against its opposition, "foreignization": "Either the translator leaves the author in peace, as much as possible, and moves the reader towards him; or he leaves the reader in peace, as much as possible, and moves the author towards him".[65] Då leaves his readers in peace, bringing the text closer to their social reality, which implies removing it from the social reality of the source text – translating is a game of loss and gain.[66]

Då's choice to integrate Danish national literature into his portrayal of Julius Caesar adds to the domestication of *Asterix* by making the world of the cartoon Gauls relatable and recognizable to a Danish audience. The reference to *Elverhøi* might be understood as compensating for instances of "cultural untranslatability",[67] references to French culture and society that would not resonate with a Danish audience. If that is the case, these must, however, be references located elsewhere in the volume or series, given that our passage is quite straightforward. In any case, it is clear that Då's translations are free, rather than literal, to quite a large extent.[68] There are minor instances in which I find it difficult to see why he felt a need to deviate from literal translation – for instance Då's tendency to let Caesar finish his remarks off with a *dixi*, as in the passage quoted above, instead of the repeated swearing by various classical gods employed by the Romans in the source text and rendered in the English translation. Moreover, the Danish translation goes further than the original in the passage in question when it comes to Caesar's awareness of his own status as a historical figure. It adds to the comedy but may raise the question of whether this is– more than a free, sense-for-sense approach to translation – a case reminiscent of what Dryden termed an "imitation", "where the translator can abandon the text of the original as he sees fit".[69]

In terms of reception, our *Asterix* panel may be understood as a case of "disjunction":

---

63 Gjørup 2000/2011.
64 Nida 1964; Bassnett 2013, 36.
65 Venuti's translation quoted from Venuti 2018, 84.
66 See e.g. Bassnett 2013, 39-40.
67 Catford 1965; Bassnett 2013, 40-43.
68 Catford 1965; Bassnett 2013, 35.
69 Dryden, in his preface to the translation of Ovid's epistles (1680); quotation from Bassnett 2013, 69.

> A transformation in which something from the reference culture is dressed in a form belonging to the reception culture, or in which something from the reception culture is endowed with a form belonging to the reference culture. Proceeding from inclusive or from exclusive selection processes, disjunction can serve to legitimize a given art form by filling it with sanctioned content (such as inscribing Christian content in pagan poetic forms) or to adapt pagan or otherwise questionable content by means of a formal approximation (usually accompanying acts of revaluation) to the reception culture.[70]

Caesar is, if not quite dressed in Christian IV's robes, then at least paraphrasing his words, and while the aim here is not to justify an art form, letting Caesar make references to *Elverhøi* effectively connects him to a Danish cultural sphere. The aim is for the Danes to recognize their own narratives and cultural conflicts in the story of the album, as well as in the general narrative of the *Asterix* series, to an extent that makes the comedy work. This use of disjunction effectively confirms that the version of Caesar presented in the Danish text becomes a kind of "hybridization", "[a] transformation in which novel cultural configurations are formed from elements of the reference and reception cultures, including intersections, distinctive syncretisms, and fusions, even of contrary and contradictory elements".[71] The absurdity of the anachronism of this hybridization furthermore, as mentioned, has a comic effect.

It is my conviction that many Danes would recognize the reference to *Elverhøi* immediately, not least when the volume came out in 1972, and that in its new context, the passage is stripped of the source's awe of royal majesty. The rejection pronounced by Då's Caesar in jesting imitation of Christian's in *Elverhøi* is stating the obvious just as much as the phrase does in *Elverhøi*. We know very well that Caesar is not one of the Gauls – that is the whole point – and we know the characteristic look of both the Gauls and Caesar well enough to see it. However, by letting Caesar negate exactly this, Då highlights how in the context of the *Asterix* volume Caesar is dealing with ordinary people rather than the great matters of state we usually associate with his person, and rather than raising these ordinary people to his majestic level, looking them in the eye and acknowledging his responsibility for their wellbeing (as the king does in *Elverhøi*), he is brought down to theirs. In the context of the comics and in the social realities of which they are a product, leaders can be scrutinized and subjected to the rules of comedy.

(Re-)assessing conquerors and rulers

In *Elverhøi*, the point of negating Christian IV's similarity to Caesar is not to degrade him by highlighting his littleness in comparison to the great Roman imperator, nor to question his power or authority. Rather, the rejection is an assertion of his and Caesar's parity, despite their immediate differences. The comparison marks first Christian IV's

---

70   Bergemann et al. 2019, 18.
71   Bergemann et al. 2019, 20.

apparent quality as a character of Heiberg's first type, underlining his obvious, recognizable distinctness and familiarity. Next, it marks the beginning of his growth and development, culminating in the emergence of him as the most complex and finest of Heiberg's three types. Christian IV thus steps forward as the prime example of the truly good ruler, transgressing his own typicality in portraying the Danish king, not a Roman emperor or imperator. His excellence relies on his depth and sense of responsibility towards his subjects rather than the size of his realm – this, I would claim, is the assertion of national identity and worthiness, which lies in Christian's confrontation with Caesar just as much as with the mythical Elf King.

When Caesar in *Asterix* not only utters historical Latin quotations but also improvises over the famous Danish reception of *Elverhøi*, Då expands the function of the Latin phrases, as defined by Anne Blair. She has suggested that while the *Asterix* volumes were originally sourcing Latin expressions that had found their way into the French language as common expressions, they gradually also came to play a role in securing the continued circulation of these phrases.[72] When Då has his version of Uderzo's and Goscinny's Caesar quote a Danish reception of *alea jacta est*, he similarly re-actualizes the Latin phrase while reminding the reader that this phrase has a particular Danish reception equally worth commemorating. In this manner Då lives up to his own ambition of letting the characters speak Danish in more than a literal sense: Då's version of Caesar confirms that we, the Danes, have a direct relationship with Caesar and the Roman culture he represents. We know Caesar, but he also knows us, our country, and our culture – even well enough to reference it. In that sense, Caesar confirms that Denmark is part of the cultural empire of Rome, while the territory was never invaded.

Caesar is an effective symbol; he evokes all the common notions of Rome – great military force, intellectualism, and worthiness. The *Asterix* volume and *Elverhøi* are, however, products of very different realities, and their attitude towards Caesar reflects this. While Caesar is an unexpected presence in the latter and not in the former, he serves in both to facilitate assessments of leadership and the relationship between leaders and their people, functioning as a standard against which ideas and ideals of leadership can be measured and discussed in both narratives. *Elverhøi* welcomes the worthiness he embodies and his authority; Christian IV insists on his majesty and confronts the legends bravely following his evocation of Caesar. But the King adds to this a closeness to his people, a mildness and attentiveness towards his subjects. In *Asterix*, Caesar stubbornly insists on evoking his authority and worthiness, but he is portrayed as a false leader there, not unlike the Elf King was in *Elverhøi*. His austerity and authority are punctured by the unimpressed Gauls, and in the particular context we have studied, the jovial local chieftain enjoys a rare moment of glory when carried on Vercingetorix' shield before the Roman imposter. When Då's version of Caesar actively rejects being Christian IV, besides being an absurd anachronism, he is openly acknowledging that he is not the kind of hands-on leader we meet in *Elverhøi*'s Christian IV or, for that matter, in *Asterix*' Vitalstatistix. In the situation we have studied, his historical status comes

---

72 Blair 2019.

out as boasting self-awareness. The repeated comic deflation of Caesar's self-acclaimed position shows the great man of the tradition to be humane and flared, encouraging the readers to question his entitlement and providing alternative ideals of leadership.

Acknowledgements

This essay was researched and written partly during my employment at Centre for Urban Network Evolutions, Grant DNRF119, partly during my time as Carlsberg Foundation Junior Research Fellow at Linacre College, University of Oxford, during which my research was supported by the Carlsberg Foundation (CF20-0380). I am grateful to the audience of the conference preceding this volume for engaging in fruitful discussion of my presentation and to Marianne Pade for her constructive reading of my text. The parts about Heiberg's *Elverhøi* form part of a larger study of reception of Roman culture in Danish literature of the nineteenth century, the main publication of which will appear in Danish.

Bibliography

Andersen, V. & Petersen, C.S. 1924. *Illustreret dansk Litteraturhistorie* 3. Copenhagen: Gyldendal.

Amalgor, E. 2015a. "Bridging the Gap between Generations. *Astérix* between Child and Adult, Classical and Modern", in: Maurice, L. 2015. *The Reception of Ancient Greece and Rome in Children's Literature Heroes and Eagles*. Leiden: Brill, 291-307.

Amalgor, E. 2015b. "Reinventing the Barbarian", in: Kovacs, G. & Marshall, C.W. 2015. *Son of Classics and Comics*. Oxford: Oxford University Press, 113-129.

Auken, S. et al. 2008. *Dansk Litteraturs Historie 2: 1800-1870*. Gyldendal: Copenhagen.

Auken, S. 2008a. "Elverhøi og Heibergskolen", in: Auken, S. et al. 2008, 280-282.

Auken, S. 2008b. "Vaudevillerne", in: Auken, S. et al. 2008, 269-274.

Baker, P., Helmrath, J. & Kallendorf, C. (eds) 2019b. *Beyond Reception. Renaissance Humanism and the Transformation of Classical Antiquity*. Berlin & Boston: De Gruyter.

Baker, P., Helmrath, J. & Kallendorf, C. 2019a. "Introduction", in: Baker, Helmrath & Kallendorf 2019b, 1-8.

Bassnett, S. 2013. *Translation*. London: Routledge.

Bergemann, L. et al. 2019. "Transformation. A Concept for the Study of Cultural Change", in: Baker, Helmrath & Kallendorf 2019b, 9-26.

Blair, A. 2019. "Les locutions latines dans *Astérix*", in: Ferrer, V., Millet, O. & Tarrête, A. 2019. *La renaissance au grand large. Mélanges en l'honneur de Frank Lestringant*. Geneva: Librairie Droz, 817-827.

Catford, J.C. 1965. *A Linguistic Theory of Translation: An Essay in Applied Linguistics*. London: Oxford University Press.

Eller, P. [no year]. "Karel van Mander 3", in: *Dansk Biografisk Leksikon på lex.dk*. https://biografiskleksikon.lex.dk/Karel_van_Mander_3, last accessed 7 February 2022.

Gamrath, H. 1991. "Litteratur om Christian IV i jubelåret 1988". *Historisk Tidsskrift* 15.6, 134-154.

Heiberg, J.L. 1826. *Om Vaudevillen som dramatisk Digtart og om dens Betydning paa den danske Skueplads. En dramaturgisk Undersøgelse*. Copenhagen: J.H. Schulz.

Heiberg, J.L. 1861. *Prosaiske Skrifter* 4. Copenhagen: C.A. Reitzels Forlag.

Heiberg, J.L. 1862. *Poetiske Skrifter* 3. Copenhagen: C.A. Reitzels Forlag.

Hertel, H. 2011. "Besættelsens kulturliv: Beskyttelsesrum, væksthus, modstandslomme og askebægerindustri". *Passage* 65, 7-23.

Lockhart, P.D. 1992. "Denmark and the Empire: A Reassessment of Danish Foreign Policy under King Christian IV". *Scandinavian Studies* 64.3, 390-416.

Lotman, J. 1972. *La struttura del testo poetico*. Milan: Musia.

Lyding, H. & B. Holm [no year]. "Elverhøi", in: *Den Store Danske på lex.dk*. https://denstoredanske.lex.dk/Elverh%C3%B8i, last accessed 24 August 2021.

Nagy, A. 2008. "Either Hegel or Dialectics: Johan Ludvig Heiberg, 'Homme de théâtre'", in: Stewart 2008, 357-394.

Nida, E. 1964. *Towards a Science of Translating. With Special Reference to Principles and Procedures Involved in Bible Translating*. Leiden: Brill.

Nielsen, N.K. 2019. "MYTE: Sagde Dalgas 'Hvad udad tabes, skal indad vindes'?", in: *Danmarkshistorien.dk*. https://danmarkshistorien.dk/leksikon-og-kilder/vis/materiale/myte-sagde-dalgas-hvad-udad-tabes-skal-indad-vindes/, last accessed 13 January 2022.

Stewart, J. 2007. *A History of Hegelianism in Golden Age Denmark* 1: *The Heiberg Period. 1824-1836*. Copenhagen: C.A. Reitzel's Publishers.

Stewart, J. (ed.) 2008. *Johan Ludvig Heiberg. Philosopher, Litterateur, Dramaturge, and Political Thinker*. Copenhagen: Museum Tusculanum Press.

Teitler, H. 2002. "Raising on a Shield. Origin and Afterlife of a Coronation Ceremony". *International Journal of the Classical Tradition* 8, 501-521.

Venuti, L. 2018. *The Translator's Invisibility. A History of Translation*, 3rd edition. Milton: Routledge.

Wenchel, K. 2008. "Lack of Money and Good Taste: Questions of Value in Heiberg's Vaudevilles", in: Stewart 2008, 395-417.

Material in other media:

Elverhøj, directed by Piv Bernth and Birgitte Price, produced for TV by Marianne Albrecthslund. Aired 22 December 1996. https://www.dr.dk/bonanza/serie/492/tv-t---90erne/39476/elverhoej-, last accessed 14 January 2022.

Christiansen, A. 2006. "Gævlingen: manden der fik Asterix til at tale dansk", Interview with Per Då, *Urban*, 2 June 2006, section 1, p. 25.

Gjørup, I. 2000. "Per Då. En mesterlig oversætter", Interview with Per Då originally published in *Strip* 12, reissued by Steffen Rayburn-Maarup 13 May 2011. https://nummer9.dk/artikler/per-da-en-mesterlig-oversaetter, last accessed 18 January 2022.

8

WRONGED IMPERIALISTS, PRIMITIVE ROMANS, AND ADVANCED BARBARIANS (AND VICE VERSA)

THE ROMANS AND THE ROMAN EMPIRE IN CLAUS DELEURAN'S *THE ILLUSTRATED HISTORY OF DENMARK – A PEOPLE'S HISTORY*

JAKOB ENGBERG

Introduction

In 1987, the cartoonist Claus Deleuran (1946-1996) began his *The Illustrated History of Denmark – a People's History*. He planned a cartoon that covered the history of Denmark from the World's creation in the middle of Ginungagap until the present day in seven volumes, a plan he still maintained in 1990.[1] By Deleuran's death in 1996, he had managed almost nine volumes, reaching 1074 AD and the death of King Svend Estridsen.

In each of volumes three to five, there are several pages devoted to the Roman Empire. This article will:

- Introduce Deleuran's work, its scope, and his style
- Analyze some examples of how Deleuran presented the Romans, the Roman Empire, and the interaction of Rome and its northern Celtic and Germanic neighbours
- Discuss Deleuran's approach, the sources and the scholarship he used, and how his text and illustrations satirized both his sources and (some of the more far-fetched) scholarly theories and stereotypical popular perceptions of Rome, the Romans, and northern 'barbarians'

---

[1] Interview from 1990, Holst 1990, 26.

Deleuran's work

Deleuran's cartoon was first published in a brand-new weekly magazine, *Kilroy*, attached to the Saturday edition of the tabloid paper *Ekstrabladet*. The first plate was printed on 10 January 1987. Peder 'Pedro' Christoffersen (1942-2020), who helped foster the magazine, had promised *Ekstrabladet*'s chief editor, Sven Ove Gade (chief editor 1976-2000), that his sales would soar since cartoons were so popular in Denmark.[2] That was not to be. Nevertheless, readers responded well and reviews were enthusiastic; this prompted a decision to gather and publish Deleuran's plates in hardcover volumes.[3]

The published volumes were ordered as follows:

1. *De ældste tider*, (The Oldest Times; to the early stone age, approximately 4200 BC)
2. *De næstældste tider* (The Second Oldest Times; the later stone age and bronze age, 4200-500 BC)
3. *Den ældre Jernalder* (The Older Iron Age; in Danish historiography this period is labelled the pre-Roman Iron Age, 500 BC to 1 AD)
4. *Den yngre Jernalder* (The Younger Iron Age; in Danish historiography this period is labelled the Roman Iron Age, 1-400 AD)
5. *Den yngste Jernalder* (The Youngest Iron Age; in Danish historiography this period is labelled the Germanic Iron Age, 400-800 AD)
6. *Vikingetiden 1* (The Age of the Vikings 1; 793-854)
7. *Vikingetiden 2* (The Age of the Vikings 2; 854-934)
8. *Vikingetiden 3* (The Age of the Vikings 3; 934-1016)
9. *Vikingetidens afslutning* (The End of the Age of the Vikings; 1016-1074)

Each of the nine volumes ends with a very unsystematic, non-exhaustive bibliography listing a small selection of both sources and scholarly literature used by Deleuran. The nine volumes were subsequently gathered into three volumes with some added appendices and an index, but otherwise unaltered. The index, containing almost 5,000 entries, was made by librarian Axel Andersen.

In volume two, Deleuran covered 3,700 years of pre-history; in each of the volumes three to five he covered 400-450 years; and in each of the volumes six to nine he managed less than 75 years, with roughly one volume published each year. Assuming, very optimistically, that he could maintain the pace of these last volumes when covering the high and late Middle Ages and subsequently modernity, it would have taken him 13 more volumes to complete the work, in around 2010. More likely, the more plentiful sources of the late Middle Ages and modernity would, coupled with his habit of making wild digressions, have resulted in further delays. An estimation of something like 50 volumes in total seems realistic, with Deleuran completing the final volume in about 2037, enabling him to retire at the age of 91. This was sadly not to be, so let us return from the world of wild projections to the world of recent Danish cartoon history.

---

2   Christoffersen 2009 and Monggaard 2023, 242.
3   Monggaard 2023, 267-271.

Plate 149: Deleuran as schoolmaster. "What I have laboured to do here, is to see through the fog of modern myths [scholarly misconceptions] and historical narratives [classical sources] and interpret the Cimbrian migration and route as a deliberate campaign initiated by conscientious though ambitious people, a campaign of conquest which failed in contrast to the campaigns of Alexander the Great."

Fig. 1.

Style

Deleuran's narrative style was very peculiar – idiosyncratic, even bordering on unique compared to other historiographic cartoonists.[4] Here follow five examples.

First, there are no main characters in his cartoon, except that Deleuran intermittently draws a caricature of himself dressed as a nineteenth-century schoolmaster who intrudes in the narrative, offering explanations, critiques of earlier scholarly theories with particular agendas in the available sources, or introductions to his own theories.[5] In Figure 1 we see him presenting his own theory regarding the Cimbri. In his interpretation, the Cimbri were a largely Germanic people from Jutland with a Celtic nobility, who deliberately sought to unite all the Celts in a single realm. According to Deleuran, this would account for their route, which has been described by scholars as erratic or hesitant, reflecting a fear of the Romans. As we shall see below, this theory contributes to Deleuran's overall agenda of presenting Celtic and Germanic societies and peoples with a higher level of sophistication than is often attributed to them in popular perceptions.

Second, his narrative is sometimes interrupted by meta-reflections on epistemology and methodology.[6]

---

4 More famous and traditional examples on ancient Rome include *Asterix*, *Alix* (late republic), and *Prince Valiant* (fifth century), and on ancient Egypt, *Nofret*.
5 E.g. plates 163-165, 168, and 198.
6 E.g. plates 3-4.

Fig. 2.

Attention to detail, Sulla on plate 147 and 149, a well-equipped Roman soldier in a red tunic, a poorer roman soldier in beige.

Third, there are frequent references – sometimes in-text citations, sometimes footnotes – to sources, scholarly theories, visual inspiration, and so on.[7] On occasion, Deleuran will even let his reader know that he looked in vain for a particular tradition that he remembered in one source before finding it in another. Exact, full or abbreviated references are mixed with casual and incomplete references, sometimes just to memory or to information provided to him by readers.[8] In an illustrative example of the latter, Deleuran links ancient Celtic and Germanic rules for inheritance, as described by Caesar and Tacitus, with how younger sons are depicted in fairytales and with early modern rules for inheritance on the island of Bornholm.[9]

---

7   E.g. plates 21, 78, 82, 122, 152, and 155-156.
8   E.g. the two adjacent plates 163-164 where we find all of this; also 122 and 168.
9   Plate 164.

126   Jakob Engberg

Plate 169: Deleuran as schoolmaster. "I retell some folklore and other kinds of traditions because I believe that traditions are as real as anything else in the World."

Fig. 3.

Fourth, there is astounding attention to visual details.[10] In the first part of Figure 2 (taken from plate 147) depicting Marius' African triumph, there is a peculiar-looking person in the background. The person is not introduced, but two plates and thus two weeks later, the observant reader is introduced to the same character now gossiping in the foreground of Marius' Cimbrian triumph. The reader is now told that Marius' officer and later enemy, Sulla, attempted to take the credit for Marius' victories. We may further notice that Sulla's skin is pale and dotted with red blemishes. This is never commented upon, but the tradition about Sulla's skin condition goes back to Plutarch, *Sulla* 2. Deleuran's depiction matches Plutarch's description. There are many possible indirect ways in which Deleuran could have picked up this detail, but a direct reading of Plutarch in translation is not unlikely. Plutarch's parallel lives were translated into Bokmål/Danish in 1876-1890 and published as some of the first volumes in a then-new and soon-to-be prolific series by the scholarly society *Selskabet til Historiske Kildeskrifters Oversættelse* (the Society for the Translation of Historical Sources, founded 1875). This translation would have been available in public libraries. That Deleuran was inspired by a direct reading is on the one hand supported by the fact that the two elements he combines – Sulla's skin and contemporary attempts to detract credit from Marius and ascribe it to Sulla – are found in close proximity in Plutarch, *Sulla* 2-3. On the other hand, there is some tension, since Plutarch traces the origin of this tradition to Marius' enemies and the Numidian king Bocchus, and only indirectly to Sulla (*Marius* 10 and *Sulla* 3 and 6), whereas Deleuran depicts Sulla as more directly active in it.

---

10   See also Stegelmann 2009.

Fifth, there is only a very rough chronological progression in Deleuran's work, which is interrupted on almost every other plate with wild, deliberate digressions describing customs, clothing, tools and implements, architectural features, related myths, folklore, and so on.[11]

In some of the methodological digressions, Deleuran stressed that this was very deliberate, since he enjoyed the digressions himself, since they provided links between distant, not-so-distant, and almost-present times and across cultures, since they reflected that the world, time, and history are not (and are not experienced as) contained in a neatly constructed historically or chronologically progressing narrative, and since – in Deleuran's words – "TRADITIONS are as REAL as anything else in the world".[12]

The Roman Empire

The Romans and the Roman Empire figure largely in volumes three to five of Deleuran's work; we have already seen some examples of this. Given Deleuran's love for digressions, there are even some references to the Romans in other volumes.[13] In the following, I will analyze some examples of how Deleuran presents the Romans and their engagement with especially its northern neighbours, as well as examining examples of the sources and scholarly works that influenced his depiction. I will focus on examples from the cartoons that cover the period from roughly 200 BC to 200 AD.

Clothing

We saw above that Deleuran works with amazing attention to detail. This is also evident in his depictions of the clothing of the Romans and their neighbours. Clothing, as we shall see also in the next section, is one of his favourite subjects; there are many books (in Danish, English, German, and Italian) on clothing found on his bibliographies (cf. the bibliographies of volumes two to six).[14] I will present just one example here. Throughout Deleuran's work, wealthy Roman soldiers are drawn in the (for popular culture) customary red tunics and capes; by contrast, less well-equipped Roman soldiers are (realistically) depicted in less expensive colours like grey, green, or beige (e.g. plate 152). This goes so much against the stereotypical image that it cannot be a coincidence. One likely inspiration could have been Peter Connolly's *Den romerske hær* (1976) – but although the illustrations here follow this pattern, they are less consistent than in Deleuran, the colour of legionaries' tunics are never discussed in the text, and the book is not in any of the bibliographies. Deleuran's inspiration could also have been one of the many books on clothing that he lists in his bibliographies. Through libraries, and

---

11 E.g. plates 103-104 on pillars.
12 "TRADITIONER er lige så VIRKELIGE som alt andet i verden", quotation from plate 169; see also plates 45, 175-176, 178, 198, 236, and 247, as well as the preface to volume five.
13 E.g. plate 8 in volume one and plates 58 and 106 in volume two.
14 Cf. the bibliographies of volumes two to six. Here we find, for example, Tilke 1955, Munksgaard 1974, Hansen 1976, and Johansen 1967.

finally with the help of Deleuran's widow, Lone Deleuran, I was able to go through all these books without finding descriptions matching this pattern. In his book-collection Lone Deleuran and I found however a book not found in his bibliography, Saxtorph 1971, which describes this pattern and is thus likely the source.

Advanced barbarians and primitive Romans, but again reversed
Deleuran is vehemently opposed to those who easily dismiss some people, cultures, and times as primitive and describe others as advanced. This is directly reflected in his depiction of the Romans and the Roman Empire in relation to its northern Celtic and Germanic neighbours.

In one example of this, Deleuran directly confronts the prejudices of the Enlightenment historian Edward Gibbon in his *Decline and Fall of the Roman Empire*. In the opening of a section in Chapter 37 on the "Conversion of the Barbarians", Gibbon contrasted how Christianity had progressed and succeeded among the *enlightened* Romans on the one hand, and among the savage and warlike barbarians from Scythia and Germania on the other. Gibbon's stereotypical depictions of Romans as advanced and enlightened and Germans as savage and primitive here comes under Deleuran's censorship. In plate 182 Deleuran depicts himself as a schoolmaster censuring Gibbon's own judgments of the conversions of barbaric chieftains and kings being based on a whim, a coincidence, a dream, an omen, the rumour of a miracle, the example of a priest, or the enchantment of a Christian wife. From the text, it is clear that Deleuran is using the Danish translation of Gibbon's work.[15] Deleuran goes on to show that the conversion of the Romans to Christianity was based on similar phenomena by relating the story of the conversion of Constantine.

In his confrontation with Gibbon's prejudice, Deleuran seemed somewhat offended. More often, as a cartoonist and author he seems to enjoy and amuse himself while playing around with traditional stereotypical perceptions of earlier times and cultures.

This is illustrated for example in plate 149, where he turns the tables on the stereotypes of advanced and primitive cultures several times.[16] First, the Celts gain the upper hand in having the more advanced clothing. Second, Deleuran let his Roman score a point by pointing to Roman architecture. But after this he explains that it was due to a lack of wood (as opposed to advanced technology) that the Romans built in stone rather than wood, and that fighting style, religious rituals, and treatment of defeated enemies were at least as cruel, savage, and barbaric among the Romans as among the Celtic and Germanic people.

Deleuran thus deliberately and humorously oscillates between confirming and dismantling ideas of Roman cultural superiority; he also points out how the ancient sources, such as Tacitus, already saw a need to create for readers a contrast between cultures and images of both negative and positive others.

---

15   Gibbon 1963, 49-53.
16   Cf. also plate 203, where the lack of a system for imperial succession leads Deleuran to describe Rome as a failed state.

Fig. 4. Plate 149: "The terms 'barbaric' and 'civilized' break down when we realize that the two parties fought with military equipment of the same level of technological sophistication and when we realize that the Celts wore trousers and tailored clothes, while the Romans still walked around with a naked ass and wore woolen blankets as in the Bronze Age. The Romans were, however undoubtedly civilized in the sense that the word *civis* means 'citizen', 'city-dweller' – they liked to live in cities around the Mediterranean, and they were good organizers."

Between the two images in Figure 5, Deleuran as a schoolmaster instructs his readers to read Tacitus' *Germania* for themselves – but to remember while reading that the difference between the Romans and the Germans was less pronounced, and that modern readers have their own skewed nineteenth- to early twentieth-century stereotypes about advanced and primitive cultures and people.

While Deleuran thus oscillates between the satire of stereotypical depictions of Celtic-Germanic savagery and acknowledgement of how culture, inventions, and ideas spread to northern Europe from the Mediterranean world, he in the process offers a satire of different nineteenth- to early twentieth-century scholarly perceptions of the relationships of Rome, the Celts, and the Germans.

In plate 175, for example, Deleuran depicts Danish Romantic-era scholars and their nationalistically motivated tendency to deny, downplay, or deride any Nordic/Germanic dependence on Mediterranean culture. He himself finds it unproblematic to acknowledge that the runic alphabet was directly adopted from the Latin (plate 188).

It is thus a major concern for Deleuran to show how we use our perceptions and depictions of the past and of other cultures to depict and understand ourselves, and to satirize this process.[17] At the same time Deleuran's depiction of the relationship between Rome and Mediterranean culture on the one hand and the Germanic cultures of Northern Europe has a dual agenda that guards against what Deleuran viewed as two historic

---

17 E.g. also plates 122, 141, 143-150, 154, 182, 188, and 203.

Plate 160: "But now back to ourselves: around 100 AD, the Roman Cornelius Tacitus, consul in the year 97, and subsequently governor in Gallia Belgica wrote his, for us, interesting work: *De origine et situ germanorum*, i.e. 'About the origins of the Germans and their land' …

Fig. 5.

The Romans saw parallels with heir own modest but noble past, before riches and city life had ruined the customs, when the nobleman had himself ploughed the lands with his spear within easy reach, the time when wives were faithful to their husbands, children obedient, and when masters dined on the same food as their slaves."

Fig. 6.

Plate 175: "But otherwise, the new Romantic-era nationalism of the nineteenth century prompted some to look down their noses at Saxo because he wrote in Latin. It was particularly wrong of him to have translated the Skaldic hymns into Latin. Some Romantic-era authors/scholars."

Plate 188: "Around this time (the time of Augustus) the Germans must have taken over the Roman version of the Phoenician alphabet and used it for creating their runic alphabet."

8 • Wronged imperialists, primitive Romans, and advanced barbarians (and vice versa)   131

Fig. 7. Plate 142: "Those who replaced the Greeks as world power, the Romans, were really quite unheroic. Rome was nothing but a provincial hamlet – and all it asked for was peace and security. Is that too much to ask for? History had however taught them that there was no one else who could get them this- except themselves."

"Roman history was permeated by haughty neighbours and arrogant lords who were always trying to snub the Romans: the Sabines did not want their daughters to marry the Romans (as mentioned in volume 2, page 48), because they were socially inferior. The Etruscans wanted to rule over them. The Gauls had plundered them and torched their city."

misconceptions of this relationship. Firstly, Deleuran really wanted his readers to find pride in their history and past, hence his desire to show that the northern "barbarians" and people in the past in general were not primitive and stupid compared to perceived Mediterranean high-culture and scientific thinking of the modern world. Secondly, Deleuran wanted to show, that all cultures, also Germanic culture depended on contact to other cultures, and he wanted through this to vaccinate his readers against the pride turning into chauvinism.[18] From these major subjects and purposes we will turn now to examining two examples of how Deleuran depicts the Roman conquest of their empire.

Romans as (not so) defensive imperialists
The denser treatment of Rome is initiated by Deleuran with plate 142. This is how the Romans are introduced in the narrative.

---

18   Interview with his widow, Lone Deleuran July 1, 2024 and Monggaard 2023, 265-266.

132   Jakob Engberg

Plate 142: "In the end, the Romans had a complex system of treaties and alliances with all cities and people in Italy, even the Greek cities (that had summoned the aid of King Pyrrhus with his elephants) – Now finally they had peace! However, they had also befriended some Greek cities in Sicily and instantly they felt threatened by Carthage! (264 BC)."

"In order to handle Carthage, the Romans had to learn how to make ships and navigate; even if they did not want to, they did it!"

Fig. 8.

We will pass over Deleuran's (satirical) stereotypical depiction of the Romans as pragmatic, practical, and un-heroic. It is clear that in the next series of plates he is interested in explaining to his readers how the Romans came to dominate, and we will examine his representation of this along with his inspirations. On the surface he depicts the Romans as seeking peace and security, as being threatened and rejected by neighbours, and as only expanding their empire when they or their allies were threatened or attacked, and war thus forced upon them. This view of how Rome expanded and gained hegemony reflects how the Roman expansion is ideologically perceived and presented in a number of classical Latin texts across such genres as historiography, poetry, and philosophy (Livy, Virgil, and Cicero). It is also adopted in a number of traditional scholarly depictions of Roman history, including some found in Deleuran's bibliography.[19]

A closer reading reveals, however, that Deleuran by no means uncritically adopts such ideological or scholarly positions. His depiction is satirical and at an ironic distance. The supposedly peaceful Romans are "demanding peace" and arming for war; how, Deleuran prompt his readers to wonder, did they come across to their supposedly

---

19   E.g. Hadas 1967, 37-40; Grimberg 1958-1961, IV, 263-275.

Fig. 9.

Plate 143: "Unfortunately, the Romans now developed a taste for being masters: they felt threatened by anyone and anybody, just in order to be able to go to war with them and subdue them. In this way the empires of the successors of Alexander's generals in the Eastern Mediterranean were also subjected to Rome."

haughty neighbours? In the ensuing narrative, Deleuran perceives this threat from their neighbours as little more than a pretext for war.

After the war with Pyrrhus, according to Deleuran Rome had peace, but "instantly they felt threatened by Carthage! (264 BC)" (plate 142).

After the Punic wars, the Romans "developed a taste for being masters: they felt threatened by anyone and anybody, just in order to be able to go to war with them and subdue them" (plate 143).

I will argue that Deleuran is here playing on the discussion between proponents and opponents of the scholarly theory of "defensive imperialism". This theory was most thoroughly and comprehensively argued by E. Badian, *Imperialism in the Late Republic* (1968). His most thorough and famous opponent is probably William Harris, *War and Imperialism in Republican Rome* (1979). I am quite certain that Deleuran did not study either of these books. A simple kind of defensive imperialism theory is, however, found in many other books, including at least two in Deleuran's bibliography: Moses Hades' *Det Romerske Imperium* (1967) and Svend Arne Jensen' *Romerriget fra Sagntid til Kejsertid* (1988). It is additionally found in Grimberg's *Verdenshistorie*, which I will later show was in all probability used by Deleuran (in spite of the fact that it is not in the bibliography). There is a further possible, even likely, influence not mentioned in the bibliography, Erik Christiansen's *Romersk historie* (1989), where we may find both sides of the Badian–Harris controversy on p. 70 (without the names of the two scholars being mentioned). We will see below that Erik Christiansen is the likely source for another satire on a scholarly theory on p. 69.

134   Jakob Engberg

Plate 144: They were loosing their old will to victory at all costs. The senate however, had not lost its pride. When the Teutonic-chieftain, Teuto-Bodus came to Rome after the aforementioned battle [Battle of Arausio] in order to offer the Romans "Peace and fellowship of arms" in return for land, the senate rejected as though it was on top of the situation.

Fig. 10.

No peace after defeat, and Italian manpower:
As we saw above, Deleuran insists that the Romans in republican times had no military technological or cultural superiority compared with their Italic neighbours, the Celts, the Carthaginians, the Iberians, or the Greeks. How, then, does he explain the expansion

of Rome? Two interconnected explanations are given for Rome's republican expansion. First, Rome formed a series of alliances with the conquered people of Italy, and these allies provided the Romans with the manpower needed for war (see again plate 142 and Figure 8). Second, Rome developed and maintained a tradition for persevering even in the face of devastating defeats; Deleuran describes this tradition by saying, for example, "The Romans had on several occasions succeeded by stubbornly denying to acknowledge defeats", and gives as examples their response to defeats at the hand of Porsenna, Pyrrhus, Hannibal, and Teuto-Bodus (plate 144).

These two explanations are interconnected: the combined manpower of Rome and her allies made perseverance possible, but in order to be a credible protector of allies, the Romans were also required to persevere. Some might, in this interconnected theory accounting for the expansion of Rome, recognize the theory of Peter Brunt in *Italian Manpower* (1971). Unknown to most, including Peter Brunt, however, the same theory had a much earlier champion. In 1942, in German-occupied Denmark, the first Roman historian at Aarhus University, Adam Afzelius, promoted this theory in his *Die Römische Eroberung Italiens*. Neither Peter Brunt nor Adam Afzelius is to be found in the bibliography of Deleuran, and I find it unlikely that he used either of them. A likely or at least possible source is, again, Erik Christiansen's *Romersk historie* (1989, 69). A presentation and critique of the defensive imperialism theory and a presentation of the link between alliance, manpower, and perseverance in face of (temporary) defeats is found on two adjacent pages in Christiansen's book.[20] I have not been able to find a similar combination, let alone proximity, in any other histories of Rome that might have influenced Deleuran. The publication of Deleuran's plates (1990) was preceded by no more than a year by Christiansen's book (1989). Christiansen had, however, used his manuscript as the syllabus for earlier courses at the Open University, and in the years prior to 1989 he delivered public lectures in both Jutland and Zealand (the home island of Deleuran).[21] A further incidental support for Christiansen as the inspiration for Deleuran is found on plate 143. Here Deleuran tells his readers that the Roman Empire existed in principle until Napoleon abolished it in 1806; this is a point Christiansen used to make in a popular lecture called "The fall of the Roman Empire – that is if it really fell", and repeated in his 1989 book.[22]

Primary sources and scholarship

In Deleuran's narrative, the reference to Napoleon's abolishment of the Roman Empire is a one-picture digression inserted in another two-picture digression on how we have received the classical authors through medieval scribes. This brings us to a further discussion of Deleuran's use of primary sources from antiquity and modern scholarship.

---

20 Christiansen 1989, 69-70.
21 Christiansen 1989, preface.
22 Unpublished lecture by Erik Christiansen, "*Romerrigets fald, hvis det ellers faldt*", 3; 1989, 178.

Deleuran's most frequent references to ancient authors are to Tacitus' *Germania* and to Jordanes' work on the Goths.[23] This provides an interesting contrast, since Deleuran says he has been reading Tacitus himself (and also advises his readers to read him), but explicitly says that he has not been reading Jordanes.[24] He makes references to many ancient authors.[25] The cases of Tacitus and Jordanes show that some were consulted by Deleuran himself (most likely in translation; see also the case with Plutarch discussed above), while others are likely quoted secondarily from quotations in scholarship.

In some instances, it is hard to tell the difference. On plate 152, a proud Vellejus Paterculus in full military kit looks directly at the reader and expresses in something resembling a direct quotation his pride in the accomplishments of the army in its summer campaign. The quotation is in fact a translated condensation of different sentences from book five, chapter 106 of *Historia Romana*. The Danish sentences are not from the only full Danish translation available at Deleuran's time, M. Adam Winding Brorson's "Det Overblevne af C. Velleius Paterculus's Romerske Historie" (1804). I have been unable to find a similar quotation in any scholarly book used by Deleuran. The source is thus unclear. Deleuran's knowledge of Latin would have made it possible for him to make his own translation.[26]

Deleuran also references ancient authors who are lost to us (e.g. Posidonius and Pomponius Mela), and only occasionally does he tell his readers that they are lost (e.g. Cassiodorus, plate 176).

On Plate 152, Deleuran makes a reference to Pomponius Mela and Pliny the Elder when discussing the possible locations of a place, most likely on the west coast of Jutland, where the Roman fleet expedition of 5 AD made a landing. He also references a source that he says he has forgotten the name of which interprets this place as Rønland, on the Limfjord. I have not succeeded in identifying Deleuran's forgotten source, but have found that possible identifications of the various locations mentioned by Pomponius Mela, Pliny, and in the fragments of Pytheas were eagerly debated in *Geografisk Tidsskrift* (1917-1918) by scholars and in a 1922 monograph by an amateur historian.[27]

Small mistakes can be very useful in identifying the material on which an author depends. For example, on plate 153, Deleuran has illustrated Augustus lamenting the defeat of Varus in 9 AD. In the illustration Augustus is banging his head against the wall, and he is depicted as unbalanced. According to Suetonius' *Augustus* (23) he butted his head against the door. In the illustration Augustus is depicted as saying "Vare, Vare"; according to Suetonius he said "Quintili Vare, legiones redde" ("Quintilius Varus, give me back my

---

23 In the index there are 13 references to Tacitus and seven to Jordanes.
24 Plate 196.
25 E.g. plate 152, Vellejus, Pliny the Elder, and Pomponoius Mela; plate 153, Augustus, Res Gaestae, and Suetonius; plate 154, Poseidonius and Paulus Diaconus; plate 158, Josephus and Matthew; plate 165, Caesar, Bellum Gallicum.
26 Interview with his widow, Lone Deleuran July 1 2024.
27 Steensby 1917-1918, 12-34; Schütte 1917-1918, 86-92; Erlang 1922. See also Ringskou & Sørensen 2022.

legions!"). The mistaken replacement of the door with a wall can be found in different places.[28] I have, however, found only one place where this mistake is combined with the mistake in how Augustus addresses Varus, and this is in Grimberg's *Verdenshistorie* (IV, 283). That this is indeed the origin of Deleuran's mistake can be supported firstly because Deleuran makes an explicit reference to Grimberg earlier on the same plate (adding a footnote where he explains that Grimberg is "a Swede, who has written a, in Danish homes very common, History of the World"), and secondly because on plate 154 he presumes that the Romans feared a new attack by the Cimbri – a supposition that Grimberg flaunts on the same page.

Conclusion

Was Deleuran's work popular, as its subtitle, *A People's History*, indicates? In terms of popularity, readership, and copies sold – of both *Ekstrabladet* and the hardcover volumes – it most certainly was. In terms of content, one may argue that many references may have been lost on most readers, or that readers were given more than they might have wanted to know about the subjects of many of his digressions. But then again, his popularity shows that popular authors, who receive and pass on their image of classical antiquity, do well in assuming much of their readers and in presenting them with a rich, complex, and diverse world.

Deleuran used a truly impressive range of sources, and he drew from both widely published (e.g. Gibbon and Grimberg) and more specialized obscure scholarship (e.g. on clothing). He was satirical and critical of some positions, theories, and constructs in both sources and scholarship – but not systematically so – and this was always tempered by his love of a good story.

Deleuran's deliberate and playful role reversals of barbaric Celts and Germans with sophisticated Romans, his loving caricatures of people of all ages, and his sarcasm towards self-assured early modern and modern scholars reveal his view of history. For Deleuran, people and cultures and economic systems and means of production are not improving or inevitably progressing in any rational way, or in accordance with some law. History is not even a logically progressing chronological, linear development. As a narrator of history, he deliberately depicts history as messy by interrupting his narrative with wild digressions. Economy and means of production are, for him, not the foundation of society, and it is not only what can be measured, weighed, and counted that exists. Folklore and myth have an equal call to reality because folklore and myth are true expressions of how people see the world and have real effects on their lives.

---

28 E.g. https://en.wikipedia.org/wiki/Battle_of_the_Teutoburg_Forest (last accessed 7 July 2021) and https://da.wikipedia.org/wiki/Varusslaget (last accessed 7 July 2021); these Wikipedia pages were of course not available to Deleuran, so they are just used to illustrate here that the door in Suetonius' anecdote is often substituted for a wall. The mistake may in general be explained by the fact that the banging of a head against a wall is a proverbial activity in several modern European (Germanic) languages, including Danish, Faroese, Swedish, German, and English.

Deleuran aims to show that people are people in spite of cultural differences and chronological progression. The past is not primitive, and we advanced; people in the past were not foolish but formed, understood, and accounted for their worlds in ways that made sense to them. The people in the past were not idealized; however, on the contrary, Deleuran aims to show that they, too, harboured many prejudices about foreign cultures and people and expressed them freely to further their own agendas. Deleuran is critical of this, but his critique is seasoned with understanding and with self-irony. He shows that later times, and indeed he as the schoolmaster, do the same: we use the past Romans as the Romans in the past used the northern barbarians to mirror our own values and norms – our dominating current of superiority and our undercurrent of critique of our own society, culture, and times.

Even when we think we are being inclusive and politically correct, for instance correcting the culturally imperialistic designations of our predecessors, we naively fall into the trap of patronizing and colonizing the past and our predecessors and elevating ourselves – and usually, we are no better at coming up with designations, depictions, or narratives that are unbiased and/or free from cultural imperialism.[29]

Bibliography

Afzelius, A. 1942. *Die römische Eroberung Italiens (340-264 v. Chr)*. Aarhus: Aarhus University Press.
Badian, E. 1968. *Imperialism in the Late Republic*. Oxford: Blackwell.
Broby-Johansen, R. 1967. *Krop og Klær*. Copenhagen: Gyldendal.
Brorson, A.W. 1804. *Det Overblevne af C. Velleius Paterculus's Romerske Historie*. Copenhagen: Selskabet til de skiønne Videnskabers Forfremmelse.
Brunt, P. 1971. *Italian Manpower 225 BC – AD 14*. Oxford: Oxford University Press.
Cahana-Blum, J. & MacKendrick, K. (eds) 2019. *We and They. Decolonizing Greco-Roman and Biblical Antiquities*. Aarhus Studies in Mediterranean Antiquity 14. Aarhus: Aarhus University Press.
Christiansen, E. 1989. *Romersk historie. Fra by til verdensrige og fra verdensrige til by*. Aarhus: Aarhus University Press.
Christoffersen, P. (Pedro) 2009. "Claus in memoriam", in: Deleuran, C., *Illustreret Danmarkshistorie for Folket 1. Del*, new edition. Copenhagen: Forlaget Politisk Revy, 3-5.
Connolly, P. 1976. *Den romerske hær*. Copenhagen: Borgen.
Deleuran, C. 2009-2010. *Illustreret Danmarkshistorie for Folket 1. Del, 2. Del og 3. Del*, new edition. Copenhagen: Forlaget Politisk Revy.
Deleuran, L. 2024. *Interview* (by J. Engberg).
Erlang, F.K. 1922. *Er Ringkjøbing Danmarks ældste og fornemste By? Hvad Nutidens Videnskab mener herom kortelig refereret*. Ringkjøbing: Bogtrykker Louis Høier.
Gibbon, E. 1963. *Det romerske riges forfald og undergang. Efter D.M. Low's udgave med udfyldende og forbindende mellemtekster, dansk oversættelse*, vols 1-4, H.C. Huus (1-2), K. Hannestad & B. Busch (3-4), Copenhagen: Rosenkilde og Bagger.
Grimberg, C.G. 1958-1961. *Verdenshistorie*. Copenhagen: Politikens Forlag.
Hadas, M. 1967. *Det Romerske Imperium*. Oversat af Leo Hjortsø. Copenhagen: Sesam.
Hansen, H.H. 1976. *Alverdens klædedragter i farver*. Copenhagen: Politikens Forlag.
Harris, W. 1979. *War and Imperialism in Republican Rome*. Oxford: Oxford University Press.
Holst, I. 2000. "En dag med Deleuran", *Strip!: Tidsskrift om tegneserier* 9, 24-28.
Jensen, S.A. 1988. *Romerriget fra sagntid til kejsertid*. Aarhus: Systime.
Munksgaard, E. 1974. *Oldtidsdragter*. Copenhagen: Nationalmuseet.

---

29 Cf. Cahana-Blum & MacKendrick 2019.

Ringskou, C. & Sørensen, B. 2022. "Raunonia, Rennumkøpingh, Ringkøbing", in: *Ringkjøbing-Skjern Museum Nyhedsbrev*, Marts 2022. https://levendehistorie.dk/nyheder/visningsside-2?Action=1&NewsId=2297&M=NewsV2&PID=378, last accessed 5 May 2022.

Saxtorph, N.M. 1971. *Krigsfolk gennem tiden*. Copenhagen: Politiken.

Schütte, G. 1917-1918. "Nordgrænsen for. Iagttagelserne hos Pytheas". *Geografisk Tidsskrift* 24, 86-92.

Steensby, H.P. 1917-1918. "Pytheas fra Massilia og Jyllands Vestkyst". *Geografisk Tidsskrift* 24, 12-34.

Stegelmann, J. 2009 "Claus Deleuran", *Den Store Danske*. https://denstoredanske.lex.dk/Claus_Deleuran, last accessed 8 July 2021.

Tilke, M. 1955. *Kostümschnitte und Gewandforme*. Tübingen: Verlag Ernst Wasmuth.

Ullmann, V. 1876-1890. *Levnedsskildringer af Plutark. I Oversættelse fra Græsk*. Copenhagen and Oslo: Selskabet til Historiske Kildeskrifters Oversættelse.

William, H. 1979. *War and Imperialism in Republican Rome*. Oxford: Clarendon Press.

9

HERCULES AND THE INCREDIBLE HULK

MYTH MEETS MARVEL'S MEGATEXT

C. W. MARSHALL

This essay offers an examination of classical reception within the field of American comics, following a run of Marvel comics published serially between July 2007 and March 2011.[1] The run constitutes an extended narrative arc, spread over 49 issues, which I read as a scholar interested in both comics and classical reception (see Kovacs & Marshall 2011; 2016). Doing so reveals thoughtful and meaningful engagement with the processes of classical myth-making that have continued without interruption since antiquity. The title of this larger arc is "The Incredible Hercules", and most issues were co-written by Greg Pak and Fred van Lente (the first four were by Pak alone). The story integrates the Greek god Heracles (who goes by the Latin form Hercules) more fully into the so-called Marvel Universe.

"The Incredible Hercules" begins in *The Incredible Hulk* (vol. 2, issue 106; w. Greg Pak, a. Gary Frank),[2] immediately following Pak's character-defining story "Planet

---

1   This essay began as a keynote address at the 2021 "Popular Receptions in Classical Antiquity" conference, held at Aarhus University. My sincere thanks go to the conference organizers for the invitation. Additional thanks are due to Jens Krasilnikoff, Tony Keen, and Charles Hatfield, as well as to Nick Lowe for a conversation long ago. This research has been supported in part by the Social Sciences and Humanities Research Council of Canada.
2   Reference to specific issues includes mention of both writer ("w.") and artist ("a."), even though the credit within the comics might have a different label (e.g. "scripts", "penciller"). Individual issues of Marvel comics, often appearing monthly, are usually numbered sequentially, with each new series with that title (often with a new issue 1) beginning, by academic convention, a new "volume". Marvel is more interested in incentivizing purchases than in helping bibliographers, and irregularities are everywhere. *The Incredible Hulk* vol. 1, for example, lasted six issues, from May 1962 to March 1963 (dates given are stated dates of publication; in reality comics often appear earlier). The series was cancelled, but Hulk continued to appear as a character, soon becoming regular in a series called *Tales to Astonish*, which was re-named *The Incredible Hulk* with issue 102 (April 1968; w. Gary Friedrich, a. Marie Severin) and continued until issue 474 (March 1999; w. Joe Casey, a. Javier Pulido). *The Incredible Hulk* vol. 2 is similarly convoluted: the series was

Hulk" (*IH* 92-105), in which Bruce Banner, as the gamma-powered, rage-fuelled Hulk, is sent to an alien planet where he survives a rags-to-riches gladiator story, leading a Spartacus-like rebellion (a narrative deserving of future attention by classical reception scholars). When Hulk returns to Earth, Marvel comics shifts the primary focus on the character into a special "event" series under the title "World War Hulk" (see Southgate 2016), and the narrative continuity of the main monthly series continues with a focus on allies and friends during the time of Hulk's return and rampage. Indeed, *IH* 106 begins with a caption that reads "Meanwhile, back on planet Earth …" (106.2.1; references in this form give issue, page, and panel numbers): this opening line, spoken by Bruce's cousin Jennifer Walters (who is also the super-powered She-Hulk), marks that this is a continuation of what has gone before, but it also signals the shift in tone and emphasis as the proper beginning to "The Incredible Hercules".

The Marvel Comics superheroes that emerged in the 1960s established a new tone for hero comics in which alternate identities were flawed and psychologically complex characters struggled, while at the same time defeating evil on a monthly basis. The Fantastic Four, Iron Man, Thor, Spider-Man, the X-Men, the Avengers: all were created at this time, and over the past decade have established themselves through cinema as a dominant narrative (perhaps *the* dominant narrative) in North American (and arguably global) popular culture. Among these characters was Bruce Banner, a milquetoast scientist who is irradiated by his own "gamma bomb" while saving a teenager from the blast site, which turns him into the green-skinned Hulk, whose strength and rage are unequalled, in *Incredible Hulk* (vol. 1) 1 (May 1962, w. Stan Lee and Jack Kirby, a. Jack Kirby). The Jekyll-and-Hyde aspects of the story were established immediately, along with conscious evocations of Frankenstein's monster and the Jewish legend of the Golem.[3] There was always a psychological component to the Hulk, with Banner's inner psyche manifesting itself externally in the creature; the Cold War resonances of the dangers of radiation and nuclear destruction remain a constant touchstone for the character (Pagnoni Burns & Marino 2016). *Incredible Hulk* 312 (October 1985; w. Bill Mantlo, a. Mike Mignola), additionally revealed Bruce as a child abused by his alcoholic father.[4] Hulk is very much

---

called *Hulk* for issues 1-11 (April 1999-February 2000), and issue 12 (March 2000) was renamed *The Incredible Hulk* (vol. 2), which ran until issue 112 (January 2008), whereupon it was renumbered *The Incredible Hercules* for issues 113-139 (February 2008-April 2010). This essay uses the abbreviation *IH* for both *The Incredible Hulk* (vol. 2) and *The Incredible Hercules*.

3   Frankenstein's Monster and Dr. Jekyll: Lerberg 2016, 24 traces an initial critical observation to the letters column of *Incredible Hulk* (vol. 1) 5 (January 1963), where Larry Tucker writes, "Physically and psychologically, he resembles Dr. Frankenstein's monster. His alter-ego, as Doctor Banner, is reminiscent of another doctor, Jekyll by name" (see Tucker 1963). See also Hatfield 2012, 117; Darowski & Darowski 2016, 9 and 15, etc. Golem: see *Incredible Hulk* (vol. 1) 134 ("Among us walks … the Golem", w. Roy Thomas, a. Herb Trimpe; December 1970) and, e.g., Pagnoni Burns & Marino 2016, 45.

4   The idea for the story may have originated from an unpublished idea by Barry Windsor-Smith, which has since been developed in *Monsters* (Windsor-Smith 2021). Accusations of plagiarism against Mantlo draw on inconsistent and one-sided evidence.

a hero for our modern nuclear age. He causes great destruction, but is motivated by fear, trauma, lack of impulse control, and a misunderstanding media. Depending on the writer, Hulk can be a childlike innocent, abused and unaware of his own abilities, an animalistic and violent force of destruction, a scientist-inventor capable of marvelous discoveries, or a hero/anti-hero struggling in every personal relationship he has.

Hercules has also been part of the "Marvel Universe" since the 1960s, with his first appearance as an opponent of the Norse god Thor, in *Journey into Mystery* annual 1 (October 1965; w. Stan Lee, a. Jack Kirby). Early appearances set him as a Greek counterpart to Thor and a super-strong, mythologically divine helper of humans in the modern world in *Thor* (vol. 1) 126 (March 1966; w. Stan Lee, a. Jack Kirby).[5] Within months, he also appeared in a story with the Hulk (*Tales to Astonish* 79 [May 1966]; w. Stan Lee, a. Adam Austin), where the warm reception of Hercules in the world contrasts with the bitter isolation of the Hulk. It is with Thor that Hercules was principally associated in these early years. While Hercules has been an Avenger, and a member of the short-lived L.A.-based 1970s superhero team the Champions, he was not given an ongoing solo title within the larger Marvel continuity. In the 1980s, Bob Layton wrote a series of short Hercules space-faring mini-series set in the distant future (*Hercules, Prince of Power*), but these were entirely separated from other Marvel characters (see Marshall, forthcoming). It was therefore a surprise to the monthly issue-buyer when the Hulk monthly series was renamed, from *The Incredible Hulk* to *The Incredible Hercules* in issue 113 (February 2008).

This was more than a marketing gimmick: "Planet Hulk" had been immensely successful, and to substitute a potentially underwhelming character as the lead, interrupting the series numbering, was a substantial publishing decision with potential economic impact that also makes an explicit claim for the place of Hercules within the Marvel Universe. The series numbering continued until issue 141. This sets the parameters for the comics I wish to examine here: *IH* 106-141, with assorted other issues that culminate in a five-issue "event" series called *Chaos War* (see Table 1); there was an 11-issue follow-up series, *Herc* (2011-12), also written by Pak and van Lente, bringing the total number of issues under consideration to 60. Events, in the context of North American hero comics, are on one level an industry mechanism designed to increase sales by encouraging readers to purchase other comics than those contained in a single title within a single narrative arc, as something 'big' happens in the world of the characters, affecting individuals in several separate books. Pak and van Lente's run on *IH* spanned four such events: "World War Hulk", "Secret Invasion", "Dark Reign", and "Chaos War" (underlined in Table 1; two further events coincided with the run of *Herc*). The first of these obviously focused around the character of the Hulk, and the last around Hercules: this patterning of events therefore points to another way that the transition to "The Incredible Hercules" was given a structural and institutional authority. These events can be headaches for readers (and scholars) trying to identify simple through-lines, and because writers are obliged to incorporate disparate narrative elements that might not

---

5   These and other stories are collected in *Thor vs. Hercules* (Marvel 2010). While a "Hercules" does appear in *Avengers* 10 (November 1964; w. Stan Lee, a. Dan Heck), this is a separate character.

have been anticipated, the presence of event series at times can derail or at least arrest significant character development. On the other hand, they do reinforce the fact that these characters share a common narrative world (or worlds) and exist as part of a larger story, and in this case, the conclusion in *Chaos War* was seen at the time as not "even so much an event comic as it is the continuing storyline that Pak and Van Lente started way back when Hercules first took over the 'Incredible Hulk' book" (Murphy 2010).

Issues	Initial collections/story arc (year)[6]
1. Incredible Hulk 106-111	World War Hulk: *The Incredible Hercules* (2008)
2. Incredible Hulk 112, Incredible Hercules 113-115, Hulk vs. Hercules: When Titans Collide	*IH: Hercules Against the World* (2008) *IH:* Secret Invasion (2009)
3. Incredible Hercules 116-120	*IH: Love and War* (2009)
4. Incredible Hercules 121-125	*IH:* Dark Reign (2009)
5. Incredible Hercules 126-131	*IH: The Mighty Thorcules* (2010)
6. Incredible Hercules 132-137	
7. Assault on New Olympus Prologue, Incredible Hercules 138-141	*IH: Assault on New Olympus* (2010)
8. Hercules: Fall of An Avenger 1-2, Heroic Age: Prince of Power 1-4	*IH: The New Prince of Power* (2010) Chaos War (2011)
9. Chaos War 1-5	
	= 49 issues (+11 for *Herc*)[7]
10. Herc 1-6, 6.1, 7-10	*Herc: Prodigal God* (2012) [Fear Itself (1-6), Spider Island (7-8)]

Table 1. Greg Pak and Fred van Lente's *The Incredible Hercules* (event titles underlined).

6   The narrative authority of the five- or six-issue story arc can be challenged, but since it represents the initial collection of the materials beyond the monthly format, it serves as a convenient touchstone. These collections have been re-packaged in larger groupings: *The Incredible Hercules: Smash of the Titans* (2009) [=1 and 2]; *The Incredible Hercules: Sacred Invasion* (2010) =3 and 4]; *The Incredible Hercules: The Complete Collection*, vol. 1 (2019) [=1, 2, and 3]; and *The Incredible Hercules: The Complete Collection*, vol. 2 (2021) [=4, 5, and 6].

7   The numbering of the collections is mine, and is admittedly problematic. *Chaos War* concludes with the words "So ends the eighth & final volume of The Incredible Hercules" (*Chaos War* 5, 24.1). It is not clear which of the preceding collections is not being counted. Possibly 1. is excluded: Hulk's name is still on the book (the cover of *IH* 112 shows "Herc" spraypainted over "Hulk", with a reprise of a famous Hulk cover by Jim Steranko, in *Incredible Hulk King-Size Special* 1 (October 1968). Apparently, Steranko's face was redrawn by Marie Severin (CBR Staff 2017) – the cover was also imitated by Kaare Andrews in *IH* (vol. 2) 34 (January 2002). Supporting this view is "The Story So Far", a one-page summary that begins with *IH* 112, found on the opening page of *IH* 141. Against this is the inclusion of *IH* 106-111 in the larger collected editions described in the previous note; Herc's initial appearance in a magnificent two-page spread of *IH* 106.21-22. It is also possible 8. is meant to be excluded. Hercules is dead by *IH* 141, and is only "summon[ed] back to this plane" (141.22.3) on the penultimate page of the collection (141.23.1). Neither answer is satisfying, and it is possibly an inconsistency that emerged through the serial publication.

The mythic scale of American comic book superheroes invites associations with Greek mythology in terms of what Charles Segal (1983) has called a "megatext", a deeply interconnected network of narratives that create a coherent, fictional universe, even if at times it contains contradictions. Resonances between these distinct narrative systems can be productive vectors of reception analysis. It is meaningful to consider the ways in which Tony Stark as Iron Man appropriates aspects of the disabled metalworking god Hephaestus, for example. A megatext can also be expanded to include figures present in other narrative systems, and this is seen in the regular presence of mythic figures (the Norse god Thor, the hero Hercules) in American comics.

The idea of a megatext looks at the corpus of myth as represented in tellings that cross language, geography, and time, but still form a meaningful "body of interrelated narratives which reveal an implicit system of logical relations" (Segal 1983, 174). It is "an artificial construct, necessarily invisible and unconscious to the society whose exemplary narratives and symbolic projections of what 'reality' is are located within that system" (*ibid.*). For Segal, this is separate from whatever religious valence a myth might convey, and indeed "the presentation of myth in Greek literature shows a high degree of what we may call the metaliterary or metalingual consciousness" (175). This does not deny a connection between myth and religion, but focuses attention primarily on widely familiar narrative structures instead. The megatext constitutes "the total corpus of myths, read synchronically" along with "the network of more or less subconscious patterns or 'deep structures' or 'undisplaced' forms which tales of a given type share with one another" (176). (I would challenge the need to read synchronically in this statement: the diachronic development of the megatext represents a series of conscious choices of engagement that are of academic interest in themselves.) Segal stresses how "[t]he remarkable coherence of the megatext of Greek myth" (176) allows "a reconstitution of its symbolic network as a whole" and "an analysis of certain logical relations" (178) in discrete mythic tellings. There emerges "a consciousness of the interrelated wholeness of the text" which means "any one of these figures may serve as a paradigm for another" (179).[8]

This approach offered productive avenues of scholarly analysis for Greek tragedy and other ancient literary forms. It was developed by Roz Kaveney, prompted by an observation from classics scholar Nick Lowe, to apply to the systemic relationship that exists between narratives within the DC and Marvel Universes: "these two continuities were the largest narrative constructions in human culture (exceeding, for example, the vast body of myth, legend and story that underlies Latin and Greek literature), and … learning to navigate them was a skill-set all of its own" (Kaveney 2008, 25). Writing in 2005, Kaveney explained:

---

[8] For an example of such a structure, see Hatfield 2012, 128-130 for the "family resemblance" between heroes and villains in American comics. The pairing of Hercules as an opponent to Thor (both gods, son of the pantheon's leader, but within separate mythologies) is a clear example of the family resemblance structure.

> Marvel Comics has accumulated well over half a century's worth of biography of its scores of superhero and super-villain characters, often attaching to those radically different alternate presents, aborted futures and past incarnations. Marvel Comics continuity is a megatext comparable in scale to that of the mythologies of the Ancient Classical European world, say – yet, in its essence and in its obsessive concerns, it is a subset of the rather smaller megatext of all the SF and fantasy genres on which it has always drawn. (2005, 5, and see 1-8)

This creates what she calls a "thick text", one that generates multi-creator narratives over time that challenge and contradict each other,[9] while still establishing a wider continuity that reflects and replicates established narrative structures, enabling "us to create a criticism which includes a sense of the particular thick text as an object positioned in the broader space of the generic megatext of which it is a part" (2005, 6). As Charles Hatfield notes with respect to the Marvel universe, the tight fictive continuity established as a process, and it is not set out prescriptively in advance (2012, 122-124, and see 116-143)

In addition to narrative continuity, meaningful connections emerge with individual creators (both artists and writers, as a start) and that collaborative narrative creation means that "all texts are not only a product of the creative process but contain all the stages of that process within them like scars or vestigial organs" (5). The consistency of the worldview within these comics megatexts offers reassurance to the reader:

> Understanding continuity is one of the pleasures of serial works of art; another is the realization that, if you don't understand quite everything that is going on, nonetheless the texture of referentiality that you are experiencing at the same time as your incomprehension is something that you can both trust and be comforted by. There is the sense that this is a creation you can trust; there is the sense that you will understand more on later readings. (Kaveney 2008, 26)

A given text will draw upon and mobilize structural features within the immediate narrative frame (a given comics run, defined either by a creator or story arc or through the title's sequential numbering), and within the wider context of the comics megatext.

On one level, "the workmanlike upkeep of continuity" (Hatfield 2012, 141) becomes an object of academic interest in itself, as the interests of the scholar overlap with those of the fan: less disparagingly, Kaveney calls this the "geek aesthetic", whereby "popular culture is consumed in an active way – sitting through films and television shows can be the start of appreciating them, not simply an end in itself" (2005, 7). Such continuity,

---

9   Kaveney 2008, 25: "Narrative universes as vast as those of the Marvel and DC continuities are not the product of any one person, even of an editor-in-chief as creative and innovative as Stan Lee of Marvel, but rather the process of slow accretion and of the desire to make sense of what were once quite random narrative choices as they came to impinge on each other. No one artist or writer is responsible for these continuities – they are collective works of art".

indeed, can extend beyond the megatext itself. As Hatfield describes, while superheroes do not constitute a modern mythology, they do draw inspiration from mythology and other non-comics literary sources (Hatfield 2012, 124-125, and see 131-132). This is another way that the idea of megatext is helpful for reception studies in popular culture: by flattening the experience of myth (through the removal of religious practice, for example) to a series of structural and narrative relationships, direct comparison of how myth impacts the creation of modern comics narrative is more naturally accomplished.

The explicit mythic dimension of the Hulk within the Marvel universe is seen, for example, in "The Last Titan" (*The Incredible Hulk – The End*, 2002; w. Peter David, a. Dale Keown). Set in a post-apocalyptic future, Bruce Banner, alter ego of the Hulk, is the last living human. The story associates Hulk with the titan Prometheus explicitly, as he protects humanity while suffering greatly as his body is regularly devoured:

> The Hulk is heir to Prometheus. The living symbol of nuclear fire, to be devoured, over and over again, but always able to rise up and be consumed once more. The last Titan. (*The End* 42.2)

The normally destructive figure of Hulk becomes a benefactor, persevering alone in the mountains with his hate. On one level, it is a failed benefaction: the only human being in existence is now Banner, and there is no sense of continuity for the species beyond him. At the same time, the constant devouring of Hulk's physical body by ravenous mutated insects (in lieu of a Zeus-sent eagle) frames his suffering in terms of divine punishment:

> Someone has to pay for that knowledge. Someone has to continue to be punished, because there are some crimes that are simply so awful, so beyond forgiveness, that punishment must continue to be exacted. That's what Hell is for, after all. Hell on Earth. (*The End* 42.2)

The panel immediately above this shows a younger Hulk, being attacked by the U.S. Army in a contemporary setting, as repeatedly occurred in the monthly *Incredible Hulk* series: the contiguous body position of Hulk under attack between the two panels points to the cyclical nature of his suffering (see Fig. 1). "The Last Titan" is a powerful story that wears its classical debts to ps.-Aeschylus on its sleeve.

Some elements of the larger story of Pak's *Incredible Hercules* have been explored by Koning (2020); my intention is to build on that discussion and provide a literary analysis of specific sections of that story. In the aftermath of *World War Hulk*, the run pursues two larger narratives, essentially alternating between one that establishes Herc's place among all the various pantheons within the Marvel universe (=3, 6, and 9 in Table 1), and one that considers his place specifically among the Olympians (=4, 5, and 7 in Table 1). Both of these major threads present Athena in a tutelary function, operating with ambiguous and ambivalent motives. While she is his patron throughout this run of *IH*, Athena is also grooming a replacement for Heracles, to be a new "Prince of Power": a Korean-American teenager named Amadeus Cho.

Fig. 1. Hulk as Prometheus (*The End*, 42.1 and 2; a. Dale Keown). © Marvel Comics and used for academic purposes.

Amadeus Cho is a new character created by Pak, who himself is Korean-American and was also raised in the Southwest.[10] A separate study could demonstrate the ways in which Cho's heroic narrative is developed in tandem with the recuperation of Hercules over the course of *IH*, both of them favoured by Athena. An implicit contrast is drawn between Hercules as the gregarious hero of physicality and his human successor of intellect: Cho is repeatedly billed as "the seventh smartest person on the planet", beginning at *Amazing Fantasy*, vol. 2, 15.2.2 (January 2006). Their relationship is nuanced in such a way that both learn from the other, as in any good buddy–cop pairing.[11] Cho is introduced in *IH* 106-111 as someone working with former Hulk allies (including some from the Champions) to defuse the tensions created by *WWH*, believing Hulk's retaliation is both justified and regulated – focused revenge and not mass terror. Ares, also established within Marvel's megatext and working on behalf of the forces opposing Hulk, pursues Herc and Cho as they seek refuge with Athena in upstate Vermont (*IH* 112-115). Following the run of *IH*, Pak wrote a 23-issue story in which Cho becomes "The Totally Awesome Hulk" (2015-2017). This in some ways cements the succession narrative I am describing: in the same way that Hercules replaces Hulk within the numeration of the main Hulk comic in 2008, so Herc's successor, Amadeus Cho, becomes the new (albeit temporary) Hulk in 2015.

Pak and van Lente also re-inscribe classical stories into the Marvel continuity: the megatext aggregates in this way by its very nature. Six mythological events are presented in initial issues of *Incredible Hercules*:

- The death of Megara and the children, set in "Thebes, 1277 B.C." (*IH* 112.5.1-4, 7.1; 113.7.6; 115.18.1-2);
- Stymphalian birds in 1271 (*IH* 112.10-12);
- Lernaean hydra in 1271 (*IH* 113.9-10, and see 113.2);
- Nessus and Deinaira in 1260 (*IH* 113.11-12);
- Shirt of Nessus in 1246 (*IH* 113.17);
- Sack of Laomedon's Troy in 1264 (*IH* 114.2-5, 9.4-10.1);
- Cerberus in 1277 (*IH* 115.17.1-2).

Subsequent storylines present other labours and parerga:

- Hercules' defeat of Kyknos in 1268 (*IH* 116.5.3-.4);
- Leaving with the Argonauts in 1289 (*IH* 117.10.1);
- Losing Hylas in 1289 (*IH* 118.11-12);

---

10   The character was created for *Amazing Fantasy* (vol. 2) 15 (January 2006) in a short story called "Mastermind Excello" (pages 2-9, w. Greg Pak, a. Takeshi Miyazawa). The issue number represents a significant choice by Pak or an editor: Spider-Man had initially appeared in *Amazing Fantasy* (vol. 1) 15 in August 1962, and the introduction of a new teenaged character here inevitably invites direct comparison.

11   See TVtropes, "Buddy Cop Show" for an overview of this trope.

- Fighting the river Achelous in 1260 (*IH* 119.12.1-3, drawing specifically on Sophocles, *Women of Trachis* 9-13);
- The apples of the Hesperides in 1268 (*IH* 121.7-8);
- The girdle of Hippolyta in 1270 (*IH* 122.9-11);
- The Nemean lion is shown to have been killed by 1290 (*IH* 126 *passim*). Indeed, with the exception of the final six panels, the entirety of issue 126 is set in 1290, as a young Hercules is told of his divine parentage by Amphitryon and is given Megara as his wife.

The use of precise dates invites the creation of a coherent narrative, and gives the impression of historicity to Hercules – there is continuity between the mythic past and the comic's present. There is a similarly detailed set of allusions to earlier comics narratives as well, as establishing scenes in a given issue evoke the art and layout of 1960s Lee/Kirby pages, for example. Both mythic history and comics history always remain important to *The Incredible Hercules*.

The selection of mythic narratives, especially in issues 112-115, is also carefully sculpted: the deaths of Megara and Deianira point to Heracles who has lost those he has loved, the specifically tragic narratives identified by Michael Silk (1985) which can so helpfully be framed in Emily Wilson's phrase as "tragic overliving".[12] The Stymphalian birds establish Herc as an archer; the hydra that he has poison arrows; the poison arrows kill Nessus; the so-called "Shirt of Nessus" (which is the title of issue 113's story) kills him as he writhes in anguish. All of this frames the current timeline of events, in which Ares coats the bullets in an assault rifle with hydra venom, so that Herc again experiences that particular torment. As Herc raves, he shouts, "**Before**, you built me a **funeral pyre** – so I could throw myself upon it! But **now I am immortal** – **mere fire** won't be **enough**! There is no escape! **There is no escaping the pain!!**" (113.22.4). The intellectual payoff here for a reader even partially familiar with the ancient sources is very satisfying. And it is the ancient paradigm that Cho chooses to follow in his attempt to restore Herc's sanity. For most of issue 114, Herc is tormented by the hydra's venom (and this is compared to his fury at the First Trojan War; Gantz 1993, 400-402), but the authors and artist Khoi Pham do not shy away from including elements from Apollodorus (*IH* 114.9.4; see Figure 2):

> But as oracles foretold deliverance from these calamities if Laomedon would expose his daughter Hesione to be devoured by the sea monster, he exposed her by fastening her to the rocks near the sea. Seeing her exposed, Hercules promised to save her on condition of receiving from Laomedon the mares which Zeus had given in compensation for the rape of Ganymede. (Apollodorus 2.5.9, tr. Frazer 1.207-209)

---

12   See Wilson 2004, 66-87 for an examination of Euripides' *Heracles*, and Gantz 1993, 1.374-466 for an overview of Heracles generally.

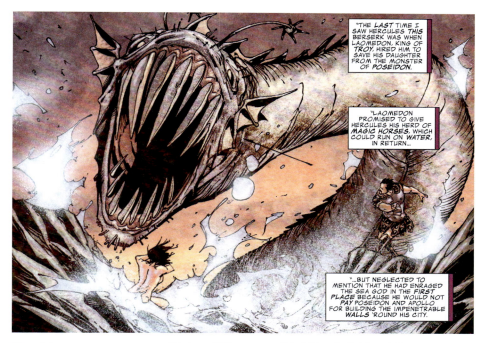

Herc fights a sea monster to save Hesione (*IH* 114.9.4; a. Khoi Pham). © Marvel Comics and used for academic purposes.

Fig. 2.

It is a single panel, half a page in size, but the inclusion of Hesione (who is provided some context for Apollodorus fans in Hercules' demand at the start of the issue, "Where … Are … My … Horses?"; *IH* 114.2-3) demonstrates the creative team has engaged directly with classical sources (Apollodorus seems to me more likely than Diodorus Siculus 4.42, where Hesione is chosen by lot). This use of classical material is thoughtful and relevant: Laomedon's omission of the way Herc will incur Poseidon's wrath becomes an analogue for the betrayal (or apparent betrayal) of Herc by Ares and the other established heroes.

In many ways, at this moment Herc is in the usual situation of the Hulk: liminally positioned, raging in madness, causing destruction, and being perceived as a threat. This is not made explicit, but for most of issue 114, the Incredible Hercules is serving the narrative function that the Hulk had played in the same wider continuity. It is during this rage that Herc sees a vision. He remembers the pain of the burning hydra venom, and asks Amadeus, fallen to the ground, "How?! How could she **do** this, Iolaus? **Again?!** That **shirt** was stained with blood poisoned by the **hydra**! The pain … **The pain!!** It's like **spikes** driven between each of my **bones!**" Confused, Cho asks himself, "'Iolaus?' Uh … … oh, YYYYEEEEEAAAAH. That's **me!**" (114.22.1-3; Figure 3). It is a moment of recognition on the part of Cho, reinforced by adjacent panels showing Cho on the ground and then a memory or maddened vision of Iolaus in the same position, also being attacked some 3200 years previously. The reader cannot hear Amadeus' tone, but the "oh yeah", extending as it does beyond the speech balloon, marks it as loud and

Fig. 3. Amadeus Cho as Iolaus (*IH* 113.22.1-3; a. Khoi Pham). © Marvel Comics and used for academic purposes.

drawn out as recognition (*anagnorisis*) dawns. Amadeus' understanding seems to point to a greater truth: as the companion of Hercules, he has become a latter-day Iolaus.

Iolaus, nephew and companion to Hercules, is also intimately involved with this particular story: in ancient art and literature Iolaus is present during this labour and is responsible for cauterizing the stumps as Herc cuts the hydra's heads. For some readers of the comic, Iolaus might be known less from classical sources,[13] and more from the television show *Hercules: the Legendary Journeys* starring Kevin Sorbo, which ran from

---

[13] Iolaus is in fact quite variable in the ancient sources himself. He is associated particularly with the second labour, against the Lernaean hydra, and as guardian of Heracles's children after his death (Gantz 1993, 1.384-386, 464-465). The second-century CE author Plutarch even presents a variant myth in which Megara survives and marries Iolaus: he has a character say, "Since we are Boeotians, we should honour Heracles and not despise someone for the age of marriage, knowing that he too made his wife Megara, when she was 33 years old, live with Iolaus, who was then 16"; *Erōtikos* 9, *Mor.* 754d–e). This is, admittedly, a weird and confused story. I know of no other source for the relative ages of Megara and Iolaus, and the story appears to be a doublet of the end of Sophocles' *Women of Trachis*, in which the dying Heracles makes Hyllus agree to marry

1994 to 1999 (five television movies and 111 episodes). Widely syndicated, the character of Iolaus (played by Michael Hurst) was familiar and mostly free of erotic interest. In establishing Cho as a latter-day Iolaus figure – someone helping Herc – the creators justify his prominence within the narrative and also establish a red herring, to allow Cho's eventual function as the successor to Hercules to remain unrecognized for the moment.

Pak and van Lente are assiduous in documenting a consistent and meaningful connection to Hercules' classical roots, while still making their story accessible to nonspecialist readers. They indicate they know what they are doing when the katabasis for Cerberus is shown (*IH* 115.17.1), with reference both to the rescue of Theseus and the usurpation of Lycus on the surface-world. This appears to ground the reader fully in the life of Heracles as presented by Euripides' play (ca. 418 BCE). Any symbolic overcoming of death is inevitably anticipatory of an eventual hardship and redemption. For the reader, this feels telegraphed, even though the means of its fulfilment is not yet clear. Given the nature of comics seriality, for the first readers of *The Incredible Hercules* the answer will not come for another two years: reading comics as they appear monthly adds a temporal dimension to the practice that is often absent today, when series are read all at once in collections.

There is also a recognition (from the seventh smartest man on the planet, no less) that mythic narratives embody inconsistencies. "Waaaaaaaait a minute…," Amadeus begins, "… I thought you started on the labors in the **first place** to **atone** for killing Megara and your sons. **Now** you're telling me the twelfth one came **before** they died? That doesn't make any –". Herc's answer is firm: "**Shut up**. You're not **listening**. This is a **myth** I'm telling you. Myths aren't some collection of dates and biographies you bicker over like a **clerk** with his **ledger**. Myths are stories that only have the meaning **you give to them**. So **listen**." (115.17.2-4). It is one of the first lessons of a first-year mythology class that consistency is not the point, but having it spoken directly by Hercules adds urgency and substance, made even poignant by the context of the larger story: a hero talking to his greatest admirer.

Though the use of specific dates continues later in the series, after this moment their valence is less important. Pak and van Lente have shown the frame within which they are operating, and it represents a new ordering of the traditional events, with the death of Megara preceding the labours, and the marriage to Deianira happening long afterwards. It is a reasonable synchronization of the events described, and it leads to one significant mythic innovation. While it is likely the traditional legend of Megara had her murder precede the labours (which then form a kind of penance), Euripides had them follow the death of Megara and the children. *The Incredible Hercules* incorporates both of these versions, with the labours following Megara's killing, but the fetching of Cerberus preceding (as in Euripides). Pak and van Lente effectively separate the journey to the underworld, which is traditionally the final and climactic labour, to a

---

Iole. The etymological overlap between Iole and Iolaus reinforces the confusion. The details are unlikely to originate with Plutarch, however, since his context presumes familiarity with a story of a young man marrying an older woman.

Fig. 4. Black Widow, now and then (*IH* 114.12.3-4; a. Khoi Pham). © Marvel Comics and used for academic purposes.

point more than a decade before the other labours begin. This information is delayed until the moment the historicity of any of these past events is undermined by Hercules himself. The classically informed reader, in making an attempt at synchronizing the story, falls into the writers' trap.

There is also a moment when the use of classical myth, Segal's megatext, is linked more deeply with the Marvel megatext, part of which we are currently reading. While he is raving from the hydra bullets, the comic shows us not only vision of Hercules' mythic past, but echoes of his comics past as well: the superhero Black Widow is seen both now, and as she appeared in 1975 when she first encountered Herc in *Champions* issue 1 (*IH* 114.12.3-4; Fig. 4), with the echo of the past presented with the stippling that was necessary because of the three-colour printing technique that was used in comics at the time. Additionally, she is illustrated wearing the costume and hairstyle she sported in 1975.[14]

This attitude to previous tellings of myth, with devices that flashback both to earlier mythic history and earlier comics history, might easily be captured with the idea of a palimpsest, a metaphor that is arguably over-used within classical studies. Nevertheless, the idea of over-writing is made explicit in the story arc "Love and War" (*IH* 121-125). Herc and Amadeus battle the Amazons, led by Hippolyta. We also learn that Greek gods led by Hera are active in the world through a megacorporation called the Olympus Group: Zeus had been killed in *Ares: God of War* issue 5 (July 2006; w. Michael Avon Oeming, a. Travel Foreman), and Hera is now filling the power vacuum. Three mythic narratives are re-written so as to accommodate the needs of this story. *IH* 123 presents a titanomachy, in which the aftermath includes Atlas holding up the sky at the location of

---

14 The same effect is seen the following page with the Champions themselves (*IH* 114.13.1-2) and Ares (13.3).

Atlas arms himself (*IH* 124.9.1; a. Clayton Henry and Salva Espin). © Marvel Comics and used for academic purposes.

Fig. 5.

Atlantis (the connected etymology is made explicit at *IH* 123.5.3). Atlantis outsources its defense contracts to the Amazons, who capture and enslave the gorgons (here a race of serpentine women, beyond Medusa and her sisters). Atlantis is the "axis mundi", and is given a political dimension as the most powerful city-state at the time. When we return to the present day, political powers have shifted, and so Atlas, mysteriously, appears on the National Mall in Washington, DC, still holding up the sky, and still bearing a grudge against Hercules. This is played for a laugh within the comic – Atlas snaps off the Washington Monument to use as a club (*IH* 124.9.1; Fig. 5) – but it allows an examination of "foundational texts" for the comic's presumptively American readership. There are four such texts, two from Greek literature, and two from American History.

Following an initial issue (*IH* 121) showing Hercules relaxing and spending time with Namora (an inhabitant of Atlantis, with whom he had shared a romantic kiss back in *IH* 111), issue 122 begins with a full-page image of Sappho fr. 31, which has been overwritten by Amadeus Cho. Cho usurps an authorial role, and by marking in red, he implies these are corrections rather than (morally neutral) edits, adopting the role of a professor. The fragment is familiar for its presentation of a love triangle, with one man caught between the attentions of two women. In the same issue a love triangle is created among Herc, Namora, and Namor the Sub-Mariner (the most long-established Marvel antihero, dating back to 1939). At the same time, Amadeus Cho is caught between Artume (the current Queen of the Amazons, who wants to use him to breed more warriors) and Delphyne Gorgon, with whom he wishes to begin a relationship. The same issue

Fig. 6. Hercules escapes with Hippolyta's girdle (IH 122.11.1-2; a. Clayton Henry and Salva Espin). © Marvel Comics and used for academic purposes.

Poseidon at gunpoint (*IH* 122.23; a. Clayton Henry and Salva Espin). © Marvel Comics and used for academic purposes.

Fig. 7.

also features a flashback myth, this time to the seizing of the girdle of Hippolyta (who is established within the comic as the predecessor of Artume). As Hercules flees (*IH* 122.11.1; Fig. 6), Amazonian arrows obscuring the moon (cf. Herodotus 7.226, Plutarch, *Sayings of the Spartans* 225b) and a strategically placed narration bubble covering his nakedness, he is nevertheless successful in his quest.

The authors are thinking about how their work might interact with specific classical texts. Sappho 31 is presented in full, and corrected to show the connections more directly, while not spelling out the double application to two love triangles in the main frame story (*IH* 121 had provided a flashback to Atlas and Heracles' deception of him to fetch the Apples of the Hesperides). The poem is arguably as familiar as any passage of poetry from antiquity might be to a modern reader, but its double deployment adds depth and nuance to the wider story. There's another important triangle in issue 122, however, and it also involves Hercules and the Sub-Mariner. The story of Atlas and Atlantis proves relevant not only as a symbolic shift of global power from the fictional city to Washington, but also because (perhaps uniquely in the entire Marvel Universe) these two both recognize the god Poseidon, one as his nephew and the other as king of an underwater society. As the cliff-hanger at the end of the issue makes clear, the Amazons have captured Poseidon and intend to kill him (*IH* 122.23; Fig. 7).

The following issue consequently begins with the Homeric Hymn to Poseidon, a short hexameter poem that would be unfamiliar to most readers. The annotations are (in my opinion) less successful, but the introduction of the poem, without a wider context, signals for some the themes of the issue, and also provides a kind of reassurance to the reader that the authors are in control of their narrative. The issue presents an account of the titanomachy, revised so that the Amazons are the immediate beneficiaries; they are also enslavers of the gorgons, creating the antagonism readers had previously encountered between Artume and Delphyne. The issue concludes by pulling back and confirming the role of Hera (and her associate Typhon, apparently now rescued from Tartarus). The reader sees the serpents that replace his legs, and Hera comfortably behind her desk at the Olympus Group, chewing on a golden apple, proclaiming that her "main corporate product … … shall be the deaths of the half-breeds Athena and Hercules!" (*IH* 123.23). This is a poor corporate business model, but not enough to stop Hera's outright villainy. The use of the racist derogatory term is striking, and given Pak's own mixed heritage, it is not accidental. The term might be thought to apply equally to Amadeus, in yet another way that he has found a path into the story of another hero. The echoes run deeper, however. Hera identifies herself as Hera Panhellenios, appropriating a cult title that is known from antiquity to belong to Zeus (it was his cult title in Aegina, for example).

Issues 124 and 125 present two American foundation texts: George Washington's Second Inaugural Address (a text chosen to coincide with the shift of the axis mundi and Atlas's supernatural shift to Washington DC) and the U.S. Constitution. These texts are interesting in a different way, but their inclusion, also edited by Cho, shows the precise shift that has already been demonstrated through Atlas in the comic. The importance for the axis mundi as (literally) what keeps the world spinning might also be tied to the omphalos, the belly-button of the ancient world, which was at Delphi. In the comic, the omphalos is an object that allows its holder to see their fondest wish, and bring it into being. After seeing the wishes of Herc, Namora, and Amadeus Cho, Artume eventually captures the omphalos, and is granted her fondest wish: a gender-flipped America, in which she is president, Amadeus Cho is her secretary, and Hercules is bound and imprisoned. The re-writing of the Constitution for *IH* 125 can therefore be seen as Artume's handiwork, overwriting reality with her will, and no longer just Amadeus' provision of a reference text for readers. If read as Cho's penmanship, a reader may instead see this as an extension of his function as amanuensis for Artume's new America. Cho and Herc set things right, and the reader is meant to accept the restoration of the patriarchal world we know as a victory.

All of this is mythmaking in the classical sense: building on previous narratives, telling a new story, but one that recognizes the specifics of geography in an attempt to explain a central feature of the world inhabited by the telling's immediate audience. The use of foundational texts offers a programmatic narrative that shows the longer tradition and provides a set of expectations from which variation and creative engagement are always possible.

I am not at this time going to dwell on Hera and the machinations of the New Olympus Group. Once it is established that Hera and other Greek gods are active in the world of the present day, the following story arc (*IH* 126-131) presents Hercules in conflict with the Olympus Group concerning Zeus. This leads to a katabasis and a trial of Zeus in the underworld, with him being tried before a jury of those he had sent there. In the underworld, Hercules encounters both Zeus and his own father Amphitryon, and consequently the katabasis leads to an investigation of the theme of fatherhood. The arc concludes with a combat between Hercules and himself – that is, "[his] own **shade**, which fell here to **Hades** upon [his] death—**after** Zeus raised the divine part of [Heracles] up to heaven" (130.22.1, with the fight at 131.3-7, 11-12, 15-17). Comics readers would be forgiven for not immediately seeing the unexpected allusion to Odysseus seeing Heracles in the underworld in *Odyssey* 11.601-604:

τὸν δὲ μετ' εἰσενόησα βίην Ἡρακληείην,
εἴδωλον: αὐτὸς δὲ μετ' ἀθανάτοισι θεοῖσι
τέρπεται ἐν θαλίῃς καὶ ἔχει καλλίσφυρον Ἥβην,
παῖδα Διὸς μεγάλοιο καὶ Ἥρης χρυσοπεδίλου.

After him [Sisyphos], I noticed mighty Heracles,
his image. He himself with the immortal gods
delights in the abundance and holds Hebe with the beautiful ankles,
the daughter of great Zeus and golden-sandaled Hera.

Since antiquity, this passage has caused interpretative problems, since the presence of an image (*eidolon*) in the underworld seems incompatible with a living and divine Heracles on Olympus. *IH* 131 confronts the apparent contradiction and turns it into a plot point. Of course, Herc is eventually able to rescue Zeus from the underworld, albeit with the consequence that Zeus now appears as a pre-pubescent child, not yet grown old enough to act on the urges he regularly describes.

As the story works towards its climax (*IH* 138-141, "Assault on New Olympus"), Hera, aided by Typhon, attempts to destroy the world, which is (again) saved by Herc, who nevertheless dies in the process. This arc's name seems designed to evoke an intermediary text that shapes its classical reception. A 1987 story, "Assault on Olympus" (*The Avengers* vol 1, #281-285; w. Roger Stern, a. John Buscema),[15] also positions Hercules, superheroes, and the Olympian pantheon in a way that needs to be interpretable for readers without a classical background. Pak and van Lente integrate a wider Marvel continuity, tying it to the Spider-Man network of stories with Aunt May volunteering in a soup kitchen of sorts and Peter Parker hitting on Hebe, Hercules' sometime wife, who is working as a receptionist at the Olympus Group.

This threatens to create another love triangle, of Spider-Man, Hercules, and Hebe the personification of eternal youth. Hebe is perhaps the most likeable character in the entire run, and is given a depth that no ancient author ever bothered to provide her with. She is introduced as a background character in a scene set in the foyer of the Olympus Group offices (*IH* 127.12-14), where she is the building receptionist. This ap-

---

15 Collected in *Avengers: Assault on Olympus*, w. Roger Stern and Bob Harras, a. John Buscema and Bob Hall (Marvel 2011).

pears initially as a slight joke, offering a where-are-they-now for a minor deity, who has been given a menial position at her mom's workplace. She is overlooked and insulted, seemingly present only to establish other characters' misogyny. She is next seen in the following issue, making her way home one day, where she has a wall of obsession with her (ex-)husband Hercules, comprising photos, beer ads, bobble-head dolls, and other memorabilia so she can dream of reuniting with him (*IH* 128.21-22). The reveal is both funny and an explanation of her actions that lead to Hera throwing her out of a skyscraper window (*IH* 129.12.1), and this provides an opportunity for the story to demonstrate Youth's powers always to regenerate.

Eventually, when Hebe meets Peter Parker, he mistakes her straightforward answers since he assumes she is a mortal teenager, like him: she says she comes from Olympus, which he thinks is the capital of Washington State (i.e. Olympia), and she corrects him that "It's the capital of everything" (*Assault on New Olympus Prologue* 12.3). She then describes her marriage to Hercules in a way that is so moving Peter kisses her, precisely as Hercules shows up (13-15). Is this Youth – beauty and vulnerability blended seamlessly while inspiring jealousy and passion? Whatever we think is happening, Hercules and Spider-Man fight for eight pages, before Hebe calls Hercules out on his double standard with regards to fidelity: "**Why** am I so **awful**? What is so **wrong** with me that you had to **flee** Olympus to be rid of me?" (24.5). She knows she is a daughter of Hera, but she does not accept his excuse, that his will cannot be tamed (25.4); the two are, for the moment, reconciled and kiss (28).

No one has thought more about Hebe as a person than Pak and van Lente, who position her simultaneously as both a naïve victim and the unconscious instigator of the thematically consistent actions that take place around her. Hera seeks reconciliation with her daughter, only to turn on her again when she realizes she continues to favour Hercules over her mother (*IH* 138.13-14), immediately before the Avengers come bursting through the doors for a big fight against those still allied with Hera. Hercules is on the side of the Avengers, and Hebe is with him.

With the announcement of Hercules' death at the end of the conflict with Hera and her new Olympians, the series ends. The monthly comic that had been *The Incredible Hulk*, in which Hulk is pushed aside in favour of another strongman, came to an end with the death of its (new) titular hero. With the defeat of the enemy, in "New Prince of Power", we see Amadeus Cho take over the Olympus Group, and attempt to become a responsible senior manager. In this new order, Hebe has been promoted to Cho's executive assistant, and she is even able to prevent Athena from entering Amadeus's office: she is bringing him tea, explicitly recapitulating her former Olympian function and now serving as "cupbearer to the chief executive" (*Fall of an Avenger* 2.21.3-4).

Athena had predicted that Amadeus would become the successor to Hercules (*IH* 126.21.6-22.1): "Even if, one day, Heracles should fall … | … There will come another," says Athena in the thirteenth century BCE, as she sees a vision of Amadeus Cho riding a moped in the twenty-first century CE. That vision is fulfilled in this arc, in multiple ways. A comics-era fulfilment of a historical/mythical event had already been intimated with a vision Athena has given to the prophet Tiresias, that Zeus "lay with [Alcmena] in

Amphitryon's form ... | ... so [she] might birth a savior for the world of gods and men from monsters and fearsome giants when they rise in revolt against heaven ..." (126.11.4). The panel does not show Herc completing any of his labours, however, but shows him battling the Hulk, in an image that appears to be taken from the same fight depicted on the cover of *IH* 107 (based on the blocking and framing, it could be Herc's return punch responding to that depicted on the cover). The promise of prophetic fulfilment within the comics narrative yokes the mythic with the comics world, but also grants a sense of larger significance to the *Incredible Hercules* storyline.

As is usual for serial superhero comics, companies are unwilling to abandon any intellectual property they might control, and so death is seldom long-lasting. Heracles receives an apotheosis at the end of *Heroic Age: Prince of Power* (4.22.1), a series that had presented Amadeus wielding Hercules' mace and running the Olympus Group. If there seems to be a sense of inevitability to the overall narrative of *Incredible Hercules*, from issues 106-141 and into *Chaos War*, it is because we have come to expect certain actions from our heroes. *IH* 116-120 had featured an arc in which Herc and Amadeus Cho, sent by Athena, team up with various immortal heroes – including the Japanese Shinto god of evil and chaos Amatsu-Mikaboshi – to form "the God Squad", on a space-faring mission to defeat the god of the alien Skrulls. Amatsu-Mikaboshi had been introduced in comics in 2006 (*Thor: Blood Oath* 6, February 2006; w. Michael Avon Oeming, a. Scott Kolins), and was a principal antagonist in the *Ares: The God of War* 2-5 (April–July 2006; w. Michael Avon Oeming, a. Travel Foreman). His presence on the God Squad is problematic in any case, but Pak and van Lente introduce him into *The Incredible Hercules* at this point in order to lay the foundation for *Chaos War*, in which Herc reforms the God Squad to combat the Chaos King, who is Amatsu-Mikaboshi. Following his death, Hercules returns with divine powers which he struggles to control, but we see him practising wisdom that has not been characteristic of his previous (comics) incarnation. His act of heroism consists of renouncing these powers, which leads to the de-powered and much more street-level story that follows in the short-lived series *Herc* (2011-12).

If the idea of a palimpsest proves inadequate to describe what is happening in the overall narrative of *The Incredible Hercules*, Pak and van Lente kindly offer an alternative: Joseph Campbell's Hero's Journey. There are many problems with the Hero's Journey (a pattern first identified in Campbell 1946), which have been discussed elsewhere (Rogers 2011; Bond & Christensen 2021). It is ahistorical and essentializing, its proponents cherry-pick examples, and it privileges a remarkably limited understanding of what constitutes heroism. At the same time, it is familiar, and it provides a model that many comics readers will know, typically filtered at least in part through its use as a patterning device in the *Star Wars* movies (see Wagner 1999).

In the story arc immediately before "Assault on New Olympus", Herc assumes the mantle of Thor in a conflict with Svartalfheim while Cho learns about the Hero's Journey (*IH* 132-137). Hercules and Thor had always been conceptually paired within the Marvel universe and had been frenemies since the 1960s, both strongman heroes but from different (but still European) pantheons. With the violence in these issues being depicted visually in a cartoonish manner, I believe this sequence is meant to be read as a critique of Campbell's reductive approach to creating a hero. The whole arc is played for humour, with Herc becoming "The Mighty Thorcules" and defending Asgard from an invasion of Dark Elves from Svartalfheim, who are led by Queen Alflyse. Herc and the child-sized Zeus are both immediately smitten. Meanwhile, Amadeus is on a bus in Utah where, mysteriously, he finds a book in the seat pocket in front of him that summarizes Joseph Campbell's stages of the Hero's Journey in brief, digestible chunks. The potted summaries read like the Wikipedia entry (and use the same terms, as it happens), but Pak and van Lente pull back the curtain to reveal how this book that Cho reads fits into the wider narrative. In a quick re-cap, all that has happened so far in *IH* is presented as if it were part of the Hero's Journey: The Call to Adventure (*IH* 106-111), Refusal of the Call (*IH* 113-115), Supernatural Aid (Athena), Crossing of the First Threshold (*IH* 116-120), and Belly of the Whale (*IH* 121-125, *IH* 126-131). These are marked explicitly, and (in the tradition of the Marvel megatext) with footnotes.

The footnotes in Marvel comics are always important, pointing readers to other issues, sometimes from the same month, but sometimes years in the past. They might indicate the last time a particular character appeared, even if it was in another title, or the last time two characters fought, for example. It is and was a system whereby a comic's editor (no doubt often ventriloquized by the author) references the wider network of continuity while helping establish an insider connection with the reader, reinforcing the superstructure of the megatext. These "new paratextual apparatuses" establish a relationship, with the result that "the reader-as-fan became the basic axiom and article of faith in so-called mainstream comic book publishing" (Woo 2020, 117). This in turn allows writers to show off their research (they knew the previous storylines of the heroes they were writing, and knew when two characters might have last seen each other), and also created links to unfamiliar texts for the readers. These links were essential in binding the megatext together, operationalizing it for a literate age in a kind of meandering thread, so that (one might imagine) one could start at any place and soon be conversant in the intricacies of previous Marvel narratives.[16]

By having Cho read these discrete steps that Hercules has taken, the authors make explicit what they have been doing, giving Herc a Hero's Journey. By placing the interpretation as a discarded book on a bus, however, they simultaneously disavow the authority of the programmatic text. (The copy Cho finds even has pictures, if you can imagine it: words and images together!) Further, the reader is authorized to see

---

16   There were other ways the megatext could be inculcated into an eager imagination. As an adolescent beginning to read comics in the late 1970s, I wondered how anyone could know all the previous Marvel stories. I began collecting *What If…?* (47 issues, 1977-1984), which offered alternate-history versions of key Marvel stories. Through this series, I learned (a) what the key Marvel storylines were, and (b) what didn't happen, which allowed me to infer what had happened in the older books that were far outside of my price range and so inaccessible. Indeed, some of these alternative narratives did anticipate changes that would be introduced into the stories of characters later.

the book as having been left there for Cho by Athena herself. Since Athena is morally ambiguous in her support for Hercules, it makes sense that, as so often, the paradigm does not exactly fit: there are two "Belly of the Whale" episodes, one involving being underwater with Namora (and so not a trial in the usual sense), and only the second being a katabasis proper. There are some genuine insights as well. For example, the book notes that the guardian of the First Threshold is often a shapeshifter of sorts: this is made literal in the relevant section of *Incredible Hercules* because the figure in question is revealed to be a Skrull, one of the shapeshifting colonializing alien species that will eventually conquer Earth.

There are two additional ways in which the Hero's Journey interacts with the larger series in a programmatic way. First, some readers might know the pattern well enough to know what is to come. Two stages in particular seem to me to be heavily foreshadowed: The Road of Trials and the Meeting with the Goddess are both applicable, and they come next, marked explicitly within this same story arc. More ominous, however, is the presence of Apotheosis on the Hero's Journey, since this anticipates both the death and return of Hercules, and does indeed point to Cho's true purpose in the narrative.

Amadeus Cho has been designated as Hercules' successor: chosen by Athena, he is to be an intellectual exemplar for the modern age, set to replace Hercules as her groomed favourite. Cho doesn't know this, but as it is announced, the prominence of the character throughout the series is explained. This, in turn, invites associations with each of the previously identified steps and Amadeus' adventures. They too, I suggest, also have analogues in Campbell's pattern, and sometimes they appear for Cho earlier than they do for Hercules. For Cho, they will also culminate with an apotheosis. How this is accomplished is outlined in *Fall of an Avenger*, the two-issue miniseries that follows *Incredible Hercules*. *Fall* sees Cho in charge of the Olympus Group, and as the inheritor of Hercules' position in the period after Herc's death. With the combined resources of the corporation, he is able to secure happiness for himself and Delphyne, and grow in power, which is what Athena intended. Now possessing divine powers through which he could advance himself, Amadeus (Loved by God?) chooses to forego all this power in order to restore Hercules to life. It is an incredible and selfless gesture, and one that helps restore the status quo ante. It is a renewed Hercules, now appearing as the god of heroes, who will lead the battle against the Chaos King (in *Chaos War* 1-5).[17] The book Amadeus finds in the bus seat pocket demonstrates, on a metaliterary level, that both Hercules and Cho are fulfilling their respective obligations to the narrative well.

The Incredible Hercules offers a great deal to scholars looking at classical reception, and operates at several levels while integrating "the Lion of Olympus" more deeply into the Marvel universe, in the character's most extended foregrounding in the 60 years he has been a Marvel character. Readers can draw conclusions about the substitution of Herc for Hulk, as a second-tier superhero replaces an iconic character at the peak of his popu-

---

17   Lund 2015 offers an overview of the series, noting that while presenting comics as a modern mythology can easily be overstated, "there are similarities in how the two genres intersect in 'Chaos War'".

larity. That placement by itself creates meaning. We see practices within Marvel comics that create mythic narratives, and these also replicate how myths generated meaning in antiquity, engaging creatively with other ancient texts and with larger mythic patterns that have shaped other narrative forms. Seeing Amadeus Cho as both an Iolaus figure and as a new Hercules deepens our appreciation of what the writers and artists understand about the characters, and through the process we come to an enriched understanding of Hercules as well. There is a narrative payoff when Hercules returns with divine powers, as it elevates the overall story to the cosmic level without cheapening the meaning or impact of the character's recent death. As the conclusion to *Chaos War* confirms, this was the story of Amadeus Cho. But it is also a story of Hercules, and it is situated in a context that ties him closely to the Incredible Hulk. Like all good creatures of myth, when thinking about the Hulk, the process of analysis deepens what it is we perceive. The transition over the course of *IH* replaces a nuclear-age hero with a bronze-age one, and ends up killing them both (though of course death in comics typically lacks the annoying permanence it has in real life). It is in the mutual entanglement of Hulk, Herc, and Amadeus Cho that the story of *The Incredible Hercules* achieves its purpose, as it weaves itself deeply into the wider tapestry which is the Marvel megatext.

Bibliography

Bond, S. & Christensen, J. 2021. "The Man Behind the Myth: Should We Question the Hero's Journey?". *LARB* 12 August 2021. https://www.lareviewofbooks.org/article/the-man-behind-the-myth-should-we-question-the-heros-journey/, last accessed 22 July 2024.

Campbell, J. 1946. *The Hero with a Thousand Faces*, 3rd ed. 2008. New York: Pantheon.

CBR Staff 2017. "15 Most Iconic Hulk Covers". *Comic Book Resources*, 21 March 2017. https://www.cbr.com/most-iconic-hulk-comic-book-covers/, last accessed 22 July 2024.

Darowski, J. & Darowski, J.J. 2016. "Smashing Cold War Consensus Culture: Hulk's Journey form Monster to Hero", in: Darowski 2016, 7-23.

Darowski, J.J. (ed.) 2016. *The Ages of the Incredible Hulk: Essays on the Green Goliath in Changing Times*. Jefferson, NC: McFarland.

Frazer, J.G. 1921. *Apollodorus: The Library*, 2 vols. Cambridge, MA: Harvard University Press.

Gantz, T. 1993. *Early Greek Myth: A Guide to Literary and Artistic Sources*, 2 vols. Baltimore: Johns Hopkins University Press.

Hatfield, C. 2012. *Hand of Fire: The Comics Art of Jack Kirby*. Jackson: University Press of Mississippi.

Kaveney, R. 2005. *From Alien to The Matrix: Reading Science Fiction Film*. London & New York: I.B. Tauris.

Kaveney, R. 2008. *Superheroes! Capes and Crusaders in Comics and Film*. London & New York: I.B. Tauris.

Keen, T. 2022. "'In our midst …an immortal!': Hercules in 1960s Marvel comics". *FA the comiczine*. http://comiczine-fa.com/features/in-our-midst-an-immortal-hercules-in-1960s-marvel-comics, last accessed 22 July 2024.

Koning, H. 2020. "The Incredible Hercules: Prince of Power," in: Blanshard, A.J.L. & Stafford, E. (eds) 2020. *The Modern Hercules: Images of the Hero from the Nineteenth to the Early Twenty-First Century*. Leiden: Brill, 199-218.

Kovacs, G. & Marshall, C.W. (eds) 2011. *Classics and Comics*. Oxford: Oxford University Press.

Kovacs, G. & Marshall, C.W. (eds) 2016. *Son of Classics and Comics*. Oxford: Oxford University Press.

Lerberg, J. 2016. "Becoming Nature's 'Monster': How the Gamma Bomb Reterritorializes the Human World", in: Darowski 2016, 24-24.

Lund, M. 2015. "Review: Marvel's Chaos War, An Epic (of Sorts)". *Sacred and Sequential*. http://www.sacredandsequential.org/2015/03/16/review-marvels-chaos-war-an-epic-of-sorts/, last accessed 22 July 2024.

Marshall, C.W. (forthcoming) "Hercules in Marvel Comics", in: Harrison, G.W.M. (ed.), *A Companion to Hercules*. Chichester: Wiley-Blackwell.

Murphy, C. 2010. "Nothing is Bad: Chaos War #1 [Review]". *Comics Alliance*. https://comicsalliance.com/chaos-war-1-review/, last accessed 22 July 2024.

Pagnoni Burns, F.G. & Merino, C.A. 2016. "A Globe-Trotting Atomic Weapon: Illustrating the Cold War Arms Race", in: Darowski 2016, 35-48.

Rogers, B.M. 2011. "Heroes UnLimited: The Theory of the Hero's Journey and the Limitation of the Superhero Myth," in: Kovacs & Marshall 2011, 73-86.

Segal, C. 1983. "Greek Myth as a Semiotic and Structural System and the Problem of Tragedy". *Arethusa* 16, 173-198.

Silk, M. 1985. "Heracles in Greek Tragedy". *Greece and Rome* 32, 1-22.

Southgate, B. 2016. "'I didn't come here for a whisper': Monsters, Violence and Heroes in *World War Hulk* and Post-9/11 America", in: Darowski 2016, 193-205.

Tucker, Larry. 1963. Letter, published in "Let's Talk about the Hulk," The Incredible Hulk vol. 1, 5 (January 1963; w. Stan Lee, a. Jack Kirby). https://readcomiconline.li/Comic/The-Incredible-Hulk-1962/Issue-5?id=18387#26, last accessed 22 July 2024.

TVtropes. N.d. "Buddy Cop Show," *TVtropes.com*. https://tvtropes.org/pmwiki/pmwiki.php/Main/BuddyCopShow

Wagner, P.M. (dir.). 1999. *The Mythology of Star Wars, with George Lucas and Bill Moyers*. Public Affairs Television. https://www.youtube.com/watch?v=pjaUeNd1kq8, last accessed 22 July 2024.

Wilson, E.R. 2004. *Mocked with Death: Tragic overliving from Sophocles to Milton*. Baltimore: Johns Hopkins University Press.

Windsor-Smith, B. (w./a.) 2021. *Monsters*. Seattle: Fantagraphics.

Woo, Benjamin. 2020. "Readers, Audiences, and Fans", in: Hatfield, C. & Beaty, B. (ed.) 2020. *Comics Studies: A Guidebook*. New Brunswick: Rutgers University Press, 113-125.

10

ANCIENT HISTORY AMPLIFIED

HERODOTUS, HEAVY METAL AND THE IRON MAIDEN

CHRISTIAN THRUE DJURSLEV

Introduction

The present paper brings the music genre of heavy metal into the conversation about classical antiquity in popular culture. I offer two case studies of how this genre riffs on the ancient world, focusing on receptions of the renowned Queen Tomyris, the "iron maiden",[1] who first appeared in the historical narrative of the ancient Greek storyteller Herodotus (1.205-214). Both case studies investigate novel receptions that, taken together, say something significant about antiquity's polyvalence and heavy metal's polyphony in popular culture.

Heavy metal is one of the most successful genres of commercial rock music. It began as a rebellious youth movement in the impoverished industrial areas of Great Britain in the late 1960s and 70s, breaking into the cultural mainstream with Metallica's *The Black Album* (1991). It thrives across continents, as it continues to evolve and expand its cultural production. Given its status as a global phenomenon, it can be said to fulfil some traditional criteria for being "popular culture",[2] such as the fact that is part of mass culture and a cultural product by "the people".[3] Yet another label of popular culture theory may be applied to heavy metal music, namely contestation of hegemony. The

---

[1] Gera 1997, 187, n. 2, gives a possible etymology of "Tomyris", connecting the name to the Turkic words for "iron" and "virgin".

[2] These definitions may be found in Grig 2017, 3, which updates *inter alios* Parker 2011.

[3] One striking example comes from the music in the fourth season of Netflix's *Stranger Things*, in which one of the characters covers Metallica's "Master of Puppets" (1986) in the last episode. This reuse of it saw the track soar into the UK top 40, at 22, as the band's first song on that list since 2008 (for the statistics, see Beaumont-Thomas 2022). Some perspective is provided by the effects of the show's inclusion of a more regular "pop" song: Kate Bush's "Running Up That Hill" (1985) became a new no. 1 hit for weeks, 37 years after its original release. Of course, this example should not stand alone; Metallica's album "72 Seasons" (14 April 2023) hit number one on charts across Europe, the US, UK, and Australia.

music genre began as a counterculture, which it remains today in rather new contexts in Britain and far beyond.[4]

More recent theoretical work foregrounds levels of authorization: although heavy metal bands tend to produce music for certain groups – their fans – these cultural products (songs, albums, concerts, merchandise, and so on) need not be authorized by an official instance, such as an institution or a music company, though they often are. In this sense, artists may escape some of the typical dichotomies, such as the culture of the elite versus the masses,[5] for anybody can theoretically participate. This participation in turn can be authorized or unauthorized: people can engage with the heavy metal universe and create something new, like a cover band, or make a passing comment on something in public fora or at a live concert.

Broadly speaking, study of heavy metal receptions may refine some of the theoretical work.[6] For example, just within this volume, Lorna Hardwick calls for "subtlety" as a guiding principle for studying classical reception, especially in literature. Of course, Hardwick does not refer to it as an absolute principle, but, if we were to privilege subtlety, some of what is studied in this volume might not qualify. This is certainly true for the present chapter, for heavy metal music is hardly subtle – quite the opposite. The genre confronts. As is well known, classics as a discipline can also be confrontational and take direct action against problematic groups,[7] so more direct receptions are worth taking into account.

In any event, the ancient worlds of heavy metal are currently receiving much scholarly attention.[8] Electrified by the emergence of heavy metal studies,[9] scholars of classical reception have undertaken a broad range of activities. The evidence is compiled in the comprehensive bibliography on the blog site of the self-styled "metal classicist" Jeremy Swist.[10] According to the general overview he supplies, researchers have pro-

---

4 See, for example, the documentary "Sirens" about the all-female Lebanese metal band Slave to Sirens, reported by Farber 2022.
5 Cf. the discussions of this topic in this volume's chapters by Andrew Faulkner, Marianne Pade, and Lorna Hardwick.
6 Heavy metal is not a typical area of interest in classical reception handbooks. See, for example, Hardwick 2003 and Willis 2017. For a succinct history of classical reception, see Maurice 2017, 5-8.
7 In her contribution, Hardwick herself mentions the Vassar-based *Pharos* website, which combats appropriations by hate groups.
8 Umurhan 2012 can be considered one of the first serious calls to arms. Fletcher & Umurhan 2020 is a good manifestation of this interest. See reviews in Djurslev 2020, Farrell 2021, and Kiilerich 2021.
9 Self-styled "Metallectuals" formed an International Society for Metal Music Studies (ISMMS) after three major conferences at the end of the 2000s. The society consolidated the field with an academic journal, *Metal Music Studies*, now in its seventh year and published three times annually. Over 2,300 items in a well-kept bibliography speak to the rapid rise of the field: https://metalstudies.org/biblio/index.php (last accessed November 2022).
10 Swist 2021.

duced detailed studies of classicizing band names and lyrical themes, thereby generating knowledge of the wide appeal of Greece and Rome to artists in this branch of music. They have charted how bands rewrite a rich array of sources principally excerpted from movies and fiction, with content ranging from mayhem, myths, and wars to gods, monsters, and hypermasculine heroes like Achilles and Alexander. Studies of language, gender, cover art, and performance have further enriched our understanding of the changing ways in which metal bands have amplified classical antiquity to address an increasingly global audience.

Two themes tend to dominate current debates among researchers: (1) the relationship between globalism and nationalism, and (2) egalitarianism in every aspect of society.[11] The former is the dynamic between national and global representations of classical antiquity, representations which Osman Umurhan and Kris Fletcher divide into the national receptions coming from the countries around the Mediterranean Sea, that is, "Mediterranean metal", and global receptions – those from elsewhere. This separation is useful because spatial differences often lead to new receptions that challenge traditional narratives of antiquity (typically in global metal) or embrace some aspects of them (typically in Mediterranean metal).[12] The second theme emphasizes the diversification of heavy metal bands and audiences, focusing on how artists make heavy metal music more egalitarian in matters of gender, race, place, and sex.[13]

Despite the impressive body of previous work, much remains to be done on either theme, let alone both together. In this paper, I aim to contribute to these discussions by exploring how bands have represented a female ruler from ancient history. In the first case study, I consider the way in which Tomyris is represented as a national hero of Romania in the track "Tomiris", the first song on the album *Naemul Dacilor* (2016) by the folk metal band Ka Gaia An from Bucharest. This study brings to the fore another reception from the region of Mediterranean metal, but outside the usual sites of Greece, Egypt, and Italy. The selection is significant, since the classical reception of the Romanian metal stage is relatively unknown, even though it is one of many important areas in ancient history. Given the Romanian lyrics and self-conducted production, the track has not been easily accessible, but it nevertheless remains notable as an instance of a classical reception. The case study thus grants wider access to a feature of this country's storytelling for the first time.

In the second case study, I explore the representation of Tomyris as a powerful female ruler and fierce fighter in the track "Tomyris" released on the album *It was Metal* (2018) by the American band A Sound of Thunder (Washington DC). I argue that the track engages in counter-discourse that subverts legitimizing discourses deployed by men on the metal stage. Such discourses pertain to an ethos of individualism, courage, strength, and violent justice retrieved from a long-lost era. The band uses the Tomyris figure to

---

11 See, for example, Umurhan 2020, 213.
12 Fletcher & Umurhan 2020, 14.
13 Ådshede & Foka 2020.

challenge such stereotypes and thereby to reclaim the ancient world as a place in which such female power was expressed.

Reception studies call for rigorous collaborative work across disciplines. In the present case, one person cannot hope to conduct a complete analysis of the range of subjects, languages, and domain-specific knowledge involved. For the first case study, I have sought specific assistance with the Romanian lyrics, and I am thankful that Flavia Teoc has supplied me with a full translation that readers may consult in Appendix 1. Ideally, a detailed focus on lyrics needs supplementing with musicological analysis, and for that task, I am grateful to my colleague Niels Christian Hansen, who has provided a full musical analysis of the track for the second case study.[14] I have otherwise consigned myself to discussing the lyrical themes, focusing on the representations of Tomyris and the reworkings of Herodotus.

Introducing the protagonist: Tomyris and the contestation of her story

In the following, I retell the Herodotean tale and consider how it continues to elicit various responses. I identify some salient features of Tomyris' contemporary reception, which anticipate the ensuing case studies about globalism–nationalism and egalitarianism. However, as a pivot for the discussion, it is impossible to avoid the award-winning cinematic blockbuster which has recently catapulted Tomyris into contemporary consciousness.

The Legend of Tomiris (2019, Kazahkfilm) is directed by Akan Sataev and chronicles the untold story of Tomyris' life at length (official runtime: 2 hours and 36 minutes). The leading role is played by Kazakhstani native Almira Tursun,[15] whose character is raised to the hard camp life by her father, Spargapeithes. When he is slain during political in-fighting among the clans of the Saka-Massagetae, Tomiris not only avenges her father, but also unites the clans and ascends the throne. She remains clan leader when she marries a man to whom she bears a son. Eventually her new family is killed by the Persian warlord Cyrus the Great (Ghassan Massoud). Tomiris does not retaliate until Cyrus crosses into her realm. Her inevitable victory over the overreaching despot follows a bloody battle.

The Legend of Tomiris provides Tomyris with an original backstory, but otherwise adheres to the principal source text of Herodotus' *Histories*. Tomyris springs fully formed from Herodotus' head to end the biography of King Cyrus of Persia, the so-called "tale of Cyrus" or *Kyros logos* (Hdt. 1.95-214).[16] Given this narrative focus, Tomyris functions

---

14   He is not responsible for any errors of interpretation that may have crept into my outline of the song below.
15   The actress has had a remarkable rise to national fame: she worked as a psychologist but was picked to play the part of Tomyris from a group of 15,000 people. In 2022, she won the Mrs Kazakhstan Globe-2022 beauty contest.
16   *The Herodotus Encyclopedia*, s.v. "Tomyris" (Rebecca Futo Kennedy).

"Tomyris", illustration by Trav Hart, 2017 – client work for ASOT, https://travhart.com/portfolio/a-sound-of-thunder/

Fig. 1.

as an antagonist, with her resistance to the Persian invader marking the climatic close of Book 1. It is the only feat recorded about her.[17]

The Herodotean narrative may be summarized as follows. The historian decides to highlight two phases of Cyrus' conquest, focusing first on the siege of the great city of Babylon and second on the invasion of a vast, if uncultivated, land controlled by the Massagetan tribe. To claim the latter, King Cyrus offers his hand in marriage to Queen Tomyris, who rejects his advances (205.1). Contrary to the opinion of his Persian counsellors, Cyrus decides to invade her territory, prompted by the war counsel of a single advisor, Croesus (207-208), a monarch of Lydia in Asia Minor captured by Cyrus. Croesus goads Cyrus to exploit the Massagetans. He emphasizes not only the fact that they cannot tolerate Persian amenities like alcohol, but also that their ruler is inferior because of her gender (207.5-6). Croesus also designs a stratagem that Cyrus deploys to draw first blood. The Persians leave a camp poorly guarded as bait for a third of the Massagetan force, who raid it and enjoy a particularly sumptuous feast. Cyrus counterattacks while the revellers sleep, capturing Sargapises, Tomyris' son (211). Tomyris requests his release by envoy, swearing an oath that she will satiate Cyrus' thirst for blood if he refuses her

---

17   Note the observation already in Giovanni Boccaccio's *On Famous Women* § 49, a Renaissance biography featuring Tomyris: "We know nothing about Tamyris (sic) except this deed, as famous as Cyrus' empire was great" (trans. Brown).

10 • Ancient history amplified   **171**

(212). Cyrus ignores her message, but releases Sargapises when the youth demands it (213). Sargapises commits suicide in the very moment of freedom, presumably ashamed of the manner of his defeat (loss and intoxication). When the news reaches Tomyris, a widow who has now also lost her son, the queen takes the field. A fierce battle ensues and, although the two sides were evenly matched (214.2), Cyrus himself is killed, and Tomyris' army eventually achieves victory.

A gory set-piece caps the tale. In the aftermath of the battle, Tomyris locates Cyrus' body on the battlefield. Like Achilles over the vanquished Hector (Hom. *Il.* 22.364-366), Tomyris gloats over the fallen Cyrus and proceeds to defile his remains. She does not drag the corpse behind a chariot, but rather submerges the severed head in a wineskin brimming with human blood. Tomyris addresses the sack with the head in direct speech, saying that, although Cyrus has ended her bloodline (1.214.3), her oath to Cyrus is fulfilled; she has given him his fill of blood (212.2-3; 214.4).

The story is such a masterfully dramatic narrative that it may seem incredible. Indeed, it is replete with highly conventional features of Herodotean storytelling.[18] For instance, this is but one of many female revenge stories in *The Histories*. Herodotus casts Tomyris in a similar role to the one he gives the vengeful wife of Candaules (1.7-14), who plays an active role in the killing of her husband at the beginning of Book 1. Moreover, the story replays key themes of Greek epic and tragedy. For example, the battle between Tomyris and Cyrus is the "most violent of battles fought among the barbarians" (1.214.1), and Tomyris' address to Cyrus' severed head reflects a tragic ending of the story. Even Herodotus himself urges caution. As the very last remark on the entire affair – a terse authorial comment – he discloses that he knew many accounts of Cyrus' demise besides the one he told; he opted for the one with Tomyris because he himself found it the "most credible" among the many versions.[19] When set against Herodotus' confident introduction to the sources for the early life of Cyrus, the variegated accounts of Cyrus' demise fall short in truth value.[20]

Such features should mean modern readers hesitate in accepting the historicity of the tale, but this has not been the case. At the time of writing, in most of the 900 reviews on *The Legend of Tomiris*' page on the Internet Movie Database (IMDb), users refer to Herodotus' absolute authority for the narrative backbone of the film. This public interest is (sadly) not prompted by some newfound passion for one of the first major historians, but rather a response to the Iranian contestation of the story. In the same forum, Iranian users argue that Cyrus was not defeated by some upstart queen, asserting that his final resting place is a tomb near the Pasargadae palace in the Fars region, a UNESCO

---

18 For a general commentary on the episode, see now Dewald & Munson 2022, 462-482. Cf. Asheri 2007, 212-218.

19 Hdt. 1.214.5. τὰ μὲν δὴ κατὰ τὴν Κύρου τελευτὴν τοῦ βίου πολλῶν λόγων λεγομένων ὅδε μοι ὁ πιθανώτατος εἴρηται.

20 Chiasson 2012 makes this case well. Regarding Cyrus' birth (Hdt. 1.95), Herodotus claims to know four versions but chooses a source of Persian origin that did not magnify (σεμνοῦν) Cyrus' deeds but told the story "how it really was" (τὸν ἐόντα λέγειν λόγον).

heritage site.[21] Within the past 45 years, the tomb has garnered increasing political and social significance, to the extent that Iran celebrates Cyrus Day (29 October) and the Persian New Year (20 March) at the site.[22] These Iranian interpretations find support in the great mass of ancient writings about Cyrus,[23] most famously an eyewitness report about Alexander the Great's visit to the tomb, preserved in the Romano-Greek authors of the early imperial period Strabo of Amesia and Arrian of Nicomedia.[24]

There is no way to resolve the conflicting ancient accounts,[25] nor the debate in the online forum. I record it as a representative example of how classical antiquity matters to national identity creation. People in public spaces often make recourse to ancient materials to augment a sense of shared identity, which is why such retrievals are rarely politically innocent. This is certainly true of modern re-uses of Tomyris' tale. To return to *The Legend of Tomiris*,[26] the Kazakhstani Ministry of Culture and Sports financially supported the production of the movie. One key producer was Aliya Nazarbayeva, the daughter of the first president of the country. This production is not a singular instance of Kazakhstani national reception. Since gaining independence in 1991, Kazakhstan has disseminated nationalistic representations of Tomyris on media, such as coins and monuments, which creates a public sphere that reinforces their invented heritage.

Kazakhstani appropriation of Tomyris matters not only because some people contest her very existence, but also because many other nations than Kazakhstan lay claim to her. She is a hero in western Turkey, Azerbaijan, and Uzbekistan – countries more than 2,000 miles apart. Admittedly, Herodotus gave a rather vague geography of her realm (1.200-204), so to make a claim to her legacy is easy. Kazakhstanis attempt to reclaim the queen for a specific purpose, but there are many other agents across a wide geopolitical landscape that make their own claims to Tomyris' legacy.

The broad contestation of Tomyris enables much remaking of her meaning. One notable instance occurs in the feminist writings of the Uzbek poet Halima Xudoyberdiyeva (1947-2018). Her last work was the *The Sayings of Tomyris* (*To'marisning Aytgani*, 1996), which give Tomyris a personal voice and a role beyond the conflict with Cyrus. Of course, the Herodotean tale lends itself particularly well to a form of radical feminism, as argued by Edith Hall, who has also contributed to this volume. In a blogpost on the *Edithorial*, Hall considers Tomyris a female leader resisting imperial oppression

---

21 *Enc. Ir.* s.v. CYRUS v. The Tomb of Cyrus (Antigoni Zournatzi). The building could be a cenotaph, of course.
22 Overview in Ansari 2021. Cf. Waters 2022, 178-183.
23 See, e.g., Plin. *HN* 6.116; Solinus § 55.
24 Aristobulus *BNJ* 139 F 51a ap. Arr. *Anab.* 6.29.4-11 and F 51b ap. Strabo 15.3.7 (730). It is also notable that Xenophon of Athens (*Cyr.* 8.6) contested the Herodotean tale by having Cyrus die peacefully abed surrounded by family. Cf. *Enc. Ir.* s.v. CYRUS iiia. Cyrus as portrayed by Xenophon and Herodotus (Robert Faulkner).
25 See already Sancisi-Weerdenburg 1985, 461, "there is no such thing as a historically reliable account of the last days of Cyrus". Cf. Briant 2003, 49.
26 Hall 2020 humorously invokes the second film of the *Borat* franchise with her blogpost title "the real Kazakh Subsequent Movie Film".

in the style of other ancient rulers, including Cleopatra of Egypt, Zenobia of Palmyra, and Boudica of Britain. Hall even commends the *Legend of Tomiris* just upon viewing the trailer; she states explicitly that she feels inspired to imagine herself "as a she-hero galloping over the Steppes with righteous wrath in my heart and a freedom agenda".[27]

To sum up, I hope to have shown how the varied tales of Tomyris illustrate her wide appeal and application in various cultures, whether national or international. This variation is notable, not least because the original Herodotean story principally highlights her antagonism with Cyrus. But as national lore and political agendas feed into the retellings of Tomyris' story, the cultural production moves far beyond Herodotus and even becomes contested territory. The results engender a polyvalent tradition that makes for a fascinating object of study in itself. In the next couple of case studies, I seek to contextualize two heavy metal receptions that contribute to this polyphony.

Tomyris as national hero of Romania: Ka Gaia An, "Tomiris" (*Naemul Dacilor*, 2016)

In this section, I explore the lyrical themes of a Romanian heavy metal track about Tomyris.[28] I analyse the lyrics with a view to the reworking of the Herodotean themes and the exposition of the song's patriotic features. I then compare the track's contents to national and ancient lore, particularly the traditions about Constanța (ancient Tomis), which reinforce the Romanian reclamation of the Tomyris figure. Lastly, I situate this particular appropriation of her story within the wider themes in Mediterranean metal.

Ka Gaia An play folk metal, which incorporates traditional folk instruments and folklore (note also the choice of band name: Gaia, 'earth mother'). The selected folklore is Dacian, insofar as the band has privileged a particular part of ancient history on their first and only album, *Naemul Dacilor* (2016,) or 'the nation of the Dacians'. The Dacians were a sub-tribe of the Thracians and eventually an independent kingdom in the Danube region; later they were integrated into the Roman Empire as a province, but the region was hardly stable. The album consists of tracks that attempt to hark back to this people, who occupied the same regions as the modern state of Romania. The album can thus be considered a concept album about putative national ancestors.

"Tomiris" is the first track on the album, indicating her role in this story. Indeed, the twice repeated lines "You are the queen of the Dacians at Pontus Euxinus / Over a mighty people with a great fate" represent her as a starting point of the Dacian people. The lyrics reinforce that connection in the first lines of the fourth verse: "Today free Dacians dance their dance close to the ember fire". The emphasis on future greatness links the Romanian present with the Dacian distant past. The present state of the country suggests that Tomyris has accomplished her mission.

---

27 Hall 2020.
28 The album and the track can be found on the band's Bandcamp site: https://kagaiaan.bandcamp.com/album/neamul-dacilor (last accessed February 2023). As already noted, a full English translation of the lyrics is available in Appendix 1.

It is primarily the second verse that contains material that can be seen to engage with the Herodotean version of the story, at least as a point of reference. The second verse refers to Tomyris' defeat of Cyrus, and it integrates some of the principal features, as follows: one line refers specifically to the oath Tomyris swore in direct speech when her son died in Cyrus' captivity ("swore by the sun"), thus highlighting the revenge theme. The name of the son is given. Cyrus is described as a "bloody Persian", no doubt referring to his excessive bloodlust and grim ending. The concluding note that Cyrus was "fortunate until he met you" stresses the very Herodotean theme of good fortune. The relevant lines, four in total, may be characterized as appropriation proper, and this effective summary is rather faithful to the reference object. Nevertheless, the band has made a slight alteration that creates a semantic shift: when the son dies, he is said to have gone to Zalmoxis and his ancestors. Zalmoxis has had many receptions, but in this case his role as a Thracian deity of the dead is probably meant.[29] The insertion makes sense, but the explicit association of the dead son with Zalmoxis is novel.

The other verses contain material that goes well beyond the Herodotean narrative. We have already seen that the attribution of Tomyris' origin to Dacia obfuscates her much more eastern associations of Herodotus and his Massagetans or, later, with the Getae (see below). In this context, it is notable that the band places her geographically at the Black Sea, with reference to its Latin name ("Pontus Euxinus"). The first verse in particular amplifies this image of a national queen, given that she reigns "from the sea to the Carpathians", a massive mountain range occupying much of Romania (eastern and southern Carpathians). Moreover, one may consider Tomyris further disjointed from the reference object of Herodotus' text insofar as the band describe the queen's looks, which Herodotus never did. The band describe her as a "tempestuous apparition with eyes of iris flowers / The wild Tomiris, with long blond locks". The physical description suggests fair skin, deep blue eyes, and blond hair, and she even rides a white horse to match. This evocative visual representation supplements the Herodotean narrative in which the Scythians ride horses, but Herodotus never mentions that Tomyris' Massagetans do so explicitly.[30] The band therefore dresses Tomyris as a stereotypical hero on horseback, as well as in a form more fitting to the Romanian reception culture, certainly in the central and eastern European contexts. Perhaps the most overt assimilation of Tomyris with modern national identity occurs in the third verse, where the flowers said to worship the queen are the colours of the Romanian flag.

That Tomyris has such potential for a national reception in Romania is corroborated by ancient authorities competing with the Herodotean version. Her kingdom is resituated at the Black Sea in the writings of the miscellanist Lucius Ampelius and the historian Ammianus Marcellinus, two Roman writers of the fourth century.[31] Lucius Ampelius states that "Cyrus conquered part of Asia and would have entered Europe,

---

29 Hdt. 4.93-96 mentions him in a completely different context. For an overview of Zalmoxis' Greek tradition, see Taufer 2008.
30 Note Hdt. 1.216.4 states that the Massagetans were said to revere horses.
31 First pointed out by Fontaine 1977, 60-61, n. 137, *ad loc*.

had he not been defeated by Tomyris, queen of Scyths",[32] thus implying a different direction of travel from Herodotus. Ammianus makes explicit the link with the Black Sea in a lengthy digression that, for more than half of Book 23, overwrites Greek and Roman accounts of previous "Persian" wars. Ammianus claims that Cyrus "crossed the strait of Bosporus with a force of legendary size, and was destroyed to the point of annihilation by Tomyris, the queen of the Scythians, that most fierce avenger of sons".[33] Accordingly, both authors associate Cyrus' death with campaigns against Europe, perhaps to realign Cyrus' ambitions with the later Persian kings Darius I and Xerxes. In this way, conquest of Europe becomes the ultimate ambition, and therefore paradigmatic, of the Asia-based emperor. That Tomyris is represented as a female bulwark of Europe against an eastern oppressor stands out.

The late antique relocation of Tomyris' realm enabled a more elaborate rewrite by the Latin historian Jordanes, active in sixth-century Byzantium. He wove Tomyris' story into his reconfiguration of one of late antiquity's most prominent nomadic tribes, the Goths. He used her link to the Getae (cf. the Massa*getae*) to establish this ethnographical connection. Jordanes' ethnogeny integrated her great military victory over Cyrus into Gothic history,[34] thus furnishing that nation with a more glorious backstory to match their meteoric rise to power around 300 AD. Jordanes essentially considers Tomyris a proto-Goth and is the first author to grant her a degree of lasting agency. He records that,

> having been rendered greater by the victory and having acquired so much booty from the enemy, queen Thomyris (sic) crossed into the part of Moesia, which is called Scythia Minor, taking its name from Greater Scythia. On the Moesian shore of the Pontus, she constructed the city of Tomi, which is named after her.[35]

Tomis is thus made the very first city foundation of the Gothic people, whom Jordanes has otherwise called a nomadic nation. Of course, the real city of Tomis was a Milesian foundation in the archaic Greek world, but Jordanes was rewriting the story of the Gothic people and therefore had a license to override existing narratives of cities and characters like Tomyris.

It lies far outside the scope of this paper to trace how the Jordanes tale came to matter to Romanian receptions of Tomyris. For the present purposes, it suffices to say that his narrative provides her with a definite space of operation within what is now Romania. For example, it is cited in the public sphere on websites, such as Wikipedia (in over 90 languages). Moreover, the idea of Tomyris as the founder is definitely widespread in the modern Romanian city of Constanca, as evidenced most clearly by 're-enactment' festivals celebrating the Romans ("Legio IIII Scythica") and the Dacians

---

32   Lucius Ampelius *Liber Memorialis* § 13.1.
33   Amm. Marc. 23.6.7. Provisional translation by Gavin Kelly for the Landmark Ammianus Marcellinus. I thank Professor Kelly for making his rendition of the text available to me.
34   Jord. *Get.* § 61.
35   Iord. *Get.* § 62 (trans. Van Nuffelen and Van Hoof; lightly modified).

during the 2010s. Locals take this event to another level. The most pertinent case is the public figure Corina Martin, who in fact played the role of Tomyris multiple times. She now works most fittingly at the honorary consulate of the Republic of Kazahkstan in Constanța, according to her Facebook page. In fact, some of the last posts on her website, TOMIRIS (2 March 2021), show that she collaborated with the Kazakhstani embassy during a public showing of the *Legend of Tomyris* in Constanța. This sort of networking between countries so far apart once again demonstrates the evocative power of the ancient world and its literature.

We may understand Ka Gaia An's "Tomiris" as an expression of the greater national interest in Tomyris.[36] As such, the song provides us with an insight into the occupation with classical antiquity on the Romanian heavy metal stage. It conforms to some key features of Mediterranean metal, as explored by Kris Fletcher and Osman Umurhan. The band makes an inclusive choice by singling out Tomyris, even if her image is doctored in an overly nationalistic way. They rework existing ancient source materials, almost certainly by intermediaries, but nonetheless, conventional story patterns are followed. Band members utilize their native language and identity to champion a nationalistic agenda, targeting a specific audience. Although the motivation behind this choice remains unclear, other musical endeavours by former Ka Gaia An members suggest a receptive domestic market for such productions.[37] Consequently, Romania's potential contribution to Mediterranean metal is ripe for exploration. It would also be productive to conduct further and comparative research into the nature of heavy metal stages across the Mediterranean world in order to explore their individual and collective significance in popularizing classical antiquity.

Tomyris as female icon for change: A Sound of Thunder, "Tomyris" (*It was Metal*, 2018)

In this section, I turn to a gendered representation of Tomyris. I first focus on the track's content and form, providing a lyrical and musical analysis. I explain how these features highlight the extent to which the band's rendition diverges from the traditional narrative to challenge prevailing gender roles in heavy metal. For example, the song departs from the traditional point of view in metal by siding with Tomyris. This departure gives us valuable perspectives on the current reshaping of traditional gender narratives in the heavy metal community.

The track about Tomyris under discussion does not appear on a concept album, but rather an album that amalgamates the interests of the band A Sound of Thunder (hereafter ASoT). ASoT consists of Nina Osegueda, Josh Schwartz, Jesse Keen, and Chris Haren, who define their genre as a blend of classic heavy metal, progressive, and

---

36 According to the *Encyclopaedia Metallum* (online), the band hails from Romania's capital, Bucharest.
37 The Bucharesti band split in 2017, but most of the members have since been active in another band, An Theos, as well as other Romania-centric bands, such as Dark Fusion (2010–).

rock.[38] They assert that they are "a fiercely independent group" that has become "Kickstarter's most successful metal band of all time".[39] Be that as it may, their production under the pressure to create content that can be crowd-funded is high and certainly gives some hint of their achievement, not least because it has sustained their activities for over a decade. The band champions progressive agendas online and makes openly political statements on a range of contested issues, including Catalan independence. These agendas are expressed across their discography, in concerts, and through wider public dissemination on social media, such as pro-women posts with their 'sister' band Womanowar, a feminist tribute to Manowar, an all-male bravado band. It is into this frame that the band projects Tomyris.

Their track "Tomyris" is an epic in theme and of substantial length (ca. 7:23 minutes). It begins with an intro, during which the music starts in one channel, and a response follows in the other. The beat is a 4/4 time signature, a beat which may help to underscore the movement at a high pace and eventual confrontation. The first verse creates a chiasmus between the lyrics and the music, establishing an expansive interface onto which the unnamed protagonist rides on horseback (the geographical location on the steppes of Scythia is noted). She is described as a "righteous queen", who can handle herself. In businesslike fashion, she rides alongside her men through a harsh environment, wielding a sword.

The lyrics turn to the antagonist, Cyrus, again with the music reinforcing the confrontation. He unsuccessfully tries to lay claim to her – possibly a reference to the Herodotean marriage proposal. The freedom of the protagonist is emphasized repeatedly, and the issue is clearly that she is avoiding the submission or enslavement to a man specifically ("not shackle herself / to any man").

The first pre-chorus voices Cyrus' ignorance of the queen's unwillingness to submit by posing the rhetorical question of how he could know that this would be the case. The music reinforces Cyrus' oblivion by the use of arpeggio and a word-painting of higher frequency, which express emotionally loaded language, as well as the language of desire.

The first chorus finally names Tomyris, stressing her power, gender, and force. The music supports the lyrical picture with backing vocals from a female chorus, deep reverberation, and echo. Particularly pronounced is the claim that "no man was her equal", which receives even more backing and extra energy from the singer. Moreover, her strength is buttressed by crash cymbals. Most important is the repeated idea that all men should know about Tomyris; that is the primary message, as the music stops for the first time to spell out each syllable of what is sung ("may all men / may all men know"). The proclamation is further underscored by an interlude that recaptures the confrontation in the intro.

The third verse turns back to Cyrus' ambitions of conquest, mentioning the trap he lays for the son and his capture. The capture is accentuated by the riffing on the guitars,

---

38   https://www.asoundofthunderband.com/about (last accessed April 2022).
39   Kickstarter is an online crowd-funding platform that allows individuals or groups to raise funds for various creative projects.

suggesting trouble (2:03-2:04). The prince lies dead in the next sentence, and his death becomes the cause of the conflict.

The second pre-chorus abruptly returns to Tomyris, who swears a religious oath in direct speech. The wording is lifted directly from the Herodotean story.

The second chorus offers a different kind of personal perspective, focusing on Tomyris' own leadership abilities and her group of powerful people ("mighty warriors"). The lyrics detail their devotion to her and reiterate that "no one could defeat her". The last part of the chorus foreshadows the eminent knowledge of her power over men – that is, Cyrus. After the line "her power would be known", there is a change in pace from compound to single metre (2:55-3:09), which might indicate that the battle is on (from horseback to a slow pace).

The fourth verse recounts the victory of Tomyris over Cyrus, emphasizing that the army killed him and that she claimed her trophy, apparently his "skull" to be drowned in "human blood". The music helps to paint the gruesome imagery: there is a hiccup for emphasis (3:14-3:17) when Cyrus lies "dead at her feet". The line "drowned in human blood" (3:20-3:23) receives extra backing vocals and a chorus. The effect of the scene is further amplified because all the solos follow immediately after. They include a power scream (3:54-3:57) and non-lyrical chorus (4:09-4:49). There is an organ solo (4:50-5:28) followed by a guitar solo (5:28-6:03), which makes the scene strange, like something from a comic book or a computer game.

The third pre-chorus (6:03-6:16) gives Tomyris the final word. She addresses Cyrus in the second person, presumably speaking to the head. Her "threat" fulfilled, she stands triumphant. The final chorus appears right away, repeating the first chorus. However, the final lines have a syncopated ending that elongates the last "may all men *know*"; "know" is distorted and drawn out long from 6:44-6:51, to suggest that Tomyris' deed stands as an everlasting monument. The outro maintains the key themes until the end at 7:23.

With "Tomyris", the band ASoT has created a compelling composition that rewrites an old tale for a new audience. They posit the glory of Tomyris to expand the "traditional masculinist narratives beyond the concern of one sex".[40] Of course, the song is conventional in other ways, especially with regard to how power is negotiated. The emphasis on a sort of hegemonic warrior masculinity remains the norm when we witness violence, war, and gore. And this may be the point. If we think of the often hostile environment in which feminist bands like ASoT and Womanowar operate, it is necessary for them to subvert the chauvinistic discourses deployed by and for men in metal. This sort of subversion is a regular strategy when an agent of change seeks to reclaim a tradition or a particular heritage. They form a counter-discourse with the same means but different meanings. In this case, ASoT's reclamation of Tomyris subverts the traditionally masculine model of individualism, courage, strength, and violent justice retrieved from a long-lost era.

In a counter-discourse reading, ASoT's rewriting of the Herodotean narrative is central. The selection of ancient source matters, for the adaptation is then based on content

---

40 Umurhan 2020, 213.

from the same storehouse of the ancient world. The selection thus destabilizes men's sole claim to a glorified past, for that past featured powerful women as well. Ancient history is not only about *klea andrōn*,[41] but also *klea gynaikōn*. Moreover, the engagement with Herodotus is also an act of resistant rewriting. Many features are naturally maintained to recreate the conflict between the two monarchs: the false marriage proposal, the killing of the son, Tomyris' promise and vengeance, and so on. But there is a key shift in narrative emphasis. Herodotus' narrative spotlights Cyrus' downfall, presenting his death as just punishment for his territorial aggression, his transgressions of cultural bounds, and his unlimited personal pride. As a female antagonist, Tomyris becomes – for Herodotus – the necessary and mocking counterpoint to Cyrus' grand ambitions for limitless empire. Indeed, for Herodotus' contemporaries, it was humiliating that Cyrus should withdraw from a woman – as Herodotus makes Croesus state – and even worse that he should lose. We can read Herodotus' story as one of male humiliation, an emasculation of the first Persian warlord, who could not control himself, just as the successive Persian kings were fated to fail. That might have been an interesting story for ASoT to tell, but instead the songwriters made a deliberate choice to platform Tomyris and her role in the story. They no doubt saw that Herodotus' representation of Tomyris suffers from her antagonism. Herodotus obfuscates Tomyris' presence and distorts her voice by letting messengers report her words; only twice do we visit her camp, and she does not meet Cyrus in person until she claims his head. Not so in ASoT's track, in which we enter the story riding by Tomyris' side.

This reading also helps to explain the relative absence of feminine traits in Tomyris. There is no stressing of her motherhood, despite the fact that her son plays a key role. In traditional terms, the ostensible marriage proposal implies that she is eligible to marry (her previous marriage is omitted), but no further elaboration on her personal thoughts and desires is offered. No other traits are attributed to Tomyris that may associate her with anything feminine.

The counter-discourse creates an apparent paradox. On the one hand, ASoT's Tomyris seeks to empower women in metal through the use of a recalibrated image of an ancient female figure. It embraces an outsider from distant lands as an extraordinary story, because it embodies an exterior position that women might sometimes find themselves occupying in the metal community. It provides a powerfully confrontational narrative and a renegotiation of that space, co-created by a female writer and performed by a powerful female voice. In this way, the track destabilizes patriarchal structures and resists the hegemony. And perhaps that is exactly what was needed when it was released in 2018's Washington DC.[42] On the other hand, that empowerment might have limitations because it is influenced by traditional ideas of masculinity that restrict

---

41   González Vaquerizo 2020.
42   Spracklen 2020, 186-187, draws attention to the heavy metal community's reaction to the ostensible legitimation of populist policies with the election of the then US president.

how much gender norms can be challenged.[43] In this sense, the Herodotean narrative seems rather more restrictive than progressive.

Of course, if we turn to the wider discography of ASoT and bands like them, it is clear that counter-discourse is but one strategy to stir change in the heavy metal community. As Gabby Riches argues, women's participation within heavy metal offers many opportunities to rethink how we do metal differently.[44] It will be stimulating to see what kind of role classical antiquity will play in shaping the genre for the future.

Coda: hail to (ancient) history!

We have explored one of the routes by which the reception of the Herodotean Tomyris entered popular culture before the Kazakhstani movie.[45] These receptions are part and parcel of popular culture, not least because the artists are independent and unauthorized by anyone but themselves. The bands are performing in a quantifiably popular music genre that has the potential to reach any audience and thus mediate content about classical antiquity.

The case studies examined the novel ways in which Tomyris is made relevant to very different contemporary causes and cultures. They show that no "characters are so monumental in their nature, so impressive in their acts, so influential in their legacy that they are immune to vagaries of fashion".[46] Tomyris, who is otherwise known to us as the bane of Cyrus, was, could, and can be much more. As people continue to engage with her legacy across media and other venues for popular culture, the potential for receptions is high.[47] This is also the case with other ancient women, such as Cleopatra and Boudica.[48]

I hope that the preceding pages also have shown something of the allure of heavy metal as a site for classical receptions beyond the academy. This is one of the finer tasks in reception studies: to take a critical look at how people across the world continue to make antiquity relevant to their own experience, thus enriching our perspectives and prompting diverse conversations about the ancient world.[49]

---

43 One of the central points of Savigny & Sleight 2015.
44 Riches 2015.
45 Historically speaking, movies have stimulated further creative work about a given topic. This is also true of movies and heavy metal music. The widely known example is Metallica's "Creeping Death" (*Ride the Lightning*, 1984), which was inspired by the green cloud of the Angel of Death in the 1956 movie *The Ten Commandments*, featuring Charlton Heston as Moses.
46 Blanshard 2018, 676.
47 So is scholarly interest; see, e.g., Carlà-Uhink & Wieber 2021; Cothran & Schubert 2020.
48 See, e.g., Swist 2020 on Cleopatra; Gillespie & Moffat 2022 on Boudica.
49 The broadening of horizons across disciplines is beautifully exemplified in initiatives like the virtual conference series "Heavy metal and global premodernity", in which scholars, artists, and fans unite to exchange ideas.

Appendix 1: Lyrics to Ka Gaia An, "Tomiris" (*Naemul Dacilor*, 2016)[50]

Năpraznica nălucă cu ochi de flori de iris,
Cu plete lungi și blonde, sălbateca Tomiris
Regina de la mare și până la Carpați,
Pe calul alb în spume, condus-ai dacii frați

The tempestuous apparition with eyes of iris flowers;
The wild Tomiris, with long blond locks.
The queen of the land from the sea to the Carpathians.
You led the Dacian brothers, riding on your white foaming horse.

Și ai jurat pe soare, Spargapus să-i răpui
Atunci când la Zalmoxe, plecat-a la strpbuni
Și l-ai învins pe Cyrus, persanul sângeros
Ce până să te știe fusese norocos

And you swore by the sun to kill the Persians
When to Zalmoxe, Spargapus went to meet his ancestors.
You defeated Cyrus the bloody Persian,
Who was fortunate until he met you.

ărută vântul rece, obrazul tău regina
Când flori albastre, roșii și galbene-ți închină
Și ești regina dacă, la Pontul Euxin
Peste-un popor puternic cu un măreț destin

The cold wind kisses your cheek, queen,
When it worships you with blue, red, and yellow flowers.
You are the queen of the Dacians at Pontus Euxinus
Over a mighty people with a great fate.

Azi joacă dacii liberi, joc lângă foc de jar
Nu-i nimeni să-i învingă hotar peste hotar
Și ești regina dacă la pontul euxin
Peste-un popor puternic cu un măreț destin.

Today free Dacians dance their dance close to the ember fire;
There is no one to defeat them in the wide world,
And you are the Dacian queen at Pontus Euxinus
Over a mighty people with a great fate.

---

50   I am grateful for the translation made by Flavia Teoc.

Appendix 2: Lyrics to A Sound of Thunder, "Tomyris" (*It was Metal*, 2018)

[Instrumental intro]

From the steppes of Scythia
Came a righteous queen
With sword in hand.
She rode beside her men
Through wild and unforgiving lands.

Yet to the west the king,
Cyrus the Great thought
that he could lay claim
To one who would not shackle herself
To any man despite his name.

[Pre-chorus:]
How could he know
That the queen he desired
Would never submit
Never kneel before his throne?

[Chorus:]
Tomyris reigned.
A woman of strength and power,
Warrior queen of the Massagetae.
No man was her equal.
Who could ever rule beside her?
Tomyris!
May all men,
May all men know.

Cyrus desired her land.
He lay a trap and captured her son.
The prince was dead by dawn.
The war between them had just begun.

[Pre-chorus:]
"I swear by the sun,
The sovereign lord,
I will give you your fill of blood."

[Chorus:]
Tomyris lead
An army of mighty warriors.
For her they fought and killed and bled.
No man could defeat her.
How could one stand beside her?
Tomyris!
Her power would be known.

Defeated by her army,
Cyrus the Great dead at her feet.
His skull the final trophy,
Drowned in human blood.

[Various solos by voices and instruments]

[Pre-chorus:]
His army dead,
"See now I fulfill my threat
You have had your fill of blood", she said.

[Repeat first chorus:]
Tomyris reigned.
A woman of strength and power,
Warrior queen of the Massagetae.
No man was her equal.
Who could ever rule beside her?
Tomyris!
May all men,
May all men know.

Bibliography

Ansari, A. 2021. "A Royal Romance: The Cult of Cyrus the Great in Modern Iran". *Journal of the Royal Asiatic Society* 31.3, 405-419.

Asheri, D. et al. 2007. *A Commentary on Herodotus. Books I–IV*. Oxford: Oxford University Press.

Beaumont-Thomas, B. 2022. "Metallica's Master of Puppets conjures UK Top 40 Hit thanks to Stranger Things". https://www.theguardian.com/music/2022/jul/15/metallicas-master-of-puppets-conjures-uk-top-40-hit-thanks-to-stranger-things?CMP=share_btn_link, last accessed 15 July 2022.

Blanshard, A.J.L. 2018. "Alexander as Glorious Failure: The Case of Robert Rossen's *Alexander the Great* (1956)", in: Moore, K.R. (ed.) 2018. *Brill's Companion to the Reception of Alexander the Great*. Leiden: Brill, 675-693.

Briant, P. 2003. *From Cyrus to Alexander – A History of the Persian Empire*. Winona Lake, IN: Eisenbrauns.

Carlà-Uhink, F. & Wieber, A. (eds) 2021. *Orientalism and the Reception of Powerful Women from the Ancient World. IMAGINES*. London & New York: Bloomsbury.

Chiasson, C. 2012. "Myth and Truth in Herodotus' Cyrus Logos", in: Baragwanath, E. & de Bakker, M. (eds) 2012. *Myth, Truth and Narrative in Herodotus*. Oxford: Oxford University Press, 213-232.

Cothran, B., Judge, J. & Schubert, A. (eds) 2020. *Women Warriors and National Heroes. Global Histories*. London & New York: Bloomsbury.

Dewald, C. & Munson, R.S. 2022. *Herodotus Histories Book 1*. Cambridge: Cambridge University Press.

Djurslev, C.T. 2020. "Review of Fletcher & Umurhan (2020)". *Bryn Mawr Classical Review*, 26 June 2020.

Farber, J. 2022. "'It's the Language of Rebellion': The Story of Slave to Sirens, the All-female Lebanese Metal Band". https://www.theguardian.com/film/2022/sep/28/slave-to-sirens-lebanese-metal-band-documentary, last accessed 28 September 2022.

Farrell, G. 2021. "Review of Fletcher and Umurhan (2020)". *The Classical Review* 71.1, 236-238.

Fletcher, K.F.B. & Umurhan, O. (eds) 2020. *Classical Antiquity in Heavy Metal Music. IMAGINES*. London & New York: Bloomsbury.

Fontaine, J. 1977. *Ammien Marcellin. Histoire, tome IV*. Paris: Les Belles Lettres.

Gera, D. 1997. *Warrior Women. The Anonymous Tractatus De Mulieribus*. Leiden: Brill.

Gillespie, C. & Moffat, D. 2022. "Feminist Anthems and Iron Age Queens: Heavy Metal's Obsession with Boudica". https://youtu.be/TvgCFVaZi9I, last accessed 13 April 2022.

González Vaquerizo, H. 2020. "Κλέα ἀνδρῶν: Classical Heroes in the Heavy Metal", in: López Gregoris, R. & Macías Villalobos, C. (eds) 2020. *The Hero Reloaded: The Reinvention of the Classical Hero in Contemporary Mass Media*. Amsterdam: John Benjamins, 51-72.

Grig, L. 2017. "Introduction", in: Grig, L. (ed.) 2017. *Popular Culture in the Ancient World*. Cambridge: Cambridge University Press, 1-36.

Hall, E. 2020. "Cyrus the Great's 2550th Death Anniversary and the Real Kazakh Subsequent Movie Film". *The Edithorial Blog*, 4 December 2020. https://tinyurl.com/4zn97tbk, last accessed 12 July 2024.

Hardwick, L. 2003. *Reception Studies*. Oxford: Oxford University Press.

Kiilerich, B. 2021. "Review of Fletcher & Umurhan (2020)". *CLARA* 7.

Maurice, L. 2017. "Introduction: The Ancient World and Popular Fiction", in: Maurice, L. (ed.) 2017. *Rewriting the Ancient World: Greeks, Romans, Jews, and Christians in Modern Popular Fiction*. Leiden: Brill, 1-15.

Parker, H.N. 2011. "Toward a definition of popular culture". *History and Theory* 50, 147-170.

Riches, G. 2015. "Re-conceptualizing Women's Marginalization in Heavy Metal: A Feminist Post-structuralist Perspective". *Metal Music Studies* 1.2, 263-270.

Sancisi-Weerdenburg, H. 1985. "The Death of Cyrus: Xenophon's *Cyropaedia* as a Source of Iranian History", in: Duchesne-Guillemin, J. & Lecoq, P. (eds) 1985. *Papers in Honour of Professor Mary Boyce*. 2 vols. Leiden: Brill, 459-471.

Savigny, H. & Sleight, S. 2015. "Postfeminism and Heavy Metal in the United Kingdom: Sexy or Sexist?". *Metal Music Studies* 1.3, 341-357.

Spracklen, K. 2020. *Metal Music and the Re-imagining of Masculinity: Place, Race, and Nation*. Bingley: Emerald Publishing.

Swist, J.J. 2020. "Vile Nilotic Rites: Cleopatra in Heavy Metal Music". *Heavy Metal Classicist Blog*, 19 November 2020.

Swist, J.J. 2021. "Ancient Studies & Metal Music Studies: From Discography to Bibliography". *Save Ancient Studies Alliance (Online)*, 11-12 December 2021.

Taufer, M. 2008. "Zalmoxis nella tradizione greca: rassegna e rilettura delle fonti". *Quaderni di Storia* 34, 131-164.

Umurhan, O. 2012. "Heavy Metal Music and the Appropriation of Greece and Rome". *Syllecta Classica* 23, 127-152.

Umurhan, O. 2020. "Coda: Some Trends in Metal's Use of Classical Antiquity", in: Fletcher & Umurhan 2020, 201-216.

Waters, M. 2022. *King of the World: The Life of Cyrus the Great*. Oxford: Oxford University Press.

Willis, I. 2017. *Reception*. London: Routledge.

Åshede, L. & Foka, A. 2020. "Cassandra's Plight: Gender, Genre, and Historical Concepts of Femininity in Goth and Power Metal", in: Fletcher & Umurhan 2020, 97-114.

11

THE UNRULY POWER OF MYTH

CLASSICAL NARRATIVES IN CONTEMPORARY DANISH ART

VINNIE NØRSKOV

In the summer of 2021, six Danish artists were installed in a beautiful beach hotel. For two weeks, they were tasked with producing a group exhibition. The process was filmed and broadcast on Danish public service television as a reality show under the name *The Artist Colony* (Kunstnerkolonien) – "*Paradise Hotel* for artists", as one Danish newspaper called it (Dahl 2020). The idea of the reality concept was to place present-day artists in a geographic setting that has inspired artists in the past. The first season in 2020 was situated in Skagen, North Jutland, where a famous artist colony dominated the small fishing town in the early twentieth century. The 2021 season brought the artists to the island of Bornholm, where each one had their own studio and worked on independent works, which were assembled in a group exhibition at the Bornholm Art Museum after two weeks. Bornholm is a holiday paradise for Danes, but also an island with many myths and stories. Some of the artists found inspiration in the stories of the 'underworld' (the island's trolls); others, mostly the older artists, were exploring their own identities and personal stories. But the young artist Sif Itona Westerberg stood out: she carved a sculpture of the ancient Greek princess Ariadne.

In this paper, I will investigate the engagement of young Danish artists with classical heritage. Contemporary art can be very elitist, and might not seem an obvious choice of subject in a volume on popular receptions of the classical heritage. However, this reality show on Danish public service television is an excellent case study in how this barrier can be, and is, broken down. The interesting dimension of the programme is that we follow the artistic processes: from the development of an idea, over various trials and errors, to the finalization of an artwork and its inclusion in an exhibition, where different works are brought together and into dialogue. This is a process that is mostly not open to the museum audience. It is also an insight that is extremely valuable when studying the use of and engagement with the classical heritage. The first case considered in this paper is thus Sif Itona Westerberg's sculpture *Ariadne*. After analyzing this work in depth, I will turn to two exhibitions at Aarhus University's Museum of Ancient Art and Archaeology. Over the last ten years I have developed an exhibition strategy based on opening the space for users to engage with the museum collections or the classical heritage in general. I will first present the exhibition programme, then go deeper into two of the exhibitions shown during this period, studying the reasons and processes behind the artist's choice of venue and their dialogue with classical antiquity.

Popular reception on reality TV

Sif Itona Westerberg is a visual artist. She studied at the Funen Art Academy and then the Royal Academy in Copenhagen, where she graduated in 2014. In 2019 she received the Carl Nielsen and Anne-Marie Carl Nielsen Talent Prize, and the following year the prestigious three-year working grant from the Danish Arts Foundation. She defines herself as a visual artist, but she is a sculptor. She carves reliefs out of prefabricated gas concrete blocks – in the first instance, for economic reasons, as the material was much cheaper than marble, but there is also a tension that she has come to appreciate between the quickly produced material and her slow, careful carving. The blocks are assembled with large metal bolts, combining a finely detailed carving technique with an industrial look. The low reliefs show large figural images of fabulous creatures in an ornamental art nouveau style, and the subjects are often from Greek mythology. Her first major solo exhibition was *The House of Dionysos*, shown at Gether Contemporary, Copenhagen, in 2020, and in autumn 2021 three series were shown at ARoS Aarhus Art Museum.

The reality show *The Artist Colony* allows its audience to follow the processes, accompanied by the artists' own thoughts about these processes. In connection with the exhibition at the Bornholm Art Museum, a short film was produced that included some of the key moments in the creation of the works by all six artists. The section on Sif Itona Westerberg focuses on her work process: we see her sitting at her desk with various images of the Ariadne figure on the wall in front of her.

"Now I am sitting drawing the model for the sculpture I want to make," she explains, and then she retells the story of Ariadne, pointing to the images on the wall, for instance when she explains that Ariadne wakes up in the morning abandoned by Theseus. Then the film shows her walking on the beach at Bornholm, and she explains how she is "playing a Greek film for her inner eye view" while on the island. And now comes the clue: Westerberg takes her point of departure in Italian author Felice Vinci's theory that Homer's *Odyssey* is set not in the Mediterranean but in the Baltic Sea (Vinci 2012). He places Ariadne's Naxos in Neksø – a village on the island of Bornholm, where the artists are staying (Vinci 2012, 35). This connection between Westerberg's interest in Greek mythology and the landscape of Bornholm legitimizes her choice of subjects. It does not matter that this theory is highly contested. As the island is populated by trolls and a strong belief in the supernatural, the story is a perfect match.

Normally, when we analyze an artwork to look for possible inspiration or reception of classical motifs, shapes, or narratives, we are lucky if the artist has written a diary or expressed in some other way how she relates to possible sources of inspiration. In the programme, Westerberg's inspiration is made clear through the drawings and photocopies on the wall (Fig. 1). Many of them can be identified. The first two above her head I

Sif Itona Westerberg at her work desk. Screenshot from *The Artist Colony* 2021.

Fig. 1.

do not recognize. Next are two images of sculptures. The first is a drawing by Raphael Morghen of Canova's sculpture of Theseus resting after killing the Minotaur, today in the collection of Thorvaldsen's Museum, Copenhagen. The next is a copy of a photograph of a sculpture by the Danish sculptor Rudolf Tegner named *The Belt of Aphrodite* in the Rudolf Tegner Museum, northern Zealand. To the left of this is a photocopy of a painting by Evelyn de Morgan from 1877, showing Ariadne resting on the beach. This image comes up as one of the first in a Google Image search on Ariadne and Naxos. In the middle, we recognize an image of a sculpture by Johann Heinrich von Dannecker in Liebighaus, Frankfurt. The round image is not identifiable, but to the right there is an engraving from 1580 by Johann Sadeler, after Bartholomeus Spranger, showing Neptune raping Caenis, in the collections of the Rijksmuseum Amsterdam and the Metropolitan Museum of Art. Here we are in another mythological narrative known through Ovid's *Metamorphoses*. Caenis was a beautiful young girl who caught the eye of Poseidon, who raped her; after the deed, he promised her a wish, and she asked to be transformed into a man so she would never be a victim again. Behind the artist's shoulder hangs a drawing of a famous Greco-Roman statue of the sleeping Ariadne in the Vatican Museum. A photocopy of a painting of Ariadne on the beach from 1853 by the German portrait painter Friedrich Horschfelt is hanging next to it. This is the image illustrating the Danish-language Wikipedia article on Ariadne. To the right is an image of a terracotta statuette of Theseus and the Minotaur in the Walters Art Museum, Baltimore, by an unknown artist from the eighteenth century, and the last image shows Cupid, but it has not been identified.

These images materialize Sif Itona Westerberg's research and Google searches; they also testify to a fascination with moving figures, both in the sense of movements that underline emotional distress, and of actual movements in actions like murder and rape.

Fig. 2. Sif Itona Westerberg drawing the wounded Amazon. Screenshot from The Artist Colony 2021.

She does not limit herself to ancient representations of Ariadne, but finds her inspiration in other narratives and figures. This becomes very clear in the first scene, where we see her drawing a figure (Fig. 2): it is a wounded Amazon, which turns out to be her main inspiration for the shape of the final sculpture. The best-known statue of this figure is in the Capitoline Museum in Rome. There are two interesting dimensions to this choice: first, the choice of the Amazon as a model lends the figure greater female strength, and second, the Amazon is a standing figure. As visible in the images on the wall, most of the illustrations of Ariadne show her reclining – left behind on the beach. One of the best known of the ancient sculptures is the sleeping Ariadne in the Vatican Museum, mentioned above and reproduced in a drawing on Westerberg's wall. Here Ariadne lifts her right arm over her head – in the same stance as the Amazon. The position of the Amazon's arm thus associates her with the sleeping Ariadne and the figure is easily transformed into the standing figure of Ariadne.

Sif Itona Westerberg's sculpture of Ariadne developed into a very personal interpretation of the figure (Fig. 3). As noted above, it is carved out of industrial concrete blocks joined with metal bolts. The sculpure is a standing female figure, lifting her right arm and inclining her head. She is wearing a dress, but it is nearly transparent, and it looks as if she is standing behind something, only letting us see her upper body. She is carrying the Ariadne thread – linking the figure to the story of Theseus on Crete, emphasized through the maze on the figure's torso. This is not the abandoned Ariadne, but the creative, solution-finding, strong Ariadne – the real hero of the story. Furthermore, her face is different: it is still classical, copying the fifth-century Polykletian head of the Amazon, but has both the horns and ears of a bull – she is the sister of the Minotaur, and here she has taken over some of the power of her brother.

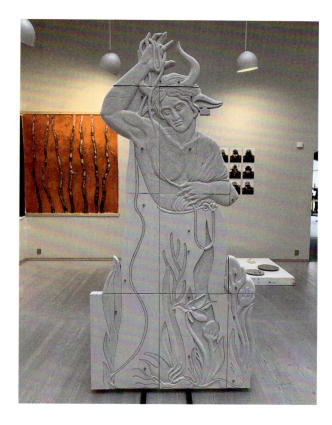

Ariadne by Sif Itona Westerberg. Bornholm Art Museum. Photo: Sif Itona Westerberg.

Fig. 3.

Danish artists and their engagement with classical myth

Sif Itona Westerberg stands out among the artists participating in the reality show for her deep fascination with ancient Greek and Roman mythologies. But she is not alone in this in Denmark. Interest in and use of classical mythology have continuously persisted in contemporary art – albeit at times it was considered old-fashioned. Well-established artists like Bjørn Nørgaard have continued to use and question the classical heritage and its connotations of ideal aesthetics and cultures in their works; Nørgaard has been a strong defender of the Royal Cast Collection at the National Gallery in Copenhagen, which in recent decades has been threatened and was nearly closed. He established a kind of vintage classicism in the 1970s in the collective Arms and Legs, which merged classicism, modernism, and contemporary disruption (Nørgaard 2004, 29). Nørgaard explains how the group worked with classical sculpture as a kind of "reference catalogue" that they knew through illustrations more than through actual contact. He remodelled the Belvedere torso without ever having seen the original, though he knew it through the cast collections and through illustrations (Nørgaard 2005, 86) – similar to the way Sif Itona Westerberg models her Ariadne through illustrations, in this case of several different sculptures. Another artist with similar concerns is the autodidact Peter Brandes, who has worked with classical narratives for the last five decades in large pottery and graphics, and is one of the most productive illustrators of translations of ancient texts in Denmark (see for instance Homer 1999, Homer 2003, Vergil 1996).

Nørgaard and Brandes were both shaped by the expressionist art movements of the 1960s. However, in the last 10 to 15 years, I have experienced increased interest among younger artists in engaging with Greek and Roman art and mythology. They see the stories as a powerful, if uneasy source that can be used to question our values and identity. In the example of Ariadne, it is the female figure that is centre stage; she is interpreted as the protagonist, the one with the solution to avert catastrophe. The story goes that Theseus, once she had saved him, left her behind on Naxos – and this was the story popular among older artists. Sif Itona Westerberg brings out a different aspect of the story, one that positions Ariadne as the saviour, underlining this through her transformation into a female version of the Minotaur. This, in combination with the placement of Naxos in Neksø, legitimizes the choice of narrative in the reality show. It is not important whether this is true or not – Vinci's reinterpretation is part of a very long tradition of connecting Northern European cultures and dynasties to the mythology of the Trojan War, as in Snorri Sturluson's poem *Edda*, for instance. And the mythology is not a 'true story' – these are narratives that connect. Graeco-Roman mythology, art, and culture were essential in connecting Denmark to the rest of Europe (Funder et al. 2019).

Classical sculpture in Danish art museums

There is a vibrant living tradition among Danish artists of appropriating and reinterpreting ancient Greek and Roman myths. It began in the eighteenth century, coinciding with the establishment of the Royal Art Academy in Copenhagen in 1754 (Fuchs & Salling 2004). This forged a close relationship between art education and engagement with subjects from Greek and Roman narratives, both literary and visual. It is no coincidence that this relationship was connected to the neoclassicism that first emerged in Denmark with the sculptor Johannes Wiedewelt. Wiedewelt was a close friend of Johan Joachim Winckelmann, and he communicated the ideas of Winckelmann's first important publication, *Gedanken über die Nachahmung der griechischen Werke der Malerei und Bildhauerei*, to the Danish audience in a publication that would today be judged a work of plagiarism (Fejfer 2003). Wiedewelt was also responsible for the first casts of classical sculpture arriving in Copenhagen. Classical sculpture as the ideal – and casts as 'training objects' – had a profound impact on art production in Denmark from this time onward, as they did all over Europe. The importance of the Danish sculptor Bertel Thorvaldsen and the establishment of a private collection of his art works, his collection of antiquities, and his collection of casts of classical sculpture as the first public museum in Denmark in 1848 is illustrative of the importance of classical heritage in Danish art and museum history. The inauguration of this museum initiated a wave of public art museums collecting and exhibiting sculptures from the classical past in casts around the country, where market towns were keen to establish institutions that would provide citizens with a general education – libraries, theatres, museums, and educational institutions. Casts of classical sculptures became the means of displaying the origin of Western art and aesthetics to the public. One of these market towns was Aarhus, where in the 1870s the art collection moved to a new building with space for more than a hundred casts of Greek and Roman sculpture. A change in attitudes to casts in the 1950s and 1960s whereby they were seen as copies led many art museums to deaccession these casts. Luckily, this happened in Aarhus only shortly after a department of Classical and Near Oriental Archaeology had been established at Aarhus University in 1949. The new professor, P.J. Riis, at once began a study collection, and the first objects were a deposit of original objects on loan from the National Museum in Copenhagen. In 1950, the collection of plaster casts of Greek and Roman sculpture moved out of the local art museum and into the basements of the university, where they were housed until the present locations were built in the late 1960s. In 1986 the collection changed its name to the Museum of Ancient Art and Archaeology, and regular special exhibitions have been on the programme ever since. When I was employed as an assistant in 1999, we aimed to have the museum mount one exhibit a year, but it was difficult to find the resources to do so. Changes in staff, organization, and economy paved the way for a rethinking of the workings of the museum.

Popular receptions in the museum

In 2004, I took over the responsibility for the museum after Pia Guldager Bilde, and in the first few years it became clear that the challenge was to resolve the tension between the desire to undertake more activities and a lack of resources. With only three employees covering two full-time positions (a part-time director, a part-time receptionist, and a full-time museum technician) and a small group of student employees, the possibilities for realizing large projects were limited.

In the following years, we moved into a different working mode that, since 2011, has developed into an exhibition strategy that opens the museum space to scholars, artists, and designers with projects that engage with the collection or classical antiquity in a number of different ways. While the starting point was a lack of resources, seen from a museological perspective the idea has proven highly relevant and timely. In 2010, the American museum consultant and director Nina Simon published her highly influential book *The Participatory Museum*, making her the most influential museologist in participatory museum models. Her basic argument is that participation makes the museum relevant. Traditional museum practices tend to constitute exclusive, one-way communication based on the knowledge paradigm lending authority to the institution. Participatory practices acknowledge different knowledge paradigms and emphasize sharing and collaboration as effective in constructing new knowledge and meaning-making for the participants. This approach must offer a range of levels of engagement and participation – meeting the user and visitor in their different needs and abilities. The model also accounts for different levels of control for the institution. It thus frames different possibilities for the institution and the user, depending on their needs and wishes. In essence, it is about power: the more control an institution wants, the more work it needs to put into a project. The more an institution opens up and gives up control, the less work it has to do.

Simon defines four types of participatory work in the museum (Simon 2010, Chap. 5):

Contributory: The institution is the project owner and has the final say and full control over the project. The institution defines the content, and requests content and participation from users. The target group is very large, and there is a wish to include as many visitors as possible.

Collaborative: The institution defines the project and the framework, but the content can be generated in partnerships. There are often specific target groups and aims for participation.

Co-Creative: The project is developed in partnership with and out of the needs of the community. The responsibility is aligned, and the institution needs to invest a lot of time and management in the project. All participants need to be dedicated, and the skills acquired are impressive.

Hosted: The institution provides a framework, through a set of rules, and helps, but the project is the responsibility of the participants. This means that the resources invested by the institution are limited, but also that the participants do not gain so many skills through the collaboration. Instead, the participants are empowered by carrying out their own project.

The model can be applied as it fits the wishes, resources, and power of the institution. In the Museum of Ancient Art and Archaeology, we have worked with different types of projects: collaborative and co-creative projects are mostly done with researchers who have vested interests in the collections, or – where the museum is a partner – the research projects. When it comes to exhibitions of contemporary art or design, these are nearly always hosted. The hosted exhibitions are very successful and generate a lot of inspiration, both for the participants and also for the visitors. We get many new suggestions for exhibitions from people who have visited one of these: they see themselves as potential participants. They bring in new audiences, and create new and interesting relationships with the connecting community, both the local community in Aarhus and also a more national art community.

In the last ten years, the Museum of Ancient Art and Archaeology has housed 14 exhibitions showing art and crafts inspired by the classical past. All these exhibitions were proposed by an artist and accepted if considered to add new perspectives to our understanding of the collections and the meaning of the classical heritage today. In the next few paragraphs, I will address two of these exhibitions, exploring what drove the artists to choose the museum as a venue and how it has influenced their art and the understanding of the role of the classical past in contemporary art.

In general, we have three types of exhibitions, defined according to the format of cooperation:

1. A single-artist exhibition around the work of the artist, often made for the museum space
2. A group of artists choose works based on a joint interest in a subject relevant to the exhibition space
3. Associations of artists or designers who choose the space and develop a joint theme

The first of the single-artist exhibitions was by visual artist Bo Mølgaard, who graduated from the Jutland Art Academy in 1989. Mølgaard engaged with the sculptures of Pergamon and the political dimensions of their location in Berlin, where they lend their name to the Pergamon Museum. These exhibitions mostly evolved out of an existing interest in classical heritage and art. The exhibition *Dialogue with Acropolis* (2013) was an example of a group of artists collaborating and cooperating with curator Hanne Pedersen and the Art Centre at Silkeborg Bad in 2012/2013 (Pedersen 2012). The artists Søren Elgaard, Karin Birgitte Lund, and Bjarke Regn Svendsen had been in residence together at the Danish Academy in Athens, where the idea was born. Again, these exhibitions tend to begin with an interest in classical art and culture. Much more demanding is the third type of exhibition, made with association partners. Several different kinds of associations have used the museum space. The first was a textile association, which used the museum as a venue for its 40th anniversary in 2014. In the introductory discussions with the group, it became clear that we needed to set up some transparent criteria to assess possible projects suggested by people approaching the museum. A first, essential criterion when evaluating whether we want to house an exhibition is the relevance of the collections or of classical antiquity in one way or another. This group of women were invited to the museum to see the place and to hear about the collections and classical antiquity in general. During the talk and the dialogue that followed in the museum space, they narrowed down a subject they could agree on, focusing on the colour blue. Working with textiles, they were deeply fascinated by emerging new knowledge about colours in antiquity, the result of research taking place at the Ny Carlsberg Glyptotek. They were especially intrigued by a specific shade of blue, also known as Egyptian Blue, and the group decided that all participants should just use a blue thread and find their inspiration in the museum space or classical antiquity. There was a certain anxiety about the outcome: how would their creations work together and in the museum space? I had no idea what the result would be, but the exhibition was fascinating and permitted very personal interpretations. It was an eye-opener as a general way of working – these personal statements and engagements with classical heritage were so rich, and worked so very differently from the way we would usually work. The exhibition thus paved the way for more of these kinds of projects.

Guirlanden

This leads me to the first of two examples, an exhibition shown in 2018 in the museum called *L* – the Roman numeral for 50. The title was chosen by the artist collective Guirlanden, a local group that celebrated its fiftieth anniversary in that year. In many ways it was ironic that a collective formed in 1968 in opposition to the institutionalization and professionalization of museums and exhibition spaces – because they wanted to be in charge themselves, claiming ownership of their art and of how it would be exhibited – chose to hold their anniversary in a museum of classical art: the quintessence of art 'civilization', the art that for centuries had been considered the most educational and thus also oppressing and limiting. However, much had changed since 1968. From its foundation the association had had an agreement with the local exhibition venue the Art Building (in Danish *Kunstbygningen*, today *Kunsthal Aarhus*) to hold a group exhibition every two to three years. This changed in 2013 as part of a further professionalization of that institution, which updated their exhibition policy so as to imply a curatorial process for all exhibitions. This was exactly what Guirlanden had reacted against in 1968: they wanted to be in charge of the exhibitions themselves. This led them to seek alternative solutions, and the Museum of Ancient Art and Archaeology became a possible venue.

As with the textile association, we had an introductory meeting with a few group members to discuss the possibilities and the process, also making clear that they needed to take the museum space and the collections as points of departure. They agreed to the conditions, and after this we had several meetings as preparation, both for the entire group to show them the museum and the collections, and also with single members who wanted more information about single objects. The group consisted of ten members and for the exhibition they had invited three guests, so in total 13 artists were present. They all made their art independently of each other, but many worked in a very site-specific way, creating works that could only be exhibited in the space. This dynamic meant that the project became a multifaceted interaction with the collections and the classical past. Many of the artists did not have a long trajectory of working with the classical past, but they took up the challenge and found inspiration from quite diverse places. Among the works that included objects in the museum were Else Plough's reconstructions of the palmette on the cornice of the Parthenon, inspired by the casts of the fragments in the collection. She drew three different reconstructions by scholars, layering them in a 1:1 drawing on transparent paper. Another was Christian Yde Frostholm's installation, which included the cast of the *Knife Grinder* in the museum. He surrounded the cast with written narratives exploring its object history and that of a bronze copy in a park in Copenhagen. It was a very sensual text–image experience, unfolding the many layers of these sculptures and their relationship and dialogues with the contexts they inhabited (Fig. 4). Other artists reflected the objects of the museum directly in their works. Anders Gammelgaard Nielsen, who is also an architect, produced a finely carved wooden Ionian pilaster capital; Bodil Sohn created 'art books' – one on the subject of the Cave of Plato and another with silhouettes of sculptures.

Interaction with the museum space was addressed by, for instance, Anne-Marie Pedersen with an installation named *Walking with Athena*. Using different-coloured

CYF Christan Yde Frostholm, *Notater om sliberen*, Guirlanden L 2018. Photo: Vinnie Nørskov.

Fig. 4.

glass and a projection of a video filmed in the Acropolis Museum in Athens of visitors walking among the sculptures there, the installation questioned the whiteness of the casts and the visitor experience.

Max Parylewics and Kim Th. Grønborg both interacted with objects in showcases, placing their works – small terracotta objects and 3D-printed sculptures created from mathematical equations – in among the ancient objects. A few artists took subjects or concepts from the present with roots in classical antiquity, such as Maja Ingerslev, who participated with photograms of flowers with names from ancient Greek. She used the real flower as a negative in the dark room, and different colours of light on photoactive paper. Her works combined nature and myth: she chose flowers with Greek names like Anemone, Crocus, and Violet, the latter the favourite flower of Athens and because of its scent also connected to Aphrodite (Fig. 5). Some flower names are named after gods or nymphs who were transformed into flowers in Greek mythology, for instance Hyacinthus and Narcissus, the daffodil. Maja was exploring transformations in nature and found inspiration in Ovid's *Metamorphoses*. In my experience, this book has been the most popular source of inspiration for the artists we have worked with, especially the narratives of the transformation of humans into nature: there seems to be a deep artistic interest in organic transformations in nature and the interrelations between man and nature. We need to rethink these categorizations, as in recent decades they have changed with the Anthropocene.

Fig. 5. Maja Ingerslev, *Metamorphoses*, Guirlanden L 2018. Photo: Maja Ingerslev.

Guirlanden's experience with the exhibition at the Museum of Ancient Art and Archaeology encouraged them to look for similar venues for future exhibitions, and in the summer of 2022 they opened the exhibition *RefeR* in the Cambridge Classical Collection.

Helle Kingbird Bjerregaard: Phaethon[1]

The single-artist exhibition is often born of an artist's idea after visiting the museum or one of our events. My last example is a 2015 exhibition by the Danish artist Helle Kingbird Bjerregaard. She had studied art history and the history of ideas at Aarhus University, and sculpture at the Royal College of Art in London. When she moved back to Denmark, she approached me and asked if she could make an exhibition at the museum. She had no clear idea, but her work with clay – exploring clay as sculpture, using her own body in artistic performances – was interesting as a contemporary sculptural practice. The project developed over about a year, and the process became an essential part of the exhibition. This is explained in a long narrative published on our website and in the course of the process, I experienced it through her stories – it was as if art and reality merged in that development. Helle Bjerregaard addressed the relationship between the personal and the archetypical, the epic and the private. The story of this exhibition blurred these borders completely.

---

1   The exhibition was entitled *Phaeton* in Danish, as this is the Danish spelling of 'Phaethon'.

Bjerregaard describes how she found the theme for the exhibition on a flight from Aberdeen to London on a starry night, reading Ovid's story of Phaethon. She was struck by the eternal human question of desire and moved by an immediate recognition. Phaethon was driven by a longing to prove his descendance from the Sun God – he wanted to know for certain that the god was his father. When the Sun God said he could have any wish fulfilled, Phaethon asked to drive the god's chariot over the sky for one day – a route to complete destruction. But the father could not deny what he had promised, even though he knew this would be the last act of his son's life. The overwhelming power of nature is forcefully described by Ovid, leading to a multitude of catastrophes on Earth when the young boy cannot handle the horses – today it is impossible to read this text without seeing mental images of burning forests all over the Earth. This was not what occupied Helle Kingbird Bjerregaard in 2015: she was intrigued by the power of desire – so that even when you know something will destroy you, you do it anyway. Reading the story on the flight that night, she had no idea about how this might materialize in the exhibition. The narrative drags us into a process of physical encounters and rejections. Two men are involved. The first she recognizes as Phaethon, a dancing star, and this became the name of one of the artworks in the exhibition. She has only one photo of him – taken by chance while pulling her phone out of her bag – and she uses it as a backdrop to the star map printed on cowskin in the exhibit:

> The only thing I have from him is an image, of his hands, that my phone makes coincidentally as I take it out of the bag, the last evening. That evening when we lose control, that evening when I lose him … like Phaethon loses the last control over the horses … by the constellation Sagittarius' knee close to the tropic of the Big Dipper.
>
> The ending is not surprising, we rode there ourselves … (Bjerregaard 2015)

The meeting is fatal: she reads him the story of Phaethon and he finds it the most beautiful he has ever heard – but clearly refuses to participate in the project, and disappears.

After meeting this first man, she decides that the subject of the exhibition will be Phaethon's ride, performed as a kind of re-enactment. Now that the dancing star is gone, she goes looking for the Sun God's son. He appears on Tinder, but it takes quite some time before they manage to meet. There are many misunderstandings, and no-shows – she has not told him about the project. When it finally happens, after half a year, it is because she has advertised on Tinder for a model for an art project and he sees the advert: they meet for her to take photos. She knows he has tattoos, but has not seen all of them – and then he takes off his T-shirt:

> It's all pretty wild. I had seen an image of some of his tattoos but the one on his back I only realize when he takes off his T-shirt. The image is a crucified Icaros figure hanging dead with outstretched wings. Impressed into his skin is the symbol (of destiny) of the young man who meets his destiny alone in space and

Fig. 6. Helle Kingbird Bjerregaard, *Phaethon* 2015. Photo: Vinnie Nørskov.

crashes to the ground. Icaros and Phaethon share their destiny, they are one and the same figure: both drifting on their travel over the sky. Icaros burned by the sun, Phaethon with the sun wagon burning the Earth, both fall lifeless from the sky … (Bjerregaard 2015)

The narrative of her search for a male muse, the erotic and sensitive experience of her meetings with both men, and their reactions to her project are an integrated part of the artworks she includes in the exhibition (Fig. 6). She transforms the narrative into physical shape in images, video, and a performance at the opening of the exhibition.

The performance is called *The Fall of Phaethon*, and here Bjerregaard worked with the wet clay in the same way as in her previous works (Fig. 7). It is an act of exploration of the sculpture. Several large round clay objects had been placed on the floor. She moved some of these large chunks of clay around, organizing them in a new pattern, and introducing a new kind of clay with different properties: fluid, lighter, and whitish. With this, she painted wings on the floor. In the end, she opened some of the round clay objects and golden and whitish fluid clay floated out – linking to the story of Phaethon falling into the Eridanus river as a falling star.

The exhibition became a process, and the installation of the four artworks and the performance captured her personal experience of the encounter with Phaethon. This was not a myth from the past; it was a lived feeling of desire, of mirroring in another human being, of being lifted up and falling down.

Helle Kingbird Bjerregaard, *Fall of Phaethon*, Phaethon 2015. Photo: Vinnie Nørskov.

Fig. 7.

Conclusion

The examples explored here show a diverse range of ways in which contemporary Danish artists engage with, discuss, and deconstruct ancient art, literature, and heritage in a present-day context. Classical myth becomes a lens through which they investigate human relations, especially human–nature relations. Our experience at the Museum of Ancient Art and Archaeology testifies to a strong attraction to the ancient transformation myths. It is not the aesthetic ideal and sculpture that attracts most artists, but the formative values of the objects and the strong narratives of life-changing events. The title of my paper – "Unruly myth" – refers to the unsettling character of so many myths: they explore the injustice and unpredictability of life through the very narratives that enable engagement with different aspects.

Curiously, the exhibition by Sif Itona Westerberg at ARoS Aarhus Art Museum in 2021 entitled *Immemorial* also included the myth of Phaethon. This exhibition was structured around three acts – or, you could say, three narratives. Two of them related to an older series, *Dionysos*, a series of reliefs showing the wine god and his companions, and playing with hybrid creatures from the medieval period combined with water basins. The third narrative was new and made for the exhibition. It was an installation called *Swan Song*, and here Westerberg explored the myth of Phaethon. The title refers to Phaethon's lover Cygnos, who transforms into a grieving swan. The installation consisted of individual and rather disconnected small figures in the dimming light of a neon installation. In the middle, a tree was on fire – the total destruction of nature by man is centre stage, whereas the protagonist, Phaethon, is not present. The two different versions of the myth as experienced in the art installations of Westerberg and Bjerregaard are striking and illustrate the fluidity and transformative nature of ancient myth. Myth is about explanations, and the artists we have worked with address these myths as stories that are continuously interpreted in new ways: they provide explanations, but they are also open to other kinds of exploration. This fluid and transformative nature of myth is essential for the present-day reinterpretation of classical art and culture. It is not what has been called "the stabilizing illusion of classicism, the idealized image of antiquity, at once timeless and the object of permanent loss, that has governed modernity's relationship with ancient Greece" (Holmes 2017, 19). It is the opposite: the recognizable, yet non-stabilized nature of myth.

Acknowledgements

I am very grateful to Sif Itona Westerberg for providing me with photographs of her work and her stay on Bornholm. I would also like to thank the artists from Guirlanden who invited me to follow them after their first exhibition at the Museum of Ancient Art and Archaeology, and Helle Kingbird Bjerregaard for allowing me to re-use images from the exhibition.

Bibliography

Andersen, T.R. 2018. "Fra 'happy hippie' til 'happy go lucky'". *Festskrift i anledning af Guirlandens 50 års jubilæum*. https://guirlanden.dk/wp-content/uploads/2018/05/Festskrift_TrineRytterAndersen.pdf, last accessed 15 February 2022.

Bencard, E.J. 2005. *Afstøbningssamlingen: død eller levende?* Copenhagen: Afstøbningssamlingens Venner.

Bilde, P.G. 2000. "From Study Collection to Museum of Ancient Art: A Danish University Museum of Mediterranean Antiquities and Plaster Casts", in: Lund, J. & Pentz, P. (eds) 2000. *Between Orient and Occident. Studies in Honour of P.J. Riis*. The National Museum of Copenhagen and Aarhus University Press, 209-231.

Bjerregaard, H.K. 2015. "Beretning om to møder". https://antikmuseet.au.dk/udstillinger/phaeton, last accessed 2 August 2024

Dahl, H. 2020. "Hip-hip-hurraaa! Et TV-program, der tager kunsten alvorligt". *Berlingske Tidende*, 16 August 2020. https://www.berlingske.dk/kultur/hip-hip-hurraaa-et-tv-program-der-tager-kunsten-alvorligt, last accessed 2 December 2021.

Den blå tråd. Exhibition catalogue. Aarhus: Antikmuseet 2014.

Fejfer, J. 2003. "Wiedewelt, Winckelmann and Antiquity", in: Fejfer, J., Fischer-Hansen, T. & Rathje, A. (eds) 2003. *The Rediscovery of Antiquity: The Role of the Artist*. Acta Hyperborea, 229-234.

Fuchs, A. & Salling, E. 2004. *Kunstakademiet 1754-2004 IIII*. Copenhagen: Det Kongelige Akademi for de Skønne Kunster & Arkitektens Forlag.

Funder, L.M.A., Kristensen, T.M. & Nørskov, V. 2019. *Classical Heritage and European Identities. The Imagined Geographies of Danish Classicism*. London: Routledge.

Holmes, B. 2017. "Liquid Antiquity", in: B. Holmes & K. Marta (eds.). *Liquid Antiquity*. Athens DESTE Foundation for Contemporary Arts, 18-59.

Homer 1999. *Homers Illiade*, tr. O.S. Due & ill. P. Brandes.

Homer 2003. *Homers Odyssé*, tr. O.S. Due & ill. P. Brandes.

Jepsen, N. 2021. "The Outcast and the Voiceless", in: Pennington 2021, 22-23.

Kiileric, B. 2021. "The Classical in Contemporary Art and Visual Culture – an Introduction". *CLARA* 8, special issue 2: *The Classical in Contemporary Art and Visual Culture*, 1-12. https://doi.org/10.5617/clara.9177.

La Cour, P. 1991. *Peter Brandes og antikken*. Odense: Kunsthallen Brandts Klædefabrik.

Lange, B. 2002. *Thorvaldsens Museum. Bygningen – farverne – lyset*. Arkitektens forlag.

Larsen, A.H., Teglhus, H. & Nørskov, V. 2008. "Danmark på museum. Museumsvæsnets opståen i Danmark", in: Høiris, O. (ed.), *Romantikkens verden*. Aarhus: Aarhus Universitetsforlag, 503-520.

Nørgaard, B. 2004. "Spejl dig i gips eller spejl dig i hvad som helst", in: Kjerrmann, P. et al. (eds) 2004. *Spejlinger i gips*. Copenhagen: Det Kongelige Danske Kunstakademi, Billedkunstskolerne, 16-29.

Nørgaard, B. 2005. "Jeg elsker gips", in: Bencard 2005, 85-88.

Nørskov. V. 2011. *Arkiv / Stativ / Trofæ. Bo Mølgaard på Antikmuseet*. Aarhus: Antikmuseet

Pedersen, H. 2012. *Dialog med Akropolis*. Aarhus: Silkeborg Bad & Antikmuseet

Pennington, L. (ed.) 2021. *Sif Itona Westerberg – Immemorial*. Aarhus: ARoS.

Sappho – Sapfo. Peter Brandes og Mille Søndergaard. Exhibtion catalogue, Lemvig Museum & Antikmuseet, Aarhus Universitet 2022.

Simon, N. 2010. *The Participatory Museum*. https://participatorymuseum.org/read/, last accessed 9 April 2023.

Vergil 1996. *Vergils Aeneide*, tr. O.S. Due & ill. P. Brandes.

Vinci F. 2012. *Homers nordiske rødder. Iliaden, Odysseen og myternes vandringer*. Copenhagen: Bindslev.

Zahle, J. 2010. "Laocoön in Scandinavia – Uses and Workshops 1587 onwards", in: Frederiksen, R. & Marchand, E. (eds) 2010. *Plaster Casts. Making, collecting and displaying from classical antiquity to the present*. Berlin: Walter de Gruyter, 143-162.

12

THE *ILIAD* AND THE TWENTY-FIRST-CENTURY APOCALYPTIC IMAGINATION

EDITH HALL

> Sing, goddess, of the dreadful wrath of Peleus' son Achilles.
> It afflicted the Achaeans with manifold causes of grief,
> and sent to Hades the brave souls of many heroes,
> leaving their bodies as spoils for dogs
> and every bird of the air. Zeus' plan was being fulfilled.[1]

So opens the *Iliad*, composed around 2,750 years ago. An erudite ancient scholar, commenting on the last phrase, "Zeus' plan was being fulfilled",[2] says that Earth begged Zeus to relieve her of the weight of the multitude of people, who were impious. So Zeus first brought about the Theban War, which destroyed large numbers, and afterwards the Trojan one, "with Momus as his adviser, this being what Homer calls the plan of Zeus, seeing that he was capable of destroying everyone with thunderbolts or floods". Momus, 'Blame', was the sinister son of Night and brother of Misery (Hesiod, *Theogony* 214); he recommended as an alternative to thunder or floods the Judgement of Paris. Thus the Trojan War came about, resulting in "the lightening of the earth as many were killed".

The scholar then quotes a fragment of the lost epic *Cypria*, which narrated the events preceding the war itself:

> There was a time when the countless tribes of humans roaming constantly over the land were weighing down the deep-breasted earth's expanse. Zeus took pity when he saw it, and in his complex mind he resolved to relieve the all-nurturing earth of mankind's weight by fanning the great conflict of the Trojan War, to void

---

1 Homer *Iliad* I.1-5, my translation.
2 Scholiast D on *Iliad* I.5. I have slightly adapted the version of West 2003, 80-83.

the burden through death. So the warriors at Troy kept being killed, and Zeus' plan was being fulfilled.[3]

A similar tradition was recounted in the early epic *Catalogue of Women*, attributed to Homer's approximate coeval, Hesiod: "high-thundering Zeus was devising wondrous deeds then, to stir up trouble on the boundless earth; for he was already eager to annihilate most of the race of speech-endowed human beings…. Hence he established for immortals, and for mortal human beings, difficult warfare … pain upon pain".[4] The fall of Troy and the notion of an apocalyptic threat to the survival of the human race have thus been linked in the mythical imagination since the archaic age.

This matters today because, ever since the first printed texts of the Homeric epics appeared in 1488, they have been seen as culturally foundational. In one sense, this status is misleading. The poems contain material inherited from an Indo-European tradition shared with Sanskrit culture, and also represent a late stage in the evolution of ancient Near Eastern mythical narrative poetry, above all the Sumerian *Epic of Gilgamesh*, in societies that had reached peaks of sophistication millennia earlier.[5] Although it also shares material with the biblical story of Noah and the flood, elements in *Gilgamesh* are related to both the *Iliad* and the *Odyssey*: like Achilles, Gilgamesh has a beloved comrade-in-arms whose death he can scarcely abide. Over the last three decades, the relatively late place occupied by the Homeric epics in the development of world literature has been proven. Yet the impact of the *Odyssey* on European and subsequently world culture has quantitatively – and some would argue qualitatively – surpassed that not only of all other ancient epics but also of the *Iliad*.

In a book published 12 years ago, I tried to explain the magnitude of the cultural responses to the *Odyssey*, transculturally across the planet, in terms of its aesthetic variety and originality, its generic hybridity, its psychological and sociological resonance, and its intellectual profundity.[6] But the twenty-first century has seen an unprecedented explosion of artworks in diverse media reconfiguring the *Iliad*. Film-makers, poets, and novelists, notably women, have rewritten the more gloomy Homeric epic and made its contents familiar as never before, except perhaps in the eighteenth century in the wake of the serial publication, between 1715 and 1720, of the evergreen English translation by Alexander Pope.[7]

This article surveys a selection of significant English-language works recently responding to the *Iliad* and suggests reasons for its recent prominence in our shared imagination: the contingent historical and political background, the transnational theme of continents in combat, the nexus of topics relating to war crimes, captivity, and migration, a shift

---

3   *Cypria* fr. 1, slightly adapted from the translation of West 2003, 82-83.
4   Slightly adapted translation of supplemented papyrus P. Berol. 10560 95-16 by Most 2018, his fragment no. 155, 256-259.
5   West 1999.
6   Hall 2008a.
7   Hall & Stead 2020, 4-5, 48-50.

from the ironic and cynical mood of much late twentieth-century postmodern culture to an appreciation of gravity, severe grandeur, and emotional authenticity, the emphasis on individual witness of harrowing events, the urgent perception that women need at last to reclaim even the most canonical, exalted, and patriarchal literary artefacts, and the sense we increasingly share of an apocalyptic era which faces the imminent prospect of our entire civilization's extinction. Many of us feel like the herald in Aeschylus' tragedy *Agamemnon*, who can scarcely believe that he has survived both the Trojan War and the hurricane that wrecked the Greek fleet on the return voyage: in a reference to the epic tradition with which this article opened, he says that it is only because Zeus "does not *yet* want completely to wipe out the human race" (677-678).

The Greek tragedy most informed by the tradition of threatened total annihilation, however, is Euripides' *Trojan Women*, used by the authors of the two most recent (and in my view best) of the *Iliad* novels discussed below, Pat Barker and Natalie Haynes. *Trojan Women* is set against the background of the ruins of Troy after the Greeks have successfully besieged it, killed off almost the entire male population, and taken the women and children captive. They are to be separated and deported into slavery. But for Troy itself, of course, there is to be no future: as the chorus sing in the closing dirge, "Like smoke on the wings of the breezes, our land, laid low in war, now vanishes into nothingness" (1297-1299). The play's apocalyptic tenor is coupled with metaphysical bleakness. It juxtaposes physically manifest Olympian god – Poseidon and Athena open the play agreeing to destroy the Greeks by shipwreck as well as Troy in its entirety – and Hecuba's explicit expressions of doubt that the gods can concern themselves with humans or even exist in their traditional form at all. She announces that the gods have "come to nothing" and that all her sacrifices have proved futile (1240-1242).

Euripides found that sense of futility in the *Iliad*'s several unforgettable images of total destruction. In book XV, the Trojan battalions pour over the bridge, led by Apollo. He kicks down the Achaeans' wall, "as easily as a child playing on the sea-shore, who has built a house of sand and then kicks it down again and destroys it" (XV.363-365). The poet describes how even the last vestiges of the Greek fortifications were obliterated after the war by Poseidon and Apollo, who inundated the shore for nine long days, before Poseidon smashed away every last beam and stone with his trident, and made the coast of the Hellespont smooth again, and covered the beach with sand (XII.15-33). The task of imagining proleptically the actual devastation of Troy is put in the mouth of the elderly King Priam, when he is pleading with his son Hector not to fight Achilles (XXII.60-71):

Father Zeus, son of Cronos, will destroy me on the threshold of old age
by a terrible fate, after I've witnessed the deaths of my sons and abduction of my daughters,
my treasure chambers plundered and little children
cast to the ground in the terrible conflict,
and my daughter-in-law dragged away at the deadly hands of the Achaeans.
I myself at the last will be torn to pieces at my front gates
by ravening dogs, when someone has taken the life from my limbs

> with the thrust or blow of a sharp bronze weapon—
> the dogs which I raised in my halls to guard its doors.
> They will drink my blood uneasily and lie there at the gate.[8]

For there is a stark tonal difference between the Homeric epics. It is not just that the *Iliad* ends with catastrophe imminent, whereas the *Odyssey* ends with the victory of Odysseus over the suitors, his reunion with wife and son, and the outbreak of peace on Ithaca. Nor is it just that there are several unambiguously comic aspects of the *Odyssey*. Its world is also much more open to the possibility of the supernatural and fantastic than the dogged realism of the *Iliad*.

Despite the epiphanies of gods and one episode involving talking horses, the *Iliad* refuses to allow its listener off the painful hook of war. As a deadly serious account of a brutal conflict, it can be transplanted to other situations involving siege or imperialism, but its consistently realist tenor is not open to the type of non-realist, magical, surreal, supernatural, and symbolic figures of the Odyssey's travelogues: a one-eyed giant, a witch who can transform humans into animals, Sirens, a journey to the underworld. In comparison with the *Odyssey*, the *Iliad* offers a constrained epistemology: it contains no serial shape-shifter like Proteus and no humans turned into animals at all. The history of staging the *Odyssey*, too, reveals that this epic can only become sufficiently dark to make it susceptible to tragic realization as a result of radical re-topicalization or surgery on the psyche of its hero.[9] When Socrates interviews a professional performer of Homer in Plato's dialogue *Ion* (535b–c), he points to some passages as especially emotive. All except one are the darkest moments in the *Iliad* (the showdown between Achilles and Hector, and the sorrows of the bereaved Andromache, Hecuba, and Priam); the only one from the *Odyssey*, revealingly, depicts its hero at his most Iliadic, leaping forth in his true warrior identity, to mow his enemies down.

Just over a century ago, the words 'apocalypse' and 'apocalyptic' acquired a new, secular meaning, relating to "a disaster resulting in drastic, irreversible damage to human society or the environment, esp. on a global scale; a cataclysm".[10] In the twenty-first century, apocalyptic fiction about the end times has become a recognized sub-genre, replete with doomsday fantasies.[11] Graphic narratives of epidemics, cataclysms, permanent war, mass starvation, and extinction have gone viral,[12] to the extent that the label 'apocalypse porn' has appeared in popular culture. There is a danger here, especially the risk that real perils are peddled as voyeuristic or sensationalist entertainment while failing to educate consumers into pre-emptive action.[13] But awareness of this mass

---

8   My translation.
9   Hall 2008b.
10 *Oxford English Dictionary* s.v. 'apocalypse', draft addition b.
11 See the excellent study by Tate 2017.
12 E.g. Wallace-Wells 2017.
13 Colebrook 2014.

psychological development can also help in analyzing more socially responsible and aesthetically ambitious cultural phenomena.

Even more strikingly associated with the twenty-first century than the word 'apocalypse' is 'Anthropocene', coined in precisely 2000. Paul Crutzen and Eugene Stoermer proposed that the changes humans had wrought in the global environment were of such geological and ecological significance that the current term used to describe our epoch, 'Holocene', had outlived its usefulness.[14] The beginning of the Holocene is placed at the end of the last glacial period. Although the idea of the Anthropocene has caught on in public discourse,[15] there remains debate about when it started. Proposals range from the mid-eighteenth-century industrial revolution all the way back to the end of the Pleistocene epoch and the agricultural revolution in Mesopotamia at least 10,000 years ago.[16] But the proposals include the period from which the *Iliad* emerged, when unprecedentedly intensive cattle farming and deforestation for shipbuilding took place. Homeric epic, although by many centuries the younger sibling of Mesopotamian epic, is often felt somehow to represent the earliest file in the archive of human destructiveness, even to be the text that inaugurated modern consciousness and breakdown of the prehistoric "bicameral mind".[17]

The second significant factor in the recent increase in cultural interest in the *Iliad* is surely the reordering of the global socio-political situation in the wake of the attacks of 11 September 2001. The US invasion of Iraq exacerbated pre-existing tensions between the USA and the entire Muslim world,[18] even though Pakistan, Indonesia, the Persian Gulf monarchies, Jordan, Egypt, and Morocco officially remained allies of the USA. The 'enemy' in George W. Bush's 'War on Terror' was expanded to include all parts of all countries in which al Qaeda and the Taliban were believed to operate, as well as the jihadi strain of Sunni nationalism. There were attempts to aid the overthrow of the Baathist regime in Syria and the Shiite ayatollahs in Iran.[19] After 9/11, the Bush administration scored successes in bringing to power previously losing sides in Afghanistan and Iraq, but the violent forces of civil conflict thereby unleashed have created dangerous instability rather than liberal democracies across the Middle East.

Although a few commercial fiction writers jumped on the Trojan War bandwagon in the wake of the 2004 movie *Troy*,[20] the first internationally important *Iliad* novel of the twenty-first century was *The Songs of the Kings* (2002) by Barry Unsworth, an Englishman and Booker Prize-winner. Alongside Aeschylus' *Oresteia* and Euripides'

---

14 Crutzen & Stoermer 2000.
15 See, e.g., Lowe et al. 2020.
16 Smith & Zeder 2013.
17 Hawkins 2009 adapts the *Iliad* to a modern context in a racily written novel informed by Julian Jaynes' theory of the bicameral mind.
18 Cole 2006, 30.
19 Cole 2006, 32.
20 E.g. Tobin 2004; Manfredi 2004; Clarke 2004; Pavlou 2005; Elyot 2005; Gemmell 2005; 2006; 2007; George 2006.

Iphigenia in Aulis (the latter of which also became suddenly popular in the wake of 9/11)[21], the novel's primary co-text is the *Iliad*, even though the events it portrays – the days leading up to the sacrifice of Iphigenia at Aulis – precede the action of the epic. In the first half, the focus is on the creation of Homeric epic, the precise mechanisms whereby truth is transformed through 'spin' into a manufactured narrative that suits the interests of history's winners.[22] Unsworth saw the Trojan legend as a series of tragic events created by 'spin-doctors' (especially Odysseus); he was motivated by his horror at the rebranding of the Labour Party by the then British government, especially by Tony Blair's lieutenants Peter Mandelson and Alastair Campbell, and the specious case made for supporting the US aggressive military policies after 9/11.[23] Unsworth's novel brushes the Trojan War story against the grain, lending voice to the ancient underclass. Unsworth himself was born into a working-class mining family in County Durham, and all his fiction demonstrates an acute sensitivity to the casual brutality of the language with which powerful people address the powerless. The date when this novel was published, a year after 9/11, certainly made the cynical warmongering exploitation of the ignorant by his obnoxious spin-doctor Odysseus seem terrifyingly topical.

It is impossible to quantify the precise instrumentality of global politics in Warner Brothers' decision to make the movie *Troy*,[24] although there is no doubt that shortly after 9/11, in November 2001, the head of the Motion Picture Association in North America, Jack Valenti, addressed a meeting attended by the presidential advisor Karl Rove and executives from all the major media conglomerates. He invited his audience to keep in mind the global scope of their industry's ideological influence: "We are not limited to domestic measures. The American entertainment industry has a unique capacity to reach audiences worldwide with important messages".[25] Decades after Hollywood had stopped producing blockbuster movies set in ancient Greece in the mid-1960s, within a few years of 9/11 no fewer than three major star-studded films about ancient Greeks had been produced. Each focuses on one of the three major military offensives against Asiatic peoples which structure Greek history: *Troy*, which was directed by Wolfgang Petersen (2004), set in the late Bronze Age and loosely based on the *Iliad*; *Alexander*, directed by Oliver Stone, which charts Alexander the Great's eastern expedition leading up to his death in 323 BCE, a narrative derived from ancient historians including Diodorus, Arrian, and Plutarch; and *300*, directed by Zack Snyder (2007), which screens the battle of Thermopylae during Xerxes' invasion of Greece in 480 BCE. The ultimate historical source for Thermopylae is Herodotus book VII, but it is distorted by the intermediary of the comic-strip illustrated novella version (1998) by the reactionary

---

21   Hall 2005.
22   Hall 2009.
23   Personal correspondence with Unsworth.
24   It is a shame that the contemporary political resonances of *Troy* receive such sparse attention in Winkler 2007, an otherwise excellent collection of essays.
25   *PR Newswire* 2001.

Promotion for the film *Troy*, directed by Wolfgang Petersen 2002.

Fig. 1.

graphic artist Frank Miller.[26] Although the success of Ridley Scott's *Gladiator* (2000) had nudged the movie industry into recalling the tradition of spectacular movies set in classical antiquity that had been so popular in the 1950s and 1960s, the emergence of an urgent new global narrative of a long war between West and East, the dividing line falling somewhere in the eastern Mediterranean, was surely a factor in the genesis of all three 'Greeks v. the East' films of 2004-2007.

Troy was written by David Benioff in 2002, soon after 9/11; a draft was circulating by November 2002 (fig. 1).[27] The filming approximately coincided with the invasion of Iraq. The most outstanding performance was by Brian Cox as the ruthless, cynical Agamemnon, determined to use Helen's elopement as the pretext for a military campaign motivated by personal greed. The director was Wolfgang Petersen, who had studied Greek at school, and had made his name with a film he both wrote and directed set during another cataclysmic war, the portrait of a German U-boat captain in *Das Boot* (1981). When reflecting on the launch of the Iraq invasion in March 2003, he said, "I couldn't believe it. I thought, it's as if nothing has changed in 3,000 years. People are still using deceit to engage in wars of vengeance". He recalled that the similarities between what happened at Troy and what was happening in Iraq became uncomfortably obvious:

26 For Miller's bellicose politics, see the interview he recorded with National Public Radio in January 2007, at http://www.theatlasphere.com/metablog/612.php.
27 Stax 2002.

> Just as King Agamemnon waged what was essentially a war of conquest on the ruse of trying to rescue the beautiful Helen from the hands of the Trojans, President George W. Bush concealed his true motives for the invasion of Iraq. … I wouldn't make a movie like Air Force One now.[28]

The ongoing military conflicts, along with the stellar cast, spectacular cinematography, and refreshing commitment to telling a tragic story in a sincere, unironic way, helped the movie – despite its failure on several scores as a reception of the *Iliad* – to achieve worldwide success.

The film certainly lies behind the subsequent penetration of the *Iliad* to a level of popular culture previously reached by hardly any other classical text except the *Odyssey* and *Aesop's Fables*. An advertisement for Amstel (2006) presented itself as a lost scene from the movie, in which some Trojans fail to drag the wooden horse through the gates and drink lager instead.[29] The *Iliad* was chosen for adaptation in 2007-2008, along with *The Jungle Book*, *The Last of the Mohicans*, *Moby-Dick*, and *The Three Musketeers*, as one of the earliest in the *Marvel Illustrated* imprint series of comic-book adaptations of literary classics.[30] The movie *Troy* is likely to have accentuated the taste for archaic 'epic' content in Heavy Metal music, and certainly informed 'Iliad', the fifth track on the debut album *Of Secrets and Lore* made by Italian band King Wraith in 2015.[31] 2018 saw the BBC/Netflix televised miniseries *Troy: Fall of a City*. The choice of Troy for the second instalment of the *Total War Saga* video game developed by Creative Assembly Sofia, released in 2020, is the most recent example.[32]

Although a few fiction writers jumped on the Trojan War bandwagon in the wake of *Troy*, the first internationally important *Iliad* novel after Unsworth's, while undoubtedly connected with the War on Terror, seems to have little connection with the movie. The Australian David Malouf's prizewinning *Ransom* (2009) retells the *Iliad* from books XXII to XXIV – the story of Priam as he goes to Achilles to plead for the return of the body of Hector.[33] Although *Ransom* was not written until the War on Terror was well underway, and did not appear until 2009, Malouf had written a poem in 1970, 'Episode from an Early War', which relates the image of the lacerated corpse of Hector to his own experience of growing up as a small child during the Second World War and the genocide of the Jews.[34] Malouf was much influenced in his reading of the *Iliad* in both poem and novel by Simone Weil's famous essay "The *Iliad*, or The Poem of Force", in

---

28 Walsh 2004. See some further statements along the same lines by Petersen, quoted in Winkler 2007, 7-8.
29 See https://www.youtube.com/watch?v=-dQSfA0EWxE&feature=youtu.be&fbclid=IwAR0OK-2zRm1T-au3a5mL349yERehkuYswOEdP-OCFfA1peSuvlDxGLrfhz.
30 Thomas, Rivera & Sepulveda 2007-2008.
31 Produced by the Italian record label Underground Symphony.
32 Published by Sega as the second instalment in the Total War Saga subseries.
33 *Ransom* was shortlisted for the 2011 International IMPAC Dublin Literary Award and received the 2009 John D. Criticos Prize.
34 Malouf 1974, 13; see Reynolds 2016.

which she had argued that "The true hero, the true subject, the centre of the *Iliad* is force. Force employed by man, force that enslaves man, force before which man's flesh shrinks away".[35] Several aspects of *Ransom* directly echo Weil's analysis, especially the emphasis on the way that neglect or violence reduce people to the status of mere object. Yet Malouf's reading of the *Iliad* is not quite so pessimistic about human moral abasement as Weil's. In a speech he delivered at the Australian National University in the same year as the novel was published, he said that he found in the epic, besides force, tenderness, civility, and "largeness of spirit" in the "all-encompassing sympathy" with which Homer treats both sides.[36]

There is a sense of apocalypse in Weil's essay: "The whole of the *Iliad* lies under the shadow of the greatest calamity the human race can experience–the destruction of a city".[37] And this apocalyptic vision of total annihilation of a community, which made the *Iliad* feel relevant to Weil at the beginning of the Second World War II, also features in *Ransom*. Somax, the ordinary Trojan who drives Priam into the Greek camp, articulates a stark vision of what will become of his nation, "later—when Troy has become just another long, windswept hilltop, its towers reduced to rubble, its citizens scattered or carried off … into exile and slavery".[38] And Malouf's story ends with an agonizing flash forward to the moment of Priam's violent death at the hands of Achilles' son, Neoptolemus.

Just two years later, Alice Oswald published her grave poetic response to the *Iliad*, *Memorial* (2011). It is the clearest example of the seriousness with which the epic has begun to be taken as poetry, although a shorter but eerily beautiful account of the death of Hector, reading *Iliad* XXII from the dying hero's perspective, had been published in 2004 by Jo Balmer, another female English classicist and poet, the year after 9/11.[39] Both poets have responded to the *Iliad*'s uncomfortable beautification of the dead bodies of young men, articulated by Priam after the passage quoted above in which he foresees his own aged cadaver being rent by his own guard dogs (XXII.71-73):

But when a young man is killed in battle
and lies mangled by the sharp bronze, everything looks seemly:
although he is dead, whatever part of him is seen appears beautiful.

Oswald focuses on the deaths of individual combatants during the Trojan War; although no explicit connection is drawn, the appalling fatalities subsequent to 9/11 provide the background to the entire 84 pages of her sombre text. Between 2003 and the publication

---

35 Weil 2005 [1940], 3. Weil's essay was first published in 1940 in *Cahiers du Sud* as "L'Iliade, ou le poeme de la force", copyright 1989 Editions Gallimard. English translation by Mary McCarthy first published in the November 1945 issue of *Politics*. See further Gold 2016.
36 Malouf 2009b, 218.
37 Weil 2005 [1940], 31.
38 Malouf 2009a, 216.
39 Balmer 2004, 41-42.

of *Memorial* in 2011, more than 162,000 Iraqis lost their lives as a result of the conflict;[40] in the same period, nearly 7,000 US and several hundred UK military personnel died in Iraq or Afghanistan. The first eight pages of *Memorial* simply consist of the capitalized names of all the named combatants who die in the *Iliad*, printed one beneath the other in the order in which their deaths are described in both the ancient and the modern poem; the relentless effect is like scrutinizing a large inscribed stone war memorial.

In the course of the poem, when each of these men's deaths is narrated, his name is capitalized again:

> And IPHITUS who was born in the snow
> Between two tumbling trout-stocked rivers
> Died on the flat dust
> Not far from DEMOLEON and HIPPODAMAS
>
> Like when a dolphin powered by hunger
> Swims into the harbour
> Thousands of light-storms of little fish
> Flit away to the water-shaken wall-shadow
> And hang there trembling[41]

Oswald notes that one of the virtues of Homer admired by ancient critics was his poetry's *enargeia* (see, e.g., Dionysius of Halicarnassus, *de Elocutione* IV.209-211), which she translates as "bright unbearable reality".[42] To recover this, she strips away the narrative parts of the *Iliad* and concentrates on just two elements, the similes and the short biographies of soldiers which often appear at the moment of their deaths. *Memorial*, she hopes, presents the *Iliad* "as a kind of oral cemetery"; the biographies, she believes, drew on ancient traditions of lament, to attempt "to remember people's names and lives without the use of writing".[43]

She has responded to the physical suffering of the Trojan War combatants. Pherecles the Trojan shipwright, for example,

> Died on his knees screaming
> Meriones speared him in the buttock
> And the point pierced him in the bladder[44]

But she also sees that these tiny biographical notices offer us brief glimpses of the bereaved. The first warrior's death in her poem, as in the *Iliad*, is that of Protesilaus,

---

40 https://www.iraqbodycount.org/analysis/numbers/2011/.
41 Oswald 2011a, 66-67.
42 Oswald 2011a, 1.
43 Oswald 2011a, 2.
44 Oswald 2011a, 19.

> He died in mid-air jumping to be first ashore
> There was his house half-built
> His wife rushed out clawing her face[45]

There are mothers like "Laothoë one of Priam's wives / Never saw her son again he was washed away".[46] There are many fathers, like Antimachus, who put the case for war:

> He opened a door in the earth
> And a whole generation entered
> Including his own young sons
> PEISANDER and HIPPOLOCHUS
> Two dazed teenagers trotting into battle
> On their father's expensive horses.[47]

There are sisters:

> What was that shrill sound
> Five sisters at the grave
> Calling the ghost of DOLON
> They remember an ugly man but quick[48]

There are men who loved socializing with their friends, like Axylus from the Hellespont, who died "In a daze of loneliness".[49] Oswald has said that as she reads Homer's obituaries, she can hear under the verse the sound of howling; she intended to pare down the epic to this bleak cry, this howl.[50] The main part of *Memorial* ends with Andromache howling for Hector, returned to Troy "sightless / Strengthless expressionless",[51] but the poem as a whole ends with the word "gone" and an image with a connotation of apocalyptic cosmic destruction:

> Like when a god throws a star
> And everyone looks up
> To see that whip of sparks
> And then it's gone.[52]

---

45 Oswald 2011a, 13.
46 Oswald 2011a, 69.
47 Oswald 2011a, 37.
48 Oswald 2011a, 33.
49 Oswald 2011a, 26.
50 Warner et al. 2016, 18.
51 Oswald 2011a, 72.
52 Oswald 2011a, 84.

This is a graver revisiting of a famous simile in which Athena "shot through the sky as some brilliant meteor which the son of scheming Kronos has sent as a sign to mariners or to some great army, and a fiery train of light follows in its wake" (*Iliad* IV.75-77).

Oswald has principles. The poem was shortlisted for the prestigious TS Eliot Poetry Prize, which she had previously won for *Dart* in 2002. But she pulled out of the competition when she researched the new sponsors of the awarding body, the Poetry Book Society (PBS); after losing Arts Council backing, the PBS won funding from an investment company which manages hedge funds. In an article explaining her motives, she said that she could not "ignore the honest muttering" in her head.[53] These convictions – that the writer has a moral, social, and political responsibility and that literature and the literary establishment are instrumental in maintaining or eroding standards of behaviour in our collective lives – are shared by most of the other writers discussed here.

Oswald's main concern was not to reappraise the *Iliad* from a feminist perspective. But *Memorial* made this point implicitly because women have not historically been much involved with creating receptions of the *Iliad*. She is one of the very few women (including Weil and an earlier Frenchwoman, Madame Anne Dacier, an exceptional Greek scholar who translated it in 1699)[54] to have historically felt equipped or daring enough to essay a translation or interpretation of this hyper-masculine, solemn, and military masterpiece. There were already suggestions in antiquity that the *Odyssey* was the product of Homer's weakened genius in old age, and was somehow more "effeminate" than the *Iliad*;[55] Richard Bentley argued that while Homer had composed the songs constituting the *Iliad* to perform at festivals in front of men, those in the *Odyssey* were designed for women.[56] William Golding agreed, saying "anyone who prefers the *Odyssey* to the *Iliad* has a woman's heart".[57]

The masculine focus of the *Iliad* was even more heightened in *Troy*, as it was in Michael Hughes' *Country* (2018), a clever and prize-winning novel, very different from those discussed in detail here, about militarized male culture; it transposed the action of the *Iliad* to the period of the Irish troubles.[58] In the film, when Achilles (Brad Pitt) is too busy worrying about Briseis (Rose Byrne) to devote himself to armed combat, Odysseus (Sean Bean) remarks cryptically to him, "women have a way of complicating things". Unfortunately, women scarcely complicate the plot of *Troy* at all. The commanding figure of Hecuba, so prominent in crucial scenes of the *Iliad*, has been entirely deleted. Helen possesses not one iota of mysterious power, and Briseis is amalgamated with both Chryseis and Cassandra. Yet alongside the reduction of the *Iliad*'s already meagre female quotient, the movie does briefly doff its cap in the direction of its more emancipated third-millennial female audience members by allowing Briseis to stab

---

53   Oswald 2011b.
54   See Wyles 2016.
55   Hall 2008a, 116-118.
56   Bentley, quoted in Grote 1869, I, 151n.
57   William Golding, in conversation, quoted in Boitani 1994, viii.
58   It won the London Hellenic Prize 2018.

Agamemnon in the neck. Her action is presented as a feisty post-feminist refusal to be complicit, when the brutal patriarchal overlord is about to take her captive, in her own victimhood. Benioff's otherwise lacklustre screenplay here dared – however briefly – to rewrite the Homeric poem in a way that enhances its presentation of female agency. It is an important moment from the perspective of the rewriting of classical texts in modern media.[59]

The first major *Iliad* novel of the remarkable cluster published in the second decade of the twenty-first century was Madeline Miller's *The Song of Achilles* (2012), which won the Orange Prize for Fiction. It is a gay love story, told from the perspective of Patroclus, who is in this novel (as in some ancient sources, though not the *Iliad*) Achilles' lover. But it is the non-Greek captive women in the Achaean camp who dominate most of the several Troy novels by women subsequent to *The Song of Achilles*. In 2014, Judith Starkston, an American writer of fantasy fiction, published *Hand of Fire*, a stirring if crudely written novel taking enormous liberties with ancient mythical traditions and centred on the mystical religious and healing powers of Briseis. Rather improbably, in Starkston's hands, she is madly in love with Achilles. Much better written is Emily Hauser's *For the Most Beautiful* (2016), which reads as if it were aimed at the Young Adult market and contains paranormal and fantasy elements as well as romance. It is told through the eyes of both Briseis and "Krisayis", a freely adapted version of Chryseis, who spies for the Trojans in the Greek camp. Hauser, a lecturer in classics, knows her Mycenaean art and archaeology well, and some of the descriptive writing is excellent.

But it only was when the heavyweight novelist Pat Barker decided to turn her hand to the Troy story that the *Iliad* found a female fiction writer of anything like sufficient technical mastery, gravitas, and emotional honesty to do Briseis and the epic justice. It is rare that a writer who has won prizes for her novels about the trauma inflicted by twentieth-century combat turns to the late Bronze-Age warfare depicted in the *Iliad*. But we should not be surprised that the definitive war epic attracted Barker's attention. She won the Booker Prize for *The Ghost Road* (1995), the final novel in her First World War trilogy, but it was only part of the monumental achievement also constituted by *Regeneration* (1991) and *The Eye in the Door* (1993), fiction on a scale and of a scope that equals the epic storytelling at which the Homeric poets excelled.

In her earlier novels, from *Union Street* (1982) onwards, Barker explored the subjective experiences of working-class women, and it is a commitment to recovering the psychological predicament of powerless women that motors *The Silence of the Girls*, which was shortlisted for two prestigious literary prizes.[60] The setting is the centre of Greek military operations, where women enslaved during the sieges of surrounding towns in Asia Minor are brutally herded into what Barker has no hesitation in calling a "rape camp". Her novel's title was suggested by the notorious ancient Greek proverb, "Silence becomes a woman". This was barked by the macho Greek hero Ajax at his concubine Tecmessa in Sophocles' tragedy *Ajax* (293), where he commits suicide after display-

---

59   Hall 2014.
60   The Women's Prize for Fiction 2019 and the Costa Novel Award.

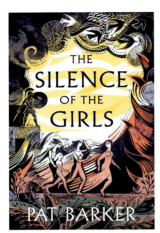
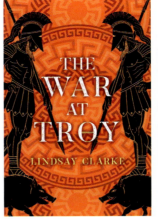

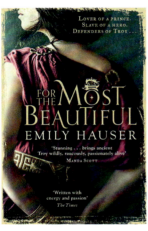
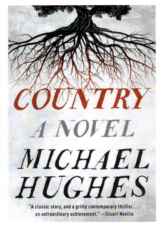
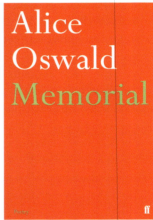
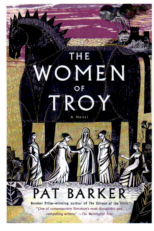
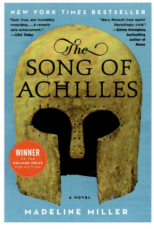
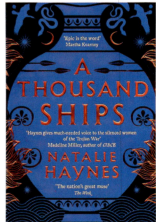

Fig. 2. Since 2011 the *Illiad* has offered serious writers a context to rethink both the historical importance of this epic, its legacy and the general uncertainty, brutality and inequality of our own era.

ing symptoms uncannily close to those which would now be diagnosed as indicating Post-Traumatic Stress Disorder.[61] Both Ajax and Tecmessa are briefly brought to vivid life in the book, and the proverb is its leitmotif. Most of the novel features Briseis as first-person narrator, painfully aware of her previous life as the young queen of nearby Lyrnessus. She was taken captive after seeing her city sacked and all her menfolk killed. Her beauty meant that she was spared being thrown to the regular soldiers for their common use. She was awarded instead to Achilles.

As in Book I of the *Iliad*, Achilles falls out with his supreme commander, Agamemnon, who expropriates Briseis from him. The actions of the subsequent 40 or so days, narrated in the *Iliad*, occupy most of the novel – Achilles' wrathful refusal to fight, the desperate attempts of his fellow officers at reconciliation, the deaths of Patroclus and Hector, Priam's visit to Achilles to request Hector's corpse, and Hector's funeral. But Barker also wants us to hear the voices of the women of Troy after it falls, and concludes with material from Euripides' *Hecuba* and *Trojan Women* to expose us to the shock and agony of Hecuba, Andromache, Polyxena, and Cassandra, as well as to the agonizing burial of baby Astyanax.

The poetry which has informed Barker's whole conception occupies fewer than 20 lines of the epic, when Briseis, restored to Achilles' tent, weeps over Patroclus' cadaver (XIX.287-300). For once we hear her voice, in direct speech, in her address to Patroclus: you comforted me, she says, when I wept for my dead husband, "for you said you would make Achilles marry me, and take me back with him to Phthia, we should have a wedding feast among the Myrmidons. You were always kind to me and I shall never cease to grieve for you". Barker makes us understand exactly the significance of Patroclus' promise.

With her celebrated frankness, she explores the appalling psychological experience of women taken in war – what Victorian translators used euphemistically to call 'spear-brides'. After months of terror, when they are finally captured and the rapes begin, the best that any woman can hope for is to be selected by as high a ranking soldier as possible, who will demand exclusive use of her. Briseis is beaten and raped anally by Agamemnon, while sex with Achilles is rough and perfunctory. But anything is better than being forced to service anyone at any time. Exactly the same principle motivates the narrator of the famous memoir *Eine Frau in Berlin* (*A Woman in Berlin*, 1959), by Marta Hillers: faced with systematic rape by numerous Red Army soldiers, women in occupied Berlin were desperate for a high-ranking Soviet officer to offer them protection, whatever the favours he demanded in return.

Briseis' account of her ordeals, and those of the other women in the camp, is relentlessly violent. Barker's dialogue is epigrammatic, pungent, and even humorous at times; a whole character can be fleshed out in a single utterance. When the Greek soldiers hand over his war prize Briseis to him – a girl in catatonic shock who has just watched four brothers die in succession – Achilles just says, "Cheers, lads. She'll do". The un-

---

61   As explored in Timberlake Wertenbaker's version *Our Ajax*, which premiered at the Southwark Playhouse in London in November 2014.

compromising accumulation of physical details, especially smells, tastes, sounds, and the tactile feel of things, conjures up the squalor of life in the dust, excrement, and gore of prehistoric tent cities. It is only occasionally relieved by a description of the exquisite fabrics the women weave and the tang of olives and fresh honey-cakes. The realism is uncompromising: women drink wine, however rancid, as anaesthetic whenever they can lay hands on it. They are often as drunk as the men.

The novel's ethical heart lies in Briseis' growing realization that the Greeks are no worse than any other warrior people, and that her only future lies with them. This is not Stockholm Syndrome: it is a pragmatic woman's rational response to a situation in which she is powerless. Because Patroclus is consistently kind to her, she begins to love him, and in due course even accepts that Achilles has certain virtues. At the end, she is not without hope: her will to survive is rewarded. This means that when, at the end of the novel, she looks at the deserted sites where the action of the *Iliad* took place, her perception of utter annihilation is more closely associated with the Greek camp than with the Trojan ruins:

> I looked down and saw, far beneath me, men like columns of black ants carrying loads up the gangways onto the ships. The huts would be empty now. I imagined the camp as it would be next winter, how the scouring winds would whistle through the deserted rooms. By next spring, or the spring after that, saplings would have taken root in the gutters, the advance guard of a forest that would one day reclaim its own. And on the beach itself, nothing left, nothing, only here and there a few broken spars bleached bone-white by the sun. And yet Troy's broken and blackened towers would still stand.[62]

It is its moral sophistication which makes Barker's novel stand out against most of the others based on or connected with the same epic. This applies even to those which, like hers, unflinchingly scrutinize the emotional cost of constant war, such as Malouf's *Ransom* and Miller's *The Song of Achilles*, or put female experience at their centre, such as Christa Wolf's much earlier *Cassandra* (1983), however dazzling, and Adèle Geras' lyrical *Troy* (2000), aimed at the Young Adult market.

Barker's was the most important novel based on the *Iliad* for decades, but just a year later, this status was challenged by Natalie Haynes' searing and fiercely feminist *A Thousand Ships* (2019), which was shortlisted for the Women's Prize for fiction the year after *The Silence of the Girls*. What makes Haynes – a highly competent classical scholar – unique as an *Iliad* adaptor is that her book's ambitious scope and grandeur make it seem truer to the vision underlying the *Iliad* than any of the comparable novels. Sublime grandeur was what ancient critics most admired in this epic, and the ancient treatise *On the Sublime* attributed to Longinus argues that this was partly to do with the extraordinary dignity of the traumatized mortals (9.7): "It seems to me that Homer, in bringing to the gods a range of suffering including internecine conflicts, grudges and

---

62 Barker 2018, 322-323.

vengeance, tears, and bondage during the Trojan War has made his men into gods in terms of strength and his gods into men". Haynes is not nervous about writing words for gods, as are most of the more realist recent novelists; she realizes that the juxtaposition of divine and tragic human perspectives is crucial to the overall elevation of the *Iliad*. She gets round the epic convention of dialogue between gods on Olympus with a sharply scripted chapter on the rivalry between Aphrodite, Hera, and Athena.

Instead of a few books of the *Iliad*, like Malouf, or one relationship, like Miller, or the experience of a single woman, like Barker, Haynes set out to imagine the experiences of numerous females – divinities as well as mortals – directly impacted by the Trojan War. She expands the stories of females who appear only briefly in the *Iliad*, such as Eris, the demi-god personifying conflict, or Laodomia, left widowed in Greece when her new husband Protesilaus was the first Greek to die at Troy, and Theano, High Priestess of Athena; she also includes females who do not appear in the *Iliad* (Penthesilea the Amazon warrior; Penelope; and Paris' first wife Oenone), and material from several other ancient texts including the *Odyssey* and Quintus of Smyrna's *Posthomerica*: the first substantial chapter narrates in free indirect discourse the hours leading up to the lonely death of Creusa in the burning ruins of Troy, but from her perspective; our main source for this is Virgil's *Aeneid* Book II. The tragedies of Euripides which Barker also used are important, providing her with a starting point for her several chapters about the relationships between the women of Troy – Hecuba, her daughters Cassandra and Polyxena, and her daughters-in-law Andromache and (the Spartan) Helen. Euripides' *Iphigenia in Aulis* inspires her painful exploration of the victimhood of this murdered youngster; Aeschylus' *Agamemnon* informs her Clytemnestra at every turn.

But Haynes is clear that her main co-text and the story it tells are epic in every sense of the word, and bookends the novel, which reads like a grand and solemn oratorio for female voices, with the words of Calliope. The cynical muse of epic is tired of Homer's relentlessly male focus and trenchantly concludes, after hundreds of gruelling pages,

> And I have sung of the women, the women in the shadows. I have sung of the forgotten, the ignored, the untold. I have picked up the old stories and I have shaken them until the hidden women appear in plain sight. I have celebrated them in song because they have waited long enough. Just as I promised him: this was never the story of one woman, or two. It was the story of all of them. A war does not ignore half the people whose lives it touches. So why do we?[63]

She has celebrated them "in song". Haynes never forgets that it is a grand and resplendent verbal medium of great tragic force and pathos, originally sung by ancient bards to the plangent lyre, that she is translating into contemporary prose fiction.

Haynes maintains a consistently elevated style, even when describing minutiae of daily life or humdrum labour. Iliadic conventions are lightly adapted to reframe the

---

63   Haynes 2019, 339.

story of women's experiences, for example the detailed arming scene, which is transferred to Penthesilea:

> First, the dark yellow chiton, a short tunic, tied at the waist with a thick brown leather belt, which also held her sword sheath. Then she added her prized leopard-skin cloak, which gave her warmth and ferocity in equal measure. These men, these Greeks would see they could not scare her, a woman who could outrun a leopard and cut him down mid-stride. The creature's paws hung below the tunic, its claws stroking the front of her thighs as she moved. She bound the straps of her leather sandals around her finely muscled calves and reached for her helmet. Hippolyta's helmet, with its high plume of blackest horsehair and its inlaid snakes, curling around her cheeks.[64]

Like Oswald and Barker, she has paid close attention to Homeric similes and metaphors:

> Achilles was the fastest creature alive, faster than the lynx that roamed the mountains, faster than Hermes who carried messages from Zeus to men. And faster than Penthesilea. She and her Amazons made straight for the Myrmidons, who scurried aside, like ants.[65]

And like Homer she varies the form of the chapters devoted to individual females; they include monologue, missive, dialogue, and narration.

Recovering the emotions of these women has been a mighty labour. Nothing in the *Iliad* prepares us for the sense of claustrophobia Haynes persuasively evokes that women, especially those with small children, must have felt when enclosed within the walls of Troy for ten long years. To compensate for the *Iliad*'s intense focus on friendships between men, she imagines a tender sisterly bond developing between the former queen Briseis and the teenaged tearaway Chryseis; the climax of this chapter is a taut reading of the conflict between the latter's father Chryses and Agamemnon, as dramatized in *Iliad* Book I, but from Chryseis' terrified perspective.

Haynes points out that the true cost in terms of female fatalities in a war of this kind must have been far greater than the *Iliad* acknowledges: since "the Myrmidons had devastated so many towns in surrounding Phrygia throughout this war", Achilles "must have killed dozens of women as he went. Not all of them had offered themselves up as slaves or concubines; some must have refused to abandon their husbands, or chosen to try to protect their children, whom he would also have killed moments later".[66] But the novel finds its sense of apocalypse not only in the multiple fatalities, but in its delicate evocation, reconfigured for our ecological crisis, of that ancient tradition that Earth had asked Zeus to destroy the human race: her Gaia recalls,

---

64 Haynes 2019, 51.
65 Haynes 2019, 53.
66 Haynes 2019, 55.

Mankind was just so impossibly heavy. There were so many of them and they showed no sign of halting their endless reproduction. Stop, she wanted to cry out, please stop. You cannot all fit on the space between the oceans, you cannot grow enough food on the land beneath the mountains. You cannot graze enough livestock on the grasses around your cities, you cannot build enough homes on the peaks of your hills. You must stop, so that I can rest beneath your ever-increasing weight. She wept fat tears as she heard the cries of newborn children. No more, she said to herself. No more.[67]

The current relevance and dramatic potential of *A Thousand Ships*, with its interlaced female voices, was quickly appreciated by Dr Magdalena Zira, a Cypriot playwright and theatre director. She translated the novel into a ten-hour script, which received a staged reading organised by an all-female team at the National Theatre in Nicosia, Cyprus, on 17 November 2019.[68] It was astonishing to hear the full story of the fall of Troy entirely in the voices of women in a country where their rights lag behind those in most northern European countries by several decades. Greek-speaking women claimed this ancient story decisively for themselves; the performance was repeated at the British Museum on 22 February 2020, just before COVID-19 put a stop to any such public gatherings.

There have been other female theatre professionals, perhaps partly inspired by Oswald's courageous response to the Iliad in *Memorial*, who have overhauled the ancient epic to bring its gender politics under scrutiny. Although Marina Carr's tragedy *Hecuba*, which premiered at Stratford upon Avon in 2015, is largely inspired by Euripides' play of the same name, she incorporates a substantial amount of material from the *Iliad* in exploring the emotions that a mother and queen losing her children and torn from her nation must undergo. In a 2019 production at the Dublin Theatre Festival, the director Lynne Parker stated that the spectacle of global migrations informed her creative decisions:

> I've been struck by how many theatre artists are talking to me about projects that attempt to deal with the desperate sense of general uncertainty. It's all-pervasive, whether because the Amazon rainforest is burning, or because hard-won gains in human rights are under threat; or because it seems that political structures are increasingly fragile. Last month I heard of three boys, found strapped under a truck in an Irish city—they were lucky to be alive, and they had no idea where or what they were emerging into. Hecuba and her daughters were enslaved and transported by ship—today people are desperate enough to seek sanctuary by clinging to the undercarriage of an aircraft …. The story …has a disturbing affinity with the global upheaval and forced migration of our modern world. Every day

---

67 Haynes 2019, 276-277.
68 The co-director was Athenetta Kasiou.

catastrophe draws closer. Syrians have suffered eight years of devastation—once they were just like us, and that's a key to our approach with this production.[69]

And Lynn Kozak, a performer, Professor of Classics at McGill University in Montreal, and author of *Experiencing Hektor: Character in the Iliad* (2016), has read the epic through a different gendered lens. Every Monday at 6pm, between January and August of 2018, she performed scenes covering the entire *Iliad* in the Bar des Pins, billed as 'Happy Hour Homer'. The effect was heightened since she was becoming more and visibly pregnant. You can see her extraordinary performances on YouTube: my favourite is the uncomfortable feast in sulky Achilles' tent in book IX.[70] Although sometimes taking a wry turn, these performances were sincere, eloquent, fierce, emotive, and tragic. This is another woman who has embraced the very status of canonical 'masterpiece' and grandeur of the *Iliad* that have in the past put it out of most of their foremothers' reach.

In an article on the global reception of ancient Greek literature published in 2015,[71] which begins with the figure of Homer and echoes of the *Iliad* in Wim Wenders' mournful 1987 movie, *Der Himmel über Berlin*, I identified four fundamental modes in which reception of ancient Greek texts operates. (1) The text may be treated as authoritative, foundational, generative, and infinitely susceptible to emulation and renewal. (2) It may create generic expectations and values which, on the contrary, are implicated in the perpetuation of a mindset which produces unnecessary human suffering: it is in the difference between the original and the new artefact or 'reception' that the importance lies. Either in form or content, it resists or reacts against the archetype; an obvious example is writing a novel consisting of monologues which forefront the female rather than male experience of the Trojan War. (3) The ancient text provides a stance or viewpoint on the world; it is a cultural phenomenon crystallizing an emotionally charged epistemology or reaction to life; it is the source of a worldview inflected by a particular psychological tone. In this type of 'tonal' reception the ancient genre is often replaced by a new medium – cinema or lyric poetry instead of epic, prose fiction instead of drama: the *Iliad*'s tragic realism, its tonal legacy, underlie almost all the recent responses to it. (4) The ancient text provides a point of departure for self-conscious thinking about aesthetics – the nature and purpose of art. Such thinking often shows the 'receiving' author engaging with an additional ancient text – one of the 'classics' of literary criticism which were written in Greek, such as Aristotle's *Poetics*, Dionysius of Halicarnassus' *de Elocutione*m, or *On the Sublime*. These four basic modes of reception – emulative, resistant, tonal, and self-consciously aesthetic – can all be present in the same artwork, interacting with and confirming, or alternatively undermining, one another.

In the twenty-first century the *Iliad* has been found to offer serious writers a context in which all four modes can operate at the same time. The works discussed here by Malouf, Oswald, Miller, Hughes, Barker, and Haynes happen all to have been nomi-

---

69   Parker 2019.
70   https://www.youtube.com/channel/UCBFoyAa8OCBP2WqSERnJ96Q.
71   Hall 2015.

nated for or to have won prestigious prizes, but all these writers would probably say that it was Homer who deserved the recognition. Oswald admires the *Iliad* and thinks it worth re-envisioning for a war-plagued planet. But she, like Barker and Haynes, omits the glory and focus on the suffering, resisting Homer's militaristic values. Her funereal tone, along with her understanding of the ancient literary critics' diagnosis of Homer's "bright unbearable reality", reveal her profound appreciation of the ancient poem's aesthetic achievement. Her *Memorial*, along with the very different but equally brilliant novels by Barker and Haynes, show that the *Iliad*, which ends with women leading the laments for a civilization on the brink of its final annihilation, is an ancient poem whose modern time has truly come.

Bibliography

Balmer, J. 2004. "Fresh meat: a Fresh Meat: A Perversion of Iliad 22", in: Balmer, J. 2004. *Chasing Catullus*. Newcastle upon Tyne: Bloodaxe.
Barker, P. 2018. *The Silence of the Girls*. London: DoubleDay.
Boitani, P. 1994 [1992]. *The Shadow of Ulysses: Figures of a Myth*, tr. A. Weston. Oxford: Clarendon Press
Clarke, L. 2004. *The War at Troy*. London: HarperCollins.
Cole, J. 2006. "Think Again: 9/11". *Foreign Policy* 156, 26-32.
Colebrook, C. 2014. *Death of the Posthuman: Essays on Extinction*, vol. I. London: Open Humanities Press.
Crutzen, P.J. & Stoermer, E.F. 2000. "The Anthropocene". *IGBP Newsletter* 41, 12.
Elyot, A. 2006. *The Memoirs of Helen of Troy*. London: Crown Publishers.
Gemmell, D. 2005. *Troy: Lord of the Silver Bow*. London: Bantam.
Gemmell, D. 2006. *Troy: Shield of Thunder*. London: Bantam.
Gemmell, D. 2007. *Troy: Fall of Kings*. London: Bantam.
George, M. 2006. *Helen of Troy: A Novel*. London: Pan.
Gold, B.K. 2016. "Simone Weil: Receiving the Iliad", in: Wyles, R. & Hall, E. (eds) 2016. *Women Classical Scholars: Unsealing the Fountain from the Renaissance to Jacqueline de Romilly*. Oxford: Oxford University Press, 360-376.
Grote, G. 1869. *A History of Greece*, 12 vols, new edition. London: John Murray.
Hall, E. 2005. "Iphigenia and her Mother at Aulis: a Study in the Revival of a Euripidean Classic", in: Wilmer, S. & Dillon, J. (eds) 2005. *Rebel Women*. London: Methuen, 3-41.
Hall, E. 2008a. *The Return of Ulysses*. London: IB Tauris.
Hall, E. 2008b. "Can the Odyssey Ever be Tragic? Historical Perspectives on the Theatrical Realization of Greek Epic", in: Revermann, M. & Wilson, P. (eds) 2008. *Performance, Iconography, Reception*. Oxford: Oxford University Press, 499-523.
Hall, E. 2009. "Greek Tragedy and the Politics of Subjectivity in Recent Fiction". *Classical Receptions Journal* 1, 23-42.
Hall, E. 2014. "Why Is Penelope Still Waiting? The Missing Feminist Reappraisal of the *Odyssey* in Cinema, 1963-2007", in: Nikoloutsos, K.P. (ed.) 2014. *Ancient Greek Women in Film*. Oxford: Oxford University Press, 163-185.
Hall, E. 2015. "Ancient Greek Literature & Western Identity", in: Hose, M. & Schenker, D. (eds) 2015. *Wiley-Blackwell Companion to Greek Literature*. Oxford: Wiley-Blackwell, 511-533.
Hall, E. & Stead, H. 2020. *A People's History of Classics: Class and Greco-Roman Antiquity in Britain and Ireland 1689-1939*. London: RTF.
Hawkins, T. 2009. *The Rage of Achilles*. Sacramento, CA: Casperian Books.
Haynes, N. 2019. *A Thousand Ships*. London: Mantle.
Lowe, C. et al. 2020. *Anthropocene Unseen: A Lexicon*. Galeta, CA: Punctum Books.
Malouf, D. 1974. *Neighbours in a Thicket: Poems*. St Lucia, Queensland: University of Queensland Press.
Malouf, D. 2009a. *Ransom*. London: Vintage.
Malouf, D. 2009b. "The Classics Today". Speech at the official launch of the new ANU Bachelor of Classical Studies and the Classics Endowment at the Australian National University in Canberra, 11 September 2009.

Manfredi, V.M. 2004. *The Talisman of Troy*. London: Pan.
Most, G.W. (ed.) 2018. *Hesiod. The Shield. Catalogue of Women. Other Fragments*. Cambridge, MA: Harvard University Press.
Oswald, A. 2011a. *Memorial*. Faber and Faber.
Oswald, A. 2011b. "Why I Pulled out of the TS Eliot Poetry Prize". *Guardian*, 12 December 2011. https://www.theguardian.com/commentisfree/2011/dec/12/ts-eliot-poetry-prize-pulled-out, last accessed 12 August 2024.
Parker, L. 2019. "Hecuba". https://www.rte.ie/culture/2019/0910/1075010-hecuba-marina-carr-and-lynne-parker-reimagine-greek-legend/, accessed 12 August 2024.
Pavlou, S. 2005. *Gene*. London: Pocket.
PR Newswire. 2001. "White House Meets with Hollywood Leaders to Explore Ways to Win War against Terror". *PR Newswire*, 11 November 2001.
Reynolds, M. 2016. "The 'Poem of Force' in Australia: David Malouf, Ransom and Chloe Hooper, *The Tall Man*", in: McConnell, J. & Hall, E. (eds) 2016. *Ancient Greek Myth in World Fiction since 1989*. London: Bloomsbury, 95-209.
Smith, B.D. & Zeder, M. 2013. "The Onset of the Anthropocene". *Anthropocene* 4, 8-13.
Stax. 2002. "The Stax Report: Script Review of *Troy*". *IGN*, 14 November 2002. https://www.ign.com/articles/2002/11/14/the-stax-report-script-review-of-troy, accessed 12 August 2024.
Tate, A. 2017. *Apocalyptic Fiction*. London: Bloomsbury.
Thomas, R., Rivera, P. & Sepulveda, M. 2007-2008. *Marvel Illustrated: The Iliad*. NYC: Marvel Comics.
Tobin, G. 2004. *The Siege of Troy*. New York: St. Martin's Press.
Wallace-Wells, D. 2017. "The Uninhabitable Earth". *New York Magazine*, July 2017. https://nymag.com/intelligencer/2017/07/climate-change-earth-too-hot-for-humans-annotated.html, last accessed 12 August 2024.
Walsh, D. 2004. "Warrior and Anti-warrior". *World Socialist Website*, 19 June 2004. https://www.wsws.org/en/articles/2004/06/troy-j19.html, last accessed 12 August 2024.
Warner, M., Rayfiel, T., Deming, S., Pinsky, R., Tarloff, E., Wagner, A., Lubow, A. & Morris, M. 2016. "A Symposium on Crying". *The Threepenny Review* 147, 18-21.
West, M.L. 1999. *The East Face of Helicon: West Asiatic Elements in Greek Poetry and Myth*. Oxford: Clarendon Press.
West, M.L. (ed. & tr.) 2003. *Greek Epic Fragments*. Cambridge, MA: Harvard University Press.
West, M.L. 2007. *Indo-European Poetry and Myth*. Oxford: Oxford University Press.
Winkler, M. (ed.) 2007. *Troy: From Homer's Iliad to Hollywood Epic*. Oxford: Blackwell.
Wyles, R. 2016. "Ménage's learned ladies: Anne Dacier (1647-1720) and Anna Maria van Schurman (1607-1678)", in: Wyles, R. & Hall, E. (eds) 2016. *Women Classical Scholars: Unsealing the Fountain from the Renaissance to Jacqueline de Romilly*. Oxford: Oxford University Press, 61-77.